Enchanted

Summer

About *Enchanted Summer*

"Enchanted Summer is a glorious, beautifully-crafted valentine to the Golden Age of Travel and the extraordinarily adventurous women who managed to discover themselves within it. In homage to those audacious female pilgrims, author Adrienne Crow takes the reader on her own irresistibly glamorous, modern day journey, which turns out be as bittersweet, revelatory and exhilarating as the long ago odyssey that inspired it."

*Linda Bloodworth-Thomason, Author of **Liberating Paris** and Creator, Writer and Producer of **Designing Women***

"When Adrienne Crow contacted me about our shared love of the book *Our Hearts Were Young and Gay* and told me her plans to follow in Cornelia and Emily's footsteps I was struck by what a wonderful idea it was for a book. I was also extremely jealous. The book had been my favorite while growing up and I believe it is the main catalyst for all of the many travel adventures I have had in my life.

Reading Adrienne's book *Enchanted Summer* reminded me of why I travel and how much joy can be found if you pack a suitcase, open your heart and walk out to meet the world."

*Kathy Kinney, Actress, Comedian and Co-Author of **Queen of Your Own Life: The Grown-up Woman's Guide to Claiming Happiness and Getting the Life You Deserve***

"Every fan of *Our Hearts Were Young and Gay* will relish Crow's 21st Century recreation of the original journey. Clearly a labor of love!"

*Nancy Allen, Author of the **Ozarks Mystery Series** and Co-Author with James Patterson of **Juror #3***

About the Author

For many more photos, backstory and tidbits about my travels with the girls, you can visit my website to check out my *Enchanted Summer* blog, and find me on Facebook and Instagram.

http://www.adriennecrow.com/
Facebook theadriennecrow
Instagram adriennecrow

Adrienne Crow grew up in Springfield, Missouri and attended Stephens College before moving to Los Angeles to work in television. For the last three years, she has been living as a nomad as she pursues her dream to be a travel writer. This is her first book.

Photo by John Stoddart, taken aboard the *Queen Mary 2*... but that's another story...

Enchanted Summer

A Journey in the Footsteps of
Our Hearts Were Young and Gay

Adrienne Crow

ISBN 978-1-7346559-0-2 eBook
ISBN 978-1-7346559-1-9 Paperback
ISBN 978-1-7346559-2-6 Audiobook
ISBN 978-1-7346559-3-3 Hardcover

Front Cover: Author's photo of the swans at Bletchley Park, Buckinghamshire, England.

Back Cover: Author photo taken in the gardens of Versailles.

Back Cover Collage, left to right:

Top Row: The Red Arrows perform a flyover of Buckingham Palace; a perfect day aboard the *Queen Mary 2;* Notre Dame Cathedral, Paris; a charming lane in Oxford.

Middle Row: Vintage photo of the timeless Big Ben and Parliament; dancing with the Foxtrot King; Cornelia and Otis Skinner on one of their voyages to Europe; Paris at sunset; the Arc de Triomphe by night.

Bottom Row: Mother Dolores Hart; 1942 copy of *Our Hearts Were Young and Gay* enjoying a rest on a garden wall; Paul Dudley White in uniform, World War I.

For Cornelia and Emily –
with many thanks for everything

Table of Contents

Prologue

Rapturous Plans

"We had been planning the trip for over a year... For months we had been exchanging letters brimming over with rapturous plans and lyric anticipation..."

This is how my favorite book begins.

Penned by Cornelia Otis Skinner and Emily Kimbrough in 1942, *Our Hearts Were Young and Gay* recounts how, in the summer of 1922, at the age of twenty-three, they traveled to Europe on their own (an adventure which was practically unheard of for unmarried women at that time).

Cornelia and Emily – who, by their own admission, were "poisonously young" – would spend four months living first in London, then Paris, finding their way into adulthood as they enjoyed a summer of independence which would greatly shape who they would become.

From the very start of their travels, the girls' journey is filled with crazy misadventures, large and small. Their ship to England runs aground before ever reaching open water. Cornelia narrowly escapes being sent to a German quarantine camp. The girls unknowingly spend the night in a French brothel. Along the way, they meet such notables as H.G. Wells and Margaret Sanger, sometimes with embarrassing results.

Told from Cornelia's marvelously witty point of view, with her droll, self-deprecating humor, this wonderfully laugh-out-loud story cast its spell on me the first time I read the book in high school. Though I'm fairly certain I was born with gypsy blood in my veins, it was Cornelia Otis Skinner and Emily Kimbrough and their book, more than anything else, which fueled my wanderlust and led me to going abroad when I was twenty-two, where I would have my own crazy series of adventures.

What makes this story especially addictive is that it is non-fiction, as Cornelia and Emily attest at the beginning of the tale:

> "Lest the reader should be in any doubt, we wish to state that the incidents in this book are all true and the characters completely non-fictitious."

I had been planning the trip for over a year. Then again, I suppose, in a way, I'd been planning it for decades.

Ever since my first reading of *Our Hearts*, I've always wished I could have been part of that world, that I could have lived inside the book, and had the same journey myself. The 1920s was the Golden Age of Travel, and everything was just so glamorous then.

Over the years I have often taken a copy of *Our Hearts* with me when I traveled. Even now when I read the book, I laugh out loud, though at this point I can practically recite it word for word. After thirty-five years, the book is still fresh and irresistible to me.

So when I realized I could live the dream of traveling with Emily and Cornelia, following in their footsteps, I began making a plan. But it would take some time to actually execute it.

The idea had come from an English writer named Tom Fremantle, a friend of a former boyfriend from Oxford. Tom has published numerous books about his travels around the world, and he has written more than once about a journey he's undertaken, following the trail of a book which resonates with him, where he recounts the author's travels and shares his own adventures along the way. His books are engaging, enlightening and wonderfully humorous.

Tom's journeys usually involve trekking across deserts and navigating jungle rivers, whereas my odyssey would be more about having tea at the Ritz and putting on evening gowns and gloves, so the comparison between my travels and his is a rather feeble one. But still, the concept is the same. And it is to Tom's book, *The Road to Timbuktu*, that I owe a debt of gratitude as a guidepost for my journey.

This notion of following in Cornelia's and Emily's footsteps began to percolate in my imagination, and by 2016, as I was taking baby steps towards pursuing a career as a writer, the idea had firmly taken hold and the stars began to align.

I took it as a sign that the calendars for 1922 and 2017 matched – meaning that, for example, July 9 (an important date in the story) fell on a Sunday in both years. I would be able to follow Cornelia's and Emily's journey, down to the exact same day of the week, ninety-five years after their travels, and seventy-five years after *Our Hearts* was published. It all had a lovely symmetry to it.

So one day in January 2017, I booked my passage on the *Queen Mary 2*, to sail for Southampton and spend the summer in London, and then in France. I began learning about the places Cornelia and Emily had visited, re-reading their book yet again, making notes, studying photos of the girls, and putting faces to the story of *Our Hearts Were Young and Gay* for the very first time. I looked up the origin of each pop culture reference in the book, researched every juicy morsel of the story, and delved into some of the mysteries within the book which I hoped to solve.

As I immersed myself in their tale, Emily and Cornelia and their world were pulled out of the past and into the present, and soon I started forming a connection to them. All of the photos and letters and bits of history brought the girls to life, and I found myself talking to them as acquaintances who were becoming my friends.

Our Hearts is a fascinating snapshot of American and European life in 1922. The world had just come through the Great War, the war to end all wars. Spirits were high and prospects bright in America, as well as in England and France. Dress hemlines were coming up, corsets were coming off, and women were just coming into the modern age, having won themselves the right to vote. It was the era of Prohibition, which only added to the thrill of the times – after all, a thing is always made more exciting when it is forbidden. Victorian restraint was a thing of the past in these Roaring Twenties, as the birth of the motion picture industry introduced to the world the smoldering sensuality of Rudolph Valentino and the coquettish self-assurance of Clara Bow. Ragtime was ushering in the Jazz Age, along with the zesty, urbane tunes of Cole Porter. These were the days of Dorothy Parker, F. Scott Fitzgerald and the Bright Young Things, and it seemed as if there was nothing but sunny skies on the horizon.

Cornelia and Emily said it best:

"…we stood, the two of us, young and hopeful in the young and hopeful 1920s."

While *Our Hearts* takes place in the summer of 1922, the book itself was actually written in 1942, just after America had entered World War II. Now middle-aged women, Cornelia and Emily began chronicling their happy tale during some of the darkest days of the war (and shortly after Cornelia's beloved father, Otis, had passed away). What would become the basis for the book began as a series of articles for *Cosmopolitan* magazine, published throughout 1942.

By the time the girls were committing to paper the joyful memories of their days in London, the city itself had just been through the Blitz. And when Cornelia and Emily wrote of their months in Paris, it was with the knowledge that Nazi troops now occupied the city. Yet there is not one hint of anything unpleasant in their book, not one whiff of the current troubles. Still, even though they chose to speak only of the world they knew in 1922, I couldn't ignore the fact that they had published this delightful story in the midst of a very volatile moment in history.

When *Our Hearts* was released, it was embraced immediately, rapidly climbing the *New York Times* bestseller list, spending five weeks at number one beginning in January 1943. The book would have multiple reprintings, and be adapted into both a popular Broadway play and a motion picture.

My life had been turned upside down. After almost two decades in the television industry, my career stalled. My sixteen-year relationship ended in crushing heartbreak. I felt untethered and adrift. And then I lost Jennifer and Sharill, two of my closest friends, along with my cousin Sarah – all beautiful souls who died way, way too young.

Nothing is forever, and no one is promised a future.

These seismic changes – these ass-kickers – lit a fire under me.

It was time to start doing all the things I had hoped to do "one day".

It was time to attempt those things I'd been too afraid to try. Like being a writer. And it was time to finally satisfy that relentless wanderlust which has resided in my soul for as long as I could remember.

It was time to take a leap of faith.

I had been brought to one of those moments of great clarity:

I could live with the fear of not knowing how – or if – it would all work out.

I could even live with failure.

But what I couldn't live with was getting to the end of my life and having to say I was too afraid to try when I had the chance.

So I sold my home and put the proceeds towards this new life I was carving out for myself. And I booked that voyage, and after those months of planning and research, in April 2017, I placed my belongings in storage in California – minus three suitcases full of what I hoped would be everything required for four months on the road.

The largest suitcase, known as the Really Big Suitcase, was dedicated only to what I would need for the first few weeks in the States, and then during my week aboard the glamorous *Queen Mary 2*.

Filled with copies of *Our Hearts* I planned to give out on the American side of the pond, along with all of my "cruisewear" – evening gowns, cocktail dresses, jewelry and opera gloves – the Really Big Suitcase would get left in the baggage office in Southampton once I reached England. I would be reunited with it only when I was boarding the *QM2* to sail back to New York at the end of my journey.

The larger of the other two suitcases contained most of my clothes, while the carry-on held my laptop, plug adapters for England and France, research materials and the requisite "the-rest-of-my-luggage-went-to-Barcelona" emergency outfit.

Most importantly, the carry-on held my faithful traveling companion: my 1942 edition of *Our Hearts*, which my mom had found in a second-hand bookstore when I was fifteen.

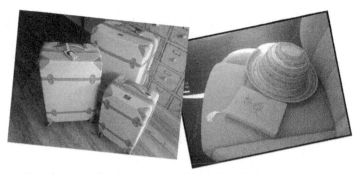

*New luggage for the trip, the closest I could get to steamer trunks; **Our Hearts** riding shotgun as we begin our journey.*

It didn't have a dust jacket and had yellowed over time, but it was in good shape. I had traveled with it for many years before allowing it to retire quietly to a bookshelf.

But on this trip, it simply had to come. I could not have made the journey without it.

Now it was time to go and live out *Our Hearts Were Young and Gay.*

Part 1

Lyric Anticipation

Quebec and New England

Chapter 1

"It was settled we could meet in Montreal at whatever hotel it is that isn't the Ritz."

It was early May 2017 when I first stepped into the book. I had crossed the border into Canada from New York, with my 1942 copy of *Our Hearts* riding shotgun in the passenger seat of my rental car. In Montreal, official starting point of my journey, I would "meet up" with Cornelia and Emily, and our travels together would begin.

The story of *Our Hearts Were Young and Gay* opens as Cornelia and Emily arrive "at whatever hotel it is that isn't the Ritz" the day before they are to board the *Montcalm*, the ship which will take them to Liverpool, England and the start of their summer in Europe.

Emily and Cornelia had become friends while attending Bryn Mawr, and had planned this trip as a post-college journey of independence. Cornelia had just turned twenty-three the day before she joined Emily in Montreal, and Emily was twenty-two and a half.

Emily hailed from Muncie, Indiana, where the Kimbrough family had made its fortune building bridges. She was petite, popular and lively, a bright and witty spirit, and a great reader of literature. She was prone to ideas which, as Cornelia explains, "were enthusiastic but lacking in accuracy," but her irreverent, almost ditzy way of seeing the world only made her all the more intriguing. Cornelia explains:

> "I loved Emily dearly but I also admired her to a point when I had occasionally to remind myself that after all she was born in Muncie, to keep from being over-awed by her. I felt I was definitely her inferior and hoped she wouldn't find out…"

Later, after my summer with the girls, I would visit Muncie, and see the house where Emily grew up, before spending the afternoon at Ball State University, reading through her papers. It was there that I would discover Emily's "version" of *Our Hearts*, a first draft of her recollections. And I would come to understand that a fair amount of the structure and phrasing I attributed to Cornelia had actually come from Emily.

It was not just one talented writer, but two, who produced the book.

Cornelia, for her part, was very much a girl of her era. Her taste in reading leaned more towards what might be considered lurid novels of the time, and

> "… it was my secret yearning to look like that macabre specimen known as a 'vamp'. I went in for 'slinky' dresses, high heels, long black earrings… and perfume so strong my school buddies used to say they could smell me coming several seconds before they saw me."

In Emily's version, she remembered Cornelia as being "quite sophisticated," noting that Cornelia seemed to carry herself like Lady MacBeth.

Bryn Mawr days: Cornelia in a school production of "Medea"; Emily's senior picture.

What Cornelia didn't touch on, in her description of herself, was her colorful family background and formative years.

Her father, Otis Skinner, was a famous and well-respected actor for almost sixty years, as well as authoring numerous plays and books. His wife, Maud, had more or less given up acting altogether by the time Cornelia was born, but she would occasionally appear on stage, and also turned her passion for the theatre to playwriting.

Born in Chicago, Cornelia spent her childhood in New York, Philadelphia and "living in a trunk," as Maud would say. Touring with Otis's theatre company would keep the family on the road for long stretches, but this probably served Cornelia well later in life when she chose to follow in her parents' footsteps, and make a career on the stage.

Otis and Maud figure prominently in *Our Hearts Were Young and Gay.* The Skinners, while wanting to give Cornelia and Emily their independence, felt it might not be a bad idea to be in Europe at the same time as the girls. So they booked their own passage out of New York, sailing on the White Star Line *RMS Celtic.* Their own travel plans would overlap with Cornelia's and Emily's in both London and Paris, which would allow them to keep tabs on the girls.

Starting at Montreal's *Le Vieux Port* (The Old Port), I meandered through the streets in the oldest part of the city, taking in the architecture and the street vibe, while looking for Cornelia's and Emily's hotel.

Of course, there was no way of knowing which hotel it was, but there were a few contenders. I would later learn from Emily's papers that she remembered the name of the hotel: it was the Mont Royal, which is now Les Cours Mont Royal, a shopping center.

Or did Emily have that right? One source of the hotel's history states that the Mont Royal was opened in December of 1922, which would have been six months after the girls sailed from Montreal. So perhaps the mystery remains.

Making my way over to the Ritz, I arrived just in time for afternoon tea. It was here that the girls were taken out on the evening before they sailed, by friends of Emily's who treated them to a lavish dinner. Emily and Cornelia had attempted to appear nonchalant about consuming quail and downing champagne, but didn't manage to pull it off. Cornelia explains:

"This was when [Emily] discovered that champagne makes her slightly deaf. Its effect upon me was to make me look distant and sad, and I hoped everyone would think I had had an unhappy love affair."

Already having decided to forego dinner with its quail and champagne, I was able to secure a table for afternoon tea even without a reservation, thanks to some creative rearranging done by the staff.

When it came time to place my order, I did include a glass of champagne as a nod to the book, and so I could toast Cornelia and Emily, and the start of our journey together. I had a quick flash of regret that I hadn't brought my 1942 copy of the book along with me from the car, as the girls' representative, but my gloomy thoughts were broken by conversation coming from the next table, where two ladies were discussing whether to have champagne. I broke in on the conversation and offered that the bubbly was very good (which it was – dry and flavorful, just right).

A little while later, after they had received and tasted their champagne, one of the ladies turned to me and agreed that it was very good. And from there we began a chat which lasted until the next tea service at 3:30pm, and I found I had made two new friends, Isabel and Marie-Helene, all thanks to champagne. I had started afternoon tea with two old friends, and ended it with two new ones.

It meant I got a late start at exploring *Le Vieux Port*, but it was totally worth it.

The Old Port is quickly becoming a revitalized, exciting area of Montreal, with shops, museums, restaurants and a marvelous bike path. My focus, though, was on its past, and locating where Cornelia and Emily had boarded the *Montcalm*. There were no historic markers, no traces from days gone by which pointed to the old passenger liner docks, but it was enough for me to know I was in the vicinity of where Emily and Cornelia had stood in rhapsodic joy, awed by the journey they were about to undertake.

"... we were sailing from Montreal, province of Quebec... and the date June 10th, the year of our Lord I shan't say which, because Emily and I have now reached the time in life when not only do we lie about our ages, we forget what we've said they are."

It hadn't taken much doing to sort out the exact date and year Cornelia and Emily sailed. This was due to the fact that on the girls' crossing to England, the *Montcalm* ran aground in the St. Lawrence River within hours of leaving port, which would incapacitate the ship. This would be the first of their many misadventures. Reportedly, the only time in its history the *Montcalm* ran aground was on June 2, 1922. Which meant Cornelia and Emily had been slightly off on the exact date the ship left for England.

But they had been spot on in asserting they lied about their ages, because in 1922, they were twenty-three (in *Our Hearts* they profess to be nineteen).

According to the *American Shipping News*'s article about the incident, it took almost two days to dislodge the *Montcalm* from the riverbed. During that time, the ship rested at a fairly substantial angle, and though the situation hadn't seemed dire enough to have the passengers taken off, a river steamer was stationed nearby in case the boat did capsize. Eventually with the help of a few tug boats, the *Montcalm* was lifted off the rocks and towed to Quebec City.

That was where I was headed now, after my lightning visit to Montreal. In Quebec, I would spend the night in the same hotel where Emily and Cornelia stayed after their adventure on the *Montcalm*. Fortunately for them (and me), the CPO line, owners of the *Montcalm*, put the girls up at the opulent (and now historic) Chateau Frontenac.

The company had booked Cornelia and Emily passage on the next ship leaving for England – the *Empress of France* – which was to sail from Quebec City in eight days' time. The CPO line would foot the bill for the girls' stay at the hotel until the ship sailed for England.

Cornelia and Emily were pretty well shattered by the time they disembarked from the limping *Montcalm*. For them, the Chateau Frontenac experience was a blur, but for me, it was a sublime affair from start to finish, as I shared in a blog I created to record my journey:

6

It took only two hours, as opposed to the girls' two days, for me to get from Montreal to Quebec City. I arrived in Old Town (le Vieux Ville) just as their captivating narrow streets lined with ancient stone buildings were beginning to turn on the lights for visitors, who were coming out for the evening to the restaurants and bars. It was love at first sight for me, even before I pulled my rental car in under the arches at the Chateau Frontenac.

This magnificent hotel, built in the late 1800s, has played host to politicians, celebrities and royalty for over a hundred years, and they have done it in a grand style worthy of their five-star ranking. For Cornelia and Emily, after the chaos of their first two days of travel, being welcomed into this "swanky hostelry," as Cornelia called it, must've been a most joyous moment.

"The clerk at the Chateau Frontenac beamed kindly upon us and gave us a large and comfortable room overlooking the terrace promenade. The place rather overwhelmed us…"

Though I was still trying to be cool about it at this point in the journey, it meant so much to me to know I was where the girls had been. And when I was given a beautifully-appointed room matching the description of theirs, I felt for the first time as if the three of us were indeed traveling together.

On June 4, 1922, aboard the *Montcalm* as it hobbled towards Quebec City, Cornelia had sent an SOS telegram to Miss Mary, a longtime, dear friend of her mother's, who lived in Les Eboulements, a village just a little over an hour away from the city. Upon arrival at the dock, Cornelia was handed a reply telegram from Miss Mary stating that she would come and fetch the girls from the hotel the next day, and take them to her home where they could wait for the *Empress of France*.

With these new plans in place, Cornelia and Emily would spend only one night at the Chateau Frontenac. And so would I.

The morning after my arrival at the hotel, I got up reasonably early and spent a few hours exploring Old Town, having tea and some sort of heavenly chocolate pastry confection at one of the darling eateries, before wandering over to the old walled part of the city.

I finished my exploration with a stroll along the terrace next to the Chateau Frontenac and took in the stately beauty of the hotel, hoping someday soon I would have a reason to return. I was enamored with the place and I really didn't want to leave. My stay in Quebec City had been way too short. But it was more important that I keep pace with the girls. I had given myself only a day and a half to check out Les Eboulements. Which meant on the drive to the village, it was a no-brainer for me to breeze right past Montmorency Falls and Ste. Anne de Beaupre – both referenced in *Our Hearts* – with barely any more recognition of them than taking my foot off the gas pedal as I sped by.

Of Les Eboulements, I posted:

My much-too-quick jaunt through Canada continued on Monday, when I drove about seventy miles east from Quebec City to the little town of Les Eboulements. In Cornelia's and Emily's day, the name "Les Eboulements" referred to two villages that resided on the same hillside. Today the former lower village is known as St. Joseph, while the upper village is Les Eboulements ("Falling Rocks").

I mention this only because Cornelia and Emily talk about staying in Miss Mary's log cabin located halfway between the upper and lower villages. This is, coincidentally enough, pretty much where the hotel I stayed in is located. It is immensely satisfying when I manage to drop into the girls' footsteps, and even more so when it happens by accident.

Cornelia wrote this about Les Eboulements:

"It was unspoiled by trippers then and I hope it still is, for the country was incredibly beautiful, the houses quaint and the natives charming."

While there didn't seem to be any trace of Miss Mary's log cabin, and doubtless some of the old houses have given way to more modern ones, Cornelia and Emily would be pleased to find that the picturesque little hamlet they knew is in many ways exactly the same.

The auberge (French for "inn") where I stayed – L'Aunthentique Auberge de Charlevoix – is owned and operated by a warm and welcoming family. Matthew (or is it Mathieu?) greeted me as if we were old friends, and we talked about his years as a tour guide, and how he brought groups of Canadians to Venice Beach (talk about culture shock!). His mother Joanne, who spoke very little English, was sweet and patient with my French, and we managed a few brief but pleasing conversations. And in the mornings, they prepared the most divine breakfasts, with crepes and cheeses made in nearby Charlevoix added to a generous plate of eggs, tomatoes, sausages and roasted potatoes. If that wasn't enough to recommend the place, directly across the street from the auberge is the town chocolaterie and ice cream shop. Just as it had been with Quebec City, it was irksome to have to leave here right away.

During my stopover, one Our-Hearts-book-nerd item I was able to check off my list was sorting out the story of the Seigneur, a local luminary, and his manoir.

The girls talk about meeting this man at his home: "The manoir, the Versailles of Les Eboulements, was a sweet old rambling frame house." After a bit of searching, and driving past the place a few times, completely oblivious, I located le Manoir. The sign "Camp Le Manoir" should have tipped me off. Turns out, the house was sold in the 1940s to the Freres du Sacre Couer who, with the addition of a few cabins, turned the place into a camp for kids. So not everything is exactly as it was when Cornelia and Emily were here.

I was just so pleased to know definitively that I had found the right place, mainly because it is tied to a significant event later in the girls' journey, to which Cornelia alludes:

> "Miss Mary later enlightened us concerning the status of [the Seigneur]. 'He holds,' she said, 'through direct descent his feudal rights by charter from the king and the people pay him their tithe. While the parish priest rules them morally, the Seigneur looks after their economic

and physical welfare.' Little wot we at the time how his supervision of the latter was going to affect us."

Two versions of grand style: the sublime Chateau Frontenac in Quebec City; the Manoir du Seigneur in Les Eboulements.

At one point in my exploration of the area, I could see mountains in the distance and wondered if they were where the girls had gone on a picnic one day with Miss Mary, where she had rolled her cigarettes with one hand. Then there were the pastures with cows like the girls would have seen, only now there were alpacas roaming in the fields as well, which no doubt Cornelia and Emily would have enjoyed. I couldn't venture to guess where Miss Mary's cabin might have been, but just in standing on the hillside, looking at the St. Lawrence, I felt close to her and her sister, Miss Bessie, and was struck (for the first of many times) by how fleeting time is. How those women in the book had looked at these same views, and had at one time been just as alive as I am now.

It reminded me of the scene in "Raiders of the Lost Ark" where the French archaeologist Belloq says to Indiana Jones about the Ark of the Covenant, "We are simply passing through history." Cornelia and Emily had passed through this little town of Les Eboulements. Just as I was doing now. And they had passed through history. Just as I would someday do as well. It wasn't a sad thought, but it was a weighty one, and it had come out of nowhere on a lovely summer day.

After staying in Les Eboulements for those eight days, Cornelia and Emily returned to Quebec City and boarded the *Empress of France* on June 13, 1922. This time there would be no mishap traveling up the St. Lawrence River, and they would make it to open water and begin their journey across the Atlantic, where the wonders of Europe were waiting for them to arrive.

I could only offer a passing nod to Quebec City on my return journey, as I turned south and headed to the border. I wrote in my blog:

All too soon, it was time to leave Les Eboulements and head to the States. But first, I stopped in and picked up some wildly tempting chocolates to take as a gift to my next interview. Even with a five-hundred-mile drive from Quebec to Connecticut, I am proud to say, that box of chocolates made it the whole way without ever being broken into. But the other box I bought for myself was gone before I got to Charlevoix.

Chapter 2

I was eager to begin my own voyage to Europe, and could hardly wait until the moment I would step aboard the *QM2* and raise a glass to the New York City skyline with my fellow passengers, as the ship pulled away from the dock and glided past the Statue of Liberty. But first things first. I still had some stops to make, and more research to do about Cornelia and Emily and their story. On my way from California to Montreal, I had broken my journey in Chicago in order to learn more about Emily from her niece, Linda.

I met Linda Kimbrough at a coffee shop and found she was pleased to talk about her Aunt Emily. Linda, a theatre and film actress, along with her brother Charles, had been inspired and emboldened by their Aunt Emily to pursue careers as actors. That little girl from Muncie, Indiana, had grown into a fearless, dynamic woman who made her nephew and niece believe anything was possible.

Linda had brought with her what few pictures she had of Emily: one of her at around age thirteen, with her brother (Linda's father, also named Charles) by a swimming pool; one of her with the group who traveled together in Emily's book, *Floating Island*, which included Linda's parents along with Cornelia (and her husband, I believe); and a photo of Emily and Sophie Yarnell, another longtime friend from Bryn Mawr, attending a dinner/fundraiser for the Urban League.

As for the rest of Linda's photos, she explained that at one time she had an extensive collection of family pictures, but they were accidentally thrown out by a work crew when they were clearing out her attic. An irreplaceable loss.

Linda shared a lot of memories about her aunt, which I related in my blog post, "And I thought I knew Emily Kimbrough":

Spending an hour with her niece, Linda Kimbrough, at Eva's Café in Chicago was an eye-opener for me about Emily. Linda admired and adored her aunt, and she shared not just fond memories, but also insights about Emily, which altered the way I view her.

Linda, of course, knew her Aunt Emily not as the girl from the book, but as a woman – and a famous one at that – who, as a divorced

mother of twin daughters (in a day when no one got divorced), worked as a magazine editor, radio broadcaster and travel writer. In fact, the first thing Linda mentioned to me was in regards to Emily's job as editor of the 'Ladies' Home Journal':
    "An early feminist, before anyone knew what that term meant, she reframed that magazine from something about taking care of your husband to something about taking care of yourself, and shifted the whole way in which women started to perceive their matrimonial vows."
    Emily, according to Linda, was indeed the gracious, effervescent woman whom I pictured her blossoming into, but she was also sharp and extremely intelligent. She did the New York Times crossword puzzle religiously (even Saturday's), and was a "profoundly killer Scrabble player". When one sat down to a friendly game during a weekend visit to Emily's country home, that guest was invariably trampled and left for dead.
    Even Emily's voice was different from what I imagined. It seems the Midwest accent from her childhood in Indiana disappeared, and her voice was deep and clipped and "upper crust". Linda relates, "She had this incredible, low, very powerful voice and when she would call you on the phone, it was frightening... She set you back on your heels. You did not relax with Emily... She was a tough lady."'
    Tough? Funny, fluttery little Emily?
    I asked Linda if she recognized her Aunt Emily in the girl portrayed in **Our Hearts Were Young and Gay**, *and she was quick to respond quite simply, "No." So why did Cornelia and Emily, writing as successful, intelligent women, choose to portray themselves as such light creatures? Linda offered this theory, "I think some of it is their sense of what would sell. They wanted to write a book that people were going to identify with, and how many people had daughters that had as much guts and sand as those two did? So I think they made a few alterations."*
    "But then of course... I didn't get to know my aunt until she was a force to be reckoned with, the kind of woman who took no prisoners and stood up for herself and framed her own career."
    What a thing it must've been for Linda and her brother Charles, as children, to be exposed to such a dazzling figure. Linda is an actress of both stage and screen (I didn't bring up her film with the brilliant Phillip Seymour Hoffman, "State and Main", even though I very much

wanted to), and Charles Kimbrough, along with decades of performing on New York stages, is probably best known for his role as anchorman Jim Dial on "Murphy Brown". Both of them give credit to their Aunt Emily for inspiring them to take the leap of faith and pursue careers in the theatre.

I wish I could've met the free-spirited, irreverent young Emily, but I would have liked even more to have known the remarkable woman she became. Even though she probably would've intimidated the heck out of me.

Author with Linda Kimbrough.

Linda shared many other interesting tidbits and anecdotes, which I didn't include in the blog post. She talked about Emily's four-course dinner parties, and how dinner every night was formal – almost Downton Abbey-like.

Emily and her brother had been raised that way by a family who had pulled themselves up by their bootstraps and worked hard for their success. Emily's grandparents and parents adopted the finest manners and strove to be like 'proper society folks'. These ideals were passed along to Emily, who embraced them herself, and lived her adult life by those same standards.

Recalling stories she knew of the time when Emily went to Hollywood to write the screenplay for *Our Hearts*, Linda told of how Emily became friends with Elizabeth Taylor's mother. Emily's twin daughters were right around the same age as Elizabeth, so the three of them had played together.

Also, Linda mentioned Cornelia, having been around her multiple times. It was heartwarming for me to have affirmation that those two girls from *Our Hearts* had maintained a close friendship throughout their lives. In Linda's recollection, Cornelia had always struck her as being somewhat in awe of Emily, just as she had been in their youth. Emily, it seemed to me, was a dominating presence. I had always imagined her to be charismatic and a little flighty – but I had never given her any credit for having grit.

A remarkable woman, no doubt, but certainly not who I had pictured. "A tough lady," according to her niece.

This new understanding of her had left me, strangely, a little shaken.

My first stop on my way down from Quebec was in Northampton, Massachusetts, at Smith College. The reason for this had to do with one of the biggest moments of Cornelia's and Emily's journey: the day they went to H.G. Wells' house for lunch. As in *the* H.G. Wells.

Otis Skinner had become acquainted with Mr. Wells on a prior visit to Europe, and now Mr. Wells had invited the Skinners and the girls to lunch one Sunday at his home in Dunmow, about an hour and a half northeast of London. Naturally, Mr. Wells' invitation was accepted with great pleasure. And the day itself would prove to be most memorable for all parties, for myriad reasons.

I shared a few of the juicy bits in my blog about my visit to Smith:

.. it is at Smith College where Margaret Sanger's papers are kept. And those who have read **Our Hearts Were Young and Gay** *will remember that when Cornelia, Emily and Cornelia's parents went to H.G. Wells' house, known as Easton Glebe, Mrs. Sanger was also a guest there that day, as Cornelia recalls:*

> "There was another American present, Mrs. Sanger, better known as Mrs. Birth Control Sanger. Mr. Wells said she was crusading for a noble cause and Emily and I, who hadn't the remotest idea of what Birth Control even meant, said, Yes, indeed, wasn't she?"

Along with Margaret Sanger, the girls met an additional guest,

"… a very distinguished gentleman with a shock of white hair. Mr. Wells [introduced the man], 'This is the greatest educationalist in all England'… And that was the nearest approach we got to an introduction to him. We never did learn his name…"

One other tidbit of information of which Cornelia and Emily were unaware that day (and they most likely never discovered, even when they were setting their story to paper) was that Margaret Sanger and H.G. Wells were lovers at the time of the girls' visit, and had been so for a couple of years. From when the pair was first introduced to each other in 1920 until Mr. Wells' death in 1946, they "carried on an infrequent, but often fervent [extramarital] love affair…," according to The Margaret Sanger Papers Project at New York University.

One can't blame Cornelia and Emily for not knowing this. Heck, I had never heard it before I stumbled upon the NYU article. And I must admit, once I found out about their relationship, I was keen to go snooping in Mrs. Sanger's papers and read some of the couple's correspondence to each other.

What actually compelled me, though, to visit Smith College was not love letters between the couple, but a photograph of them with Otis Skinner, which appears on the Sanger collection website.

Otis Skinner, Margaret Sanger and H.G. Wells at Easton Glebe.

*In **Our Hearts Were Young and Gay**, Cornelia and Emily write about taking photographs during their visit that day, and that Emily was the only one with a camera. What is the likelihood that Otis Skinner and Margaret Sanger ever visited Easton Glebe simultaneously beyond this one occasion? Next to nil, one would assume. Which leads me to believe that the photo in the Margaret Sanger collection was taken on the day of the girls' visit, by Emily.*

But that is still not the main reason for my visit.

According to Cornelia,

"Emily managed to get one successful exposure and while it is not a thing of particular beauty… some day someone may recognize the Great Educationalist and be able to enlighten us concerning his identity."

Could it be that this photo of the Mystery Man still existed?

Knowing that Margaret Sanger had at least one photo from the day led me to hope that she might have received and kept others which were sent to her by Emily, or Maud Skinner (who was an early supporter of Mrs. Sanger's). It seemed worth a shot to poke around in the archives. So, I paid a visit to the Special Collections Department of the Nielson Library.

The Sanger collection is extensive, but so well organized that it didn't take long to narrow down the search. While I didn't end up putting my hands on any love letters, within twenty minutes I was looking at the picture I had seen on the website of Sanger, Wells and Otis.

And then, a couple of envelopes beneath it, in that same folder, it was there: the mythical photo of The Great Educationalist.

Or at least I have to believe that is what it is. The photo appears to be Cornelia and Emily sitting on the steps in the garden with Mr. Wells' son, Frank, along with Frank's friends (they are mentioned briefly in the book), and a man with a shock of white hair.

I had been looking for a needle in a haystack.

And it was there.

Sometimes you get lucky.

So who is The Great Educationalist after all? That's a story, and a conundrum, for another day, which involves the H.G. Wells Society, conflicting dates and a sudden, dramatic demise.

Cornelia (bottom center) and Emily (top right) with Frank Wells (bottom right), son of H.G. Wells, along with two of Frank's friends from university and The Great Educationalist (top left).

Following my visit to Smith College, I drove to Hartford, Connecticut, where I would be staying for the next three nights. The place I booked seemed decent enough, with a mixed bag of individual travelers and families, and a longer-stay resident with a lovely dog who all of the staff fussed over. The staff was nice, but everyone I encountered at the front desk seemed extremely overworked and stressed.

After my long day and drive, I was so thankful to be where I could just relax for the night and prepare for the big day tomorrow. So when I got to my room and there were no sheets on the bed, or towels, and the whole place smelled of pee (not dog pee, but human pee), I was none too happy.

But when I went to the desk, the poor woman working there was on an interminable phone call and seemed on the verge of a breakdown. I didn't dare ask for a room change. I just simply waited patiently until she was able to get off the phone, and then calmly requested towels and sheets. She apologized profusely as she rustled up some linens for me. I told her it was all fine.

Because really, in the grand scheme of things, it was.

After all, nothing – not even a pee smell – could dampen my spirits, when I considered what the next day would bring: I was finally going to be introduced to Cornelia Otis Skinner, by someone whom I was thrilled to be meeting as well.

Chapter 3

Thursday, May 25 was one of my biggest days. I would be visiting the Abbey of Regina Laudis to meet Mother Dolores Hart, as my blog post explains:

*When I first got the idea to follow in the footsteps of **Our Hearts Were Young and Gay**, I couldn't have imagined all of the remarkable, diverse places this journey would take me. But almost from the beginning of my research, there has been one marvelous (and sometimes surprising) discovery after another.*

I was able to learn a lot about Emily Kimbrough through her niece Linda, but Cornelia Otis Skinner doesn't have any living blood relatives for me to speak with about her. Thankfully and most wonderfully, though, Cornelia has Mother Dolores Hart. In 1958, the two starred together in the Broadway play, "The Pleasure of His Company", where Dolores played Cornelia's daughter. The play ran for over a year, and Dolores formed a deep bond with her on-stage mom. Both women were nominated for Tony awards in 1959 for their work in the play.

When I initially discovered Dolores Hart's connection with Cornelia, I had mailed a letter to Mother Dolores, asking if she might share her memories of Cornelia with me. Soon after I received a call from Mother Lioba at the Abbey, informing me that Mother Dolores would be glad to speak with me about Cornelia, and that she was very happy I was doing this project.

I was, quite simply, overjoyed.

How many times had I seen the 1960 film "Where the Boys Are" and wished I could be "Merritt", the character Dolores Hart had played?

"And now Dolores Hart thinks what I'm doing is cool," I gushed to myself.

Ever since the conversation with Mother Lioba, I had been eagerly awaiting my day at the Abbey.

I'd even gone out shopping in search of a suitable outfit to wear for my visit. What I ended up purchasing was a lovely sleeveless dress with a full skirt and a large blue and white floral print. It wasn't until later, upon reflection, that I realized I'd chosen a vintage-looking dress in the style that "Merritt" from "Where the Boys Are" would've worn. Here is what I wrote about my day at the Abbey in my blog post:

Many of you already know Dolores Hart's story: Talented, beautiful rising star in Hollywood, gave Elvis Presley his first screen kiss, appearing in films alongside Anthony Quinn, Montgomery Clift and Myrna Loy, just to name a few. Then in 1963, she stunned the world by walking away from her successful showbiz career to become a nun.

A brief bio on Cornelia: Considered to be the offspring of theatre royalty, Cornelia found that many times she wasn't hired for a role because producers felt it was too small and beneath her pedigree. So, harnessing her sharp wit and talent for writing, Cornelia started creating monologues for herself, and began performing them wherever she could find a willing audience. Soon she had built a career by starring in her own one-woman shows (I hope desperately to someday come across a script for her "The Six Wives of Henry VIII" because it sounds like it was brilliant!). By 1958, when she was starring in "The Pleasure of His Company", Cornelia was considered Broadway royalty in her own right.

Dolores Hart, age 20, beat out over five hundred other actresses from both coasts for the role of "Jessica", and found herself working alongside not just Cornelia but other legends of the theatre like Cyril Ritchard and Charles Ruggles. For her first appearance on Broadway, she couldn't have gotten luckier. What could have been a terribly intimidating experience turned into a joyful one, mostly due to the reception she received from Cornelia.

"I knew I was working with a mountain of a woman, but when I first met her, she was so endearing. She never put me off with a feeling that she was 'the one', and I was just coming in on it. She was just a dear mother in the part, and, 'Ah, it is so nice to have you with us, and if there is anything I can do, let me know.'"

Back in Chicago, when I had interviewed Linda Kimbrough, I had asked her if she had ever met Cornelia, and Linda said she had been around her occasionally, and that Cornelia had always struck her as being shy. I asked Mother Dolores about this.

"Shy? I could see where, in front of people she didn't know, that she would be reserved. She knew us very well, so she had a certain freedom with us, but with others, I could see that. She had such a stability. She was never full of herself in any way. I've seen some of the bigwigs walk onto a set and turn it into a circus just because they were there. She didn't demand attention. She was just so completely a lady."

Growing up in the theatre and her decades on stage had made Cornelia a consummate professional, as unflappable as she was talented. Mother Dolores shared a story about one night when the lights went out on stage during a scene between her and Cornelia. Without missing a beat, Cornelia whispered to Dolores to follow her lead, and then launched into a monologue about how the electricians had been messing with the lights and she must check all of the sockets to get them working again. She moved around the set, improvising lines about what could possibly be the trouble, until the lights finally came back on.

"Her doing that monologue while the house was dark really struck me, and it struck me that possibly one of the reasons she could do that – and no other actress could do that – was because of her monologues. She could put it together, and she could do something like that in the dark. She kept the audience with her. She had it in her bones. I just don't know how many actresses could have pulled that off."

Mother Dolores appreciated and enjoyed Cornelia's spirit, sense of humor and wit, but what she remembers with the most fondness is her "play mom's" kindness. Off stage, Cornelia looked after her young co-star, giving Dolores furnishings for her apartment, inviting her to parties in her townhouse, and becoming a doting and affectionate surrogate mother.

The men who played Dolores's father and grandfather in the play, Cyril Ritchard and Charlie Ruggles, also developed a similar, paternal affection for her.

"I think probably that was one of the most saving experiences in my life in the theatre, working in that show, because it put me into a family that I never experienced [in my own life]. They treated me like *their grandchild, like their child, very sweet and very giving to me on that line. And that was a whole year of my life."*

*What a magnificent woman that girl from **Our Hearts Were Young and Gay** turned out to be. Just as I felt after talking with Linda Kimbrough about her Aunt Emily, I wish so much that I could have met Cornelia – even if only just to say thank you to her for bringing me together with my wonderful new friend, Mother Dolores Hart. Thank you, Cornelia.*

It was a rainy, raw day in Connecticut when I visited the Abbey, but it didn't matter in the slightest. Mother Dolores had invited me to come to the noon services that day, and then have lunch in the guest refectory. The day we were to meet was Ascension Day, and the Abbey would be celebrating the Feast of the Ascension.

I said an enthusiastic yes to all of it.

The Abbey of Regina Laudis is set in beautiful countryside between some of those picture postcard New England towns, less than an hour from Hartford. Originally I had planned to arrive early and explore the grounds in the public areas of the Abbey, but the muddy weather made this out of the question.

Once I parked the car, I gathered up the chocolates I had managed not to eat on the drive from Canada, and went to the "front door", which was inside a charming atrium filled with a variety of plants and adorned with some beautiful stained glass windows which had been crafted by Mother Praxedes, a gifted artisan.

I rang the bell and went inside to the little foyer. Soon the portress – an extremely gracious elderly nun – came and spoke to me from the other side of a window opening in the wall which was fitted with small wooden bars. The nuns at the Abbey of Regina Laudis are cloistered nuns, and often their interactions with the public are done through screens, or grilles. I had wondered if this would be how I would meet Mother Dolores, but I wasn't too concerned about having a conversation through a grille, once I read about it on the Abbey's website:

"Someone unfamiliar with the monastic grille may at first perceive the grille as an unwelcoming barrier, yet experience shows that clearly-defined boundaries allow for meaningful encounter and exchange. For us it is analogous to a cell's semipermeable membrane, that in protecting the cell, selectively allows molecules to pass in or out for the life of the organism."

I informed the nun who had answered the bell that I was there to see Mother Lioba, and she picked up the phone and dialed somewhere in the Abbey.

A few moments later, Mother Lioba appeared. She was young, vivacious, and engaging, and gave me a warm welcome. I presented her with the chocolates for the nuns, and she gave me a quick rundown of the day, pointing out where I would find the chapel and the guest refectory, where I would have lunch and also meet with Mother Dolores in the afternoon.

I got to the chapel a little before the Sext (the noon service) was to start, so I could look at the fourteen hand-carved cherry wood stations of the cross, which I had read about on the website. Crafted by Mother Placid Dempsey over a twenty-year period, these beautiful carvings seemed right at home in the dark, warm, intimate chapel, which had been built in 1947.

A few other visitors and guests of the Abbey began to make their way in and be seated for the service. I took a few quick photos, then sat down as the nuns began to arrive on the other side of the screen, and take their places.

I scanned the faces to see if I could spot Mother Dolores, but I couldn't be sure. I was getting so excited to finally meet her that I had a hard time focusing, but I did my best to be in the moment, and take in the beauty of the singing of the psalms.

Lunch followed immediately after the service. The guest refectory turned out to be what one might call "humble". It was a small room with two tables forming an "L" shape, which could just manage to seat eight of us on small stools. The group consisted of a mother and her two daughters, a couple of solo pilgrims, a few young women who were doing internships at the Abbey, and myself.

Everyone was very kind, and the conversation was interesting, but I couldn't help feeling out of place. All of the other women were there as worshippers, to share in the faith. I was there to interview a former actress. Luckily, the conversation stayed mostly on the work the girls were currently doing at the Abbey, which consisted of a number of daily chores (the Abbey has a working farm, with cattle, sheep and other livestock), as well as helping with an early harvest.

Lunch itself was a treat by even fine dining standards. As it was Ascension Day, the nuns had prepared a true feast. We had prime rib with potatoes and peas, and a gorgeous custard for dessert. The other visitors told me that this was in fact a feast for them, and that normally meals are much simpler – soup, salad, bread and cheese.

I suddenly understood fully how fortunate I was to have been invited to visit on this day, and I felt deeply honored.

There was a bit of time between the conclusion of lunch and when I was to meet with Mother Dolores, which I used to explore the Abbey gift shop and purchase some tea towels and homemade soaps shaped like roses.

It was then time to meet Mother Dolores. I went back to the refectory, got myself situated on a stool, with my notes in hand and the app on my phone ready to record, and I waited.

A few minutes later, Mother Dolores came in, on the other side of the screen I had thought of only as a pass-through to the pantry area.

So, we would be speaking through a screen.

No worries.

Mother Dolores, like all of the nuns at the Abbey was dressed in the full traditional nun's habit, with a white button down sweater over it, and atop her veil she wore a beret adorned with a couple of small pins. We introduced ourselves and then sat down for that interview which I would share in my blog.

For a little over an hour, I asked her questions and then listened, but only part of my brain could focus on her words. I couldn't help but search the face of this engaging eighty-something-year-old woman, looking for that girl Merritt whom I had loved since I was a girl myself.

Earlier in the spring, I had picked up Mother Dolores's autobiography, *Ear of the Heart*, and read about her uncertain childhood, her experiences in showbiz, her friendship with Elvis Presley, and, of course, her year on Broadway with Cornelia.

As it turns out, it was during the time she was doing the play with Cornelia that the young star Dolores Hart first began visiting the Abbey, which would within a few years – to everyone's, including her fiancé's, great surprise and shock – become her permanent home. Dolores had even used Cornelia as her alibi, telling friends that those weekends she disappeared from the city were being spent at Cornelia's summer house in upstate New York.

Now here I was, speaking with this gentle, gracious lady about a world she had left decades ago. At first, I couldn't find Merritt in her, but as we continued to talk, and Mother Dolores recalled stories she wanted to share from the play, the young, hopeful actress Dolores Hart began to emerge.

She beamed as she remembered some of the great kindnesses Cornelia did for her, and it was clear to see that their year together on Broadway meant a lot to Mother Dolores, which was why she had been genuinely pleased to talk with me, and was so encouraging of my project (I suspect I'm the only person who has ever asked her about Cornelia).

I had brought Mother Dolores a copy of *Our Hearts* which I had inscribed with a message of thanks. And I also had my copy of her autobiography which I asked her if she would sign, and she said yes.

When the interview was over, she stepped away from the screen and out the back of the little room she had been sitting in, and came around through a door into the refectory. She wrote the following inscription in my book:

"May 25, 2017
Ascension
Pax
Dear Adrienne,
     It was a pleasure to talk with you and is a joy to have
     you now as a friend.
                         Love, Mother Dolores Hart OSB"

"Dolores Hart considers me a friend!" I yelped inside my head. On the outside, I did my best to play it cool, but I was over the moon.

Then I asked if we could take a picture, and we took one with my phone and then with hers. We talked about the recorder app I had used, and I downloaded it onto her phone and showed her how to use it. Because that's the sort of thing we friends do for one another.

And then it was time to go. We said our goodbyes, with Mother Dolores inviting me to come back any time – wondrous! On that happy note, I left the refectory and scuttled out into the rain to the car.

The day had exceeded my expectations, despite the weather, and I was in fine fettle as I pulled my rental car into the hotel parking lot. Even that smelly room of mine wouldn't be able to bring me down.

As I was turning off the ignition, I got a call from Mother Lioba. It seemed that right after I left the Abbey, Mother Dolores had gone into her office, dug through her archives (which are substantial), and pulled out some things she wanted to share with me. Mother Lioba asked if I could come back there on Saturday morning, to which I said yes, absolutely.

We hung up and I just sat for a moment in wonderment. This marvelous day had just gotten even better. Sharing her stories with me had clearly meant something to Mother Dolores, and that thought gave me such joy. I went up to my room and called my parents to fill them in on the day's triumph.

After I spoke with my mom and dad, I checked out my photos from the day, excited to post my picture with Mother Dolores.

What a disappointment it was!

The lighting was bad, casting some dreadful shadows which weren't flattering to either of us. My hair was a mess from the rain, and overall the angle was bad.

Still, it was all I had, and I certainly wasn't brazen enough to try for another selfie when I saw Mother Dolores again, so I went ahead and posted my displeasing picture of us, before setting to work on my blog post and reliving the day.

In Chicago, I had been "set back on my heels," as Linda Kimbrough would say, by what she had told me about her Aunt Emily. My perception of Emily Kimbrough had been far from who she was, or at least who she turned out to be. It had been necessary to recalibrate my thinking, and view Emily in a whole new way as I was re-reading *Our Hearts* for the umpteenth time.

It still seems funny to imagine being intimidated by zany little Emily, but I'm pretty certain I would have been. And actually, I admire and respect her all the more for becoming a woman of great substance. With Cornelia, while I had gained a new perspective on who she was, how I had envisioned her as a grown woman hadn't been changed that drastically.

That somewhat awkward girl in the book, who had tried so hard to be glamorous and sophisticated and was forever failing, became not just the famous Broadway actress of great talent and wit. She had also blossomed into an elegant, gracious and caring lady, and someone I would have wanted to emulate.

Chapter 4

The following day was centered around my next-to-last pre-voyage research stop. It was time for me to learn more about *Our Hearts'* leading men. This involved me driving from Hartford to Boston, to the Harvard medical library, where I had arranged to view some of the papers of two of the University's most notable graduates, Dr. Paul Dudley White and Dr. Joe Aub. My blog post explains the men's connection to the girls and recounts the highlights:

It turned out to be a stroke of good luck for Cornelia and Emily that the Montcalm ran aground, and they had to switch vessels. Sailing to Europe on the Empress of France, not only did the girls have nicer accommodations on a fancier ship, but they also met two young doctors on board who would prove to be the closest thing they had to beaus during their travels.

Writing about them in 1942, Cornelia explains,

"Their names were Paul White and Joseph Aub and they are now among Boston's most distinguished physicians, but at that time were freshly hatched out of medical school."

Cornelia wasn't overstating it when she used the word distinguished for these men. In their later lives, both Joseph Aub and Paul White became extremely important figures in the field of medicine.

Joe Aub was an endocrinologist focusing not just on cancer research, but he also was an early authority on industrial contamination, collaborating with the World Health Organization to promote industrial safety. He would hold high positions at Massachusetts General Hospital, and serve as the Chairman of the Department of Medicine at Harvard.

Paul Dudley White was a cardiologist and a founder of the American Heart Association. He became President Eisenhower's physician following the President's heart attack in 1955. White was a strong advocate of preventive medicine and exercise, and he developed protocols for diagnosing patients which are still used today. He was nominated for a Nobel Peace Prize, and later was commemorated on a U.S. stamp. Part of the Charles River Greenway in Boston was named the Dr. Paul Dudley White Bike Path in his honor.

*In **Our Hearts**, these renowned doctors are just Joe and Paul, two nice young men who spend time with Cornelia and Emily during the crossing to Europe. I won't give away the story here, but the doctors come to Cornelia's rescue when disaster strikes. Later, when the girls are in Paris, the two doctors show up again and take them out for a day at Versailles, followed by dinner, a show and dancing back in Paris that evening. It turns out to be one of the high points of the girls' entire summer abroad.*

I felt it was important to spend some time getting to know these two men, so on May 26th, right in the midst of Commencement Weekend at Harvard, I paid a visit to their Countway Library of Medicine, which houses collections of both doctors' papers.

*In Joe's papers, I found a fascinating set of correspondences having to do with the movie adaptation of **Our Hearts**, and Joe's refusal to sign a very aggressive release form from Paramount Pictures. There are copies of letters Joe sent, along with letters he received from Paul and Emily, as they tried to work out a solution and a response to the studio's request. In the end, Paramount had to make due with a watered-down version of a release, along with a character in their movie which didn't resemble either Paul or Joe.*

(The film rendition of *Our Hearts* came out in 1944, and was well received. Today it enjoys a seven-out-of-ten-stars rating on the Internet Movie Database. So perhaps it seems unkind of me to say I have never cared for the movie.

They did their best. And by "they", I mean everyone in the cast and on the crew, including Cornelia and Emily, who co-wrote the script for the film. But some books don't translate well to film, and *Our Hearts* is one of them. Which is why the riotously funny narrative story had to be doctored up with an occasional wacky visual scene depicting an event which never took place.

In her book, *We Followed Our Hearts to Hollywood*, Emily would write about the experience she and Cornelia had during the production of the film. Needless to say, their journey to Hollywood together, two decades after their summer of independence, was filled with its own hilarious mishaps and missteps. But what intrigued me the most – and validated my stance on the subject – was that, in the beginning, when the idea was floated of making *Our Hearts Were Young and Gay* into a film, Cornelia's and Emily's first reactions were swift and decisive: "You can't make that book into a film."

Turns out, Hollywood can be very persuasive.)

"Dr. White never threw away anything," a member of the library staff had told me.

She was right. Paul Dudley White's collection of papers was comprehensive, to say the least. Just from the few boxes of material I looked through, covering only personal papers from 1920 to 1924, I came across receipts from his tailor, hotel bills, and an intriguing letter from some London solicitors regarding a box of cigars Paul had given to a waiter at a hotel he had stayed in, which had sparked an altercation between the waiter and a doorman, and the doorman having to appear in court for assault.

But the prize I was eager to get my hands on was his photo album from 1920 to 1922. Wearing purple surgical gloves (it is a medical library, after all), I gingerly turned the album's pages and at about halfway through, I came upon some photos entitled "Europe". It began with a picture of the St. Lawrence River, with the caption, "Leaving the dock at Quebec, June 13, 1922…"

A solid start, but then in the next page there were photos of terra firma. Paul hadn't taken any pictures aboard the ship. And I was so hoping for a photo of the girls with their beaus!

Paul's journey to Europe seems to have been a solo trip, or at least one where he wasn't traveling with Joe (in fact, Joe departed the Empress of France at Cherbourg, while Paul continued on to England). Paul traveled to a few cities in Germany before spending what seemed to be quite a while in Andorra. Just another reason he is such an interesting and impressive person – after all, how many people do you know who have traveled to Andorra?

As I neared the end of the album, my hopes were fading fast. But then as I turned to the next to last page, there it was.

The caption read, "The garden at Versailles". And there were Joe, Cornelia and Paul, right in the middle of their wonderful day out together. I thrilled at finding a photo which ties directly to the book, but I was overjoyed that I finally had a picture of Joe as a young man, which up until that moment had eluded me.

In the garden at Versailles, Joe Aub, Cornelia and Paul Dudley White.

After those well-spent hours at Harvard, I headed back to Hartford to rest up for my bonus visit to the Abbey.

The next morning, I arrived at the Abbey early enough to walk around before my visit with Mother Dolores. The day was full of sunshine, and it was warm and beautiful. I strode past beekeepers hives and the red barn-like men's guest house to the open-air theatre which sits on the property. The theatre was built in 1982, and numerous Hollywood stars – friends of Mother Dolores – have come over the years to perform in plays. It is mainly due to Mother Dolores that the theatre exists, and it has become a staple of the community, with numerous productions and events taking place there. It's an attractive rustic structure which looks perfectly in place tucked into the woods.

I then went back to the refectory to meet Mother Dolores. This time, she came right into the room with me, carrying not only her scrapbook from the show, but a bound copy of the script of *The*

Pleasure of His Company, complete with her handwritten notes in the margins. We spent over an hour looking through the scrapbook, with her apologizing that I had to make a second trip, and how she should have thought ahead and brought these out for our first meeting.

Just too, too kind.

She clearly didn't know how delighted I was to be getting this extra visit with her.

This time, I didn't record our conversation. It wasn't an interview, but a chat between friends. I looked at the marvelous pictures of her with Cornelia and the other cast members as she recalled details and backstories to some of the photos. She even offered to have copies made for me if I needed them.

As we talked, she again began to have that glow of remembrance of her youth. She was tapping into a part of her life which she might not often share, or perhaps even think about. There is no question that Mother Dolores has never regretted her life choices, but she also carries with her a fondness for that time in her life before she was a nun, when she was the talented, beautiful, rising star, flourishing in a career she had always dreamed of and worked so hard to achieve.

We came to a plastic sleeve containing the Playbill program for the show, with a picture of Cornelia and Cyril Ritchard on it.

As she took it out of the sleeve, she said, "You should have this."

"I couldn't possibly take it," I protested, "You've saved it for sixty years."

She said, "I have two of them, and I don't need both, so please take it. I would like for you to have it."

I offered no further protest. I was just so deeply touched by her kindness, to give someone barely knew such a special souvenir from her past.

But that is who Dolores Hart is. I was right to revere her all these years.

After we finished looking at the scrapbook, we went through her script (her mom had preserved all of Dolores's scripts from her plays and films, having each one bound in leather). As she turned the pages, Dolores would come across a line or passage which might trigger a memory about her cast mate or something that happened once during a scene. It was a happy year in her life she was recalling, and I was glad to spend as much time there as she wanted to.

The Pleasure of His Company is the story of Jessica, a young woman on the brink of getting married to a nice, rather dull young man (played by a tasty young George Peppard), when her estranged, world-traveling father shows up to attend the wedding (where he also tries unsuccessfully to romance Jessica's mother – Cornelia's character – away from her current husband). Jessica is immediately taken with her father's exuberance and the exciting life he leads, and in the end she decides to go off traveling with him, canceling her wedding, or at least postponing it until she returns.

The play was later made into a movie, with Debbie Reynolds playing Jessica. Mother Dolores shared with me the story which she also recounts in her book about how the Broadway cast had all been told about the plans for the movie, and that they would play their same roles on screen. Soon after, Debbie Reynolds attended the show one evening, and came backstage to congratulate Dolores on a wonderful performance, telling her that she was going to play the role of Jessica in the movie exactly the way Dolores just had.

That was how Dolores learned they were re-casting everyone's parts, except for Charlie Ruggles, who would stay in the role of Jessica's grandfather.

(Sidenote: Charlie Ruggles played Cornelia's father, Otis Skinner, in the 1944 movie version of *Our Hearts Were Young and Gay*. In *The Pleasure of His Company*, Ruggles played the father of Cornelia's character. Small world.)

Mother Dolores and I talked about the play, and I told her, knowing the storyline now, I understood why she had beaten out all of those other actresses for the role. It was the same reason I had loved her "Merritt" for decades. Dolores Hart made free-thinking, independent women a palatable idea in an era when women were just beginning to stretch their wings and create lives of their own. Her characters were smart, unapologetic, and likable. I told her it was a wonderful thing that the play, which was co-written by Cornelia, ended with Jessica choosing the unknown over the safe bet.

Mother Dolores turned to me and told me I could have been Jessica.

Which was about the most wonderful thing she could have said to me. It made me feel that, in some small way, we are kindred spirits – she and I, and Cornelia, all of us.

As for that movie version of *The Pleasure of His Company* – Hollywood changed the ending, so that Jessica marries her predictable fiancé.

Of course they did.

I guess there is that one tiny consolation: at least Dolores Hart did not have to play out the dumb ending.

Once we finished looking at the script, I knew it was time for me to get going. As I was packing up my belongings, Mother Dolores suggested that we might want to get another picture – the lighting hadn't been very good the other day.

And with that, she deftly steered me over to a bright spot near the window, where we would have the best angle of the light. I got a photo of us together, then one of her alone, and she was right on the money – the images turned out great. You can take the actress out of Hollywood… but she'll never forget how to find her light.

That's a movie star for you.

Author with Mother Dolores; Publicity photo of Cornelia and ingénue Dolores Hart with "The Pleasure of His Company" co-star Cyril Ritchard, and Dolores' dog, Pogo.

This time when I left, we hugged goodbye. And that is when a wondrous, inexplicable thing happened. All of this time, I had been trying to see Merritt in the woman I was speaking with, but I hadn't ever truly managed to find her completely. Though she glowed in the remembrance of those Hollywood days, it had been Mother Dolores speaking with me.

But as I was hugging her, I had the strangest sensation that I was hugging that ingénue from "Where the Boys Are". It was her energy, her spirit, and I would've sworn that if I had pulled back and looked at her just then, I would have been looking at the twenty-two-year-old Merritt. In that moment, she wasn't Mother Dolores, the nun in the habit. She was Dolores Hart, the girl I had loved for decades. And I was finally getting to meet her.

My weeks of roadtripping and research had been an enjoyable and extremely worthwhile run-up to my journey, but now I was filled with Cornelia's and Emily's "lyric anticipation". I was just a few days away from sailing on the *QM2* to England, and I was about to come out of my shoes with excitement.

After dropping off my rental car in Philadelphia, I took the train to New York City.

Arriving into Grand Central Station is a magical way to come into New York, and to me it felt very much in keeping with the tone of my journey with the girls.

I would be staying a few nights at the Hotel Edison, an Art Deco hotel in the theatre district – an appropriate home base for researching Cornelia (and her father, too, for that matter). As my cab from Grand Central closed in on the hotel, we got caught in traffic a couple of streets over from the Edison. I happened to glance up and notice that we were stopped directly in front of the Music Box Theatre, where *The Pleasure of His Company* had been performed. I took it as a good omen.

Monday, May 29, Memorial Day, was more of a spring day than a summer day – cloudy, cool, and mostly rainy. I decided it was a good day to stay in and continue getting caught up on social media.

I worked in my room until late morning, when the housekeeping staff started circling, whereupon I took my laptop down to the pretty Art Deco lobby and found a corner to work in.

Soon, the place began filling up with people eager to check in and others waiting to leave. I struck up a conversation with Sandra and Richard, who were over from Glasgow on a quick getaway and were soon heading to the airport and back to Scotland. We talked for around an hour about this and that, and I told them about my book project (I inflicted this on a lot of helpless folks during my travels – for me, it was like taking out insurance that I would actually have to eventually write the book, because I had gassed on about it to so many people).

They were enthusiastic about my project, and asked me to keep them posted on my progress. By the time they left for the airport, I'd found that I had some cool new friends.

After saying goodbye to Sandra and Richard, I worked for a while longer, then decided to venture out for a stroll around town.

I started with a long jaunt up to Emily's apartment on East 73rd St. It felt good to be a pedestrian after all those days in the car. As always, the city was buzzing with energy, and I felt invigorated, even as I fought my way through the masses of tourists swarming around midtown. As I reached Central Park and turned up 5th Avenue, the crowds thinned and I was able to study the architecture and the people, and walk at an unhurried pace.

Arriving at Emily's building, I mentally went through the notes I had written down the evening before, based on Linda Kimbrough's description of it.

The building itself couldn't be mistaken for anything other than the Edwardian mansion it had once been, before being converted into apartments. There was the side garden which she had shared with her friend Sophie. Peeking in the front door, I could see the beautiful lobby Linda had mentioned.

Secretly I was hoping a resident might come in or out, and I could schmooze a quick look around, but no one appeared. Even still, my visit to Emily's home made me feel newly connected to the purpose of this whole project.

I whispered to Emily that we would be leaving soon for England, and then I headed back to the theatre district.

When I had been searching for those who had worked with Cornelia, I had gone through her profile page on the Internet Broadway Database, which lists the plays she performed in, and at which theatres. As I ambled through the theatre district, I looked for and found a number of the theatres where both she and Otis had performed.

I spent some time at the Music Box, trying to take a picture of it which would match the publicity photo I'd come across of Cornelia, Dolores and Cyril Ritchard are walking in front of it.

It felt good to be with Cornelia, and with the Merritt-aged Dolores Hart. I sent good thoughts to my new friend down in Bethlehem, and as I had with Emily, I told Cornelia that we would be boarding the ship for Europe in a few days' time.

Being with Cornelia and Emily in New York was a different experience than being with them at the Ritz or the Chateau Frontenac, because in those places, I had been with the girls. Here in New York, I was with Cornelia and Emily, the women. Women close to my age, whom I had come to know a little bit about. It was unique in my trip, and I was quite pleased to be spending time with these "forces to be reckoned with".

I went back to the hotel to write my blog post about Joe, Paul and my trip to Harvard. In doing so, and comparing it to what I had written about my visit to Smith College, I realized that I tend to refer to the people from *Our Hearts* in the same way Cornelia and Emily do.

H.G. Wells is always Mr. Wells, but in speaking about Drs. Paul Dudley White and Joe Aub, I always call them by their first names.

The staff at the Harvard Medical Library must have thought me rude, or at least devoid of manners, for the way I was so informal about two of their venerable and revered doctors. To the Harvard medical community, they are Dr. White and Dr. Aub. But to me, they are forever those two darling, dashing young men, Paul and Joe.

The day before I was to board the ship for England, I had planned to spend in the Performing Arts Library, which houses a large collection of Cornelia's papers. But it turned out that, when I had originally put in my request for what materials I wished to view (many of which are stored off-site), I had made an error and didn't order everything I was interested in looking through. But the library had been able to gather a few of the most important items for me.

There were Cornelia's scrapbooks from the years when *Our Hearts* had been published, and from when it was being made into a movie. Along with these scrapbooks were two other spanning the time when she was performing in *The Pleasure of His Company* with Dolores Hart.

"Another cloudy, rather gloomy day," I noted to myself as I walked up to Lincoln Center, where the Performing Arts Library is located. After a brief detour into the Metropolitan Opera gift shop, I got to the library and made my way to the collections viewing room.

The first scrapbook, part of my request error, had nothing to do with *Our Heart Were Young and Gay* nor *The Pleasure of His Company*. But I was pleased to discover it contained 8 x 10 glossies of Cornelia in all of her costumes from her one woman show, *The Six Wives of Henry VIII* – the play I would have given anything to see. There was no accompanying script, but the captivating photos of Cornelia as the six wives left me in no doubt that she had created a brilliant show.

Cornelia was a marvelous writer, not just for her wit, but for her overall ease with words and her understanding of her subject. I remember reading her biography of Sarah Bernhardt when I was in high school, and to this day it stands out as one of the best biographies I've ever read – it was engaging, capturing not just the woman but the time she lived in, and giving us not just a list of the events and actions in her life, but who she was, her mindset, her approach to the world.

Cornelia brought Sarah Bernhardt to life.

What an example for me to follow. It's hard not to get a little overawed by this humble, gracious lady who was teeming with great talent.

The scrapbooks for both *Our Hearts* and *The Pleasure of His Company* were essentially collections of press clippings, with few photos, but they gave me some good information.

Cornelia kept scrapbooks for all the productions she was involved in. She seemed to save everything written about each production, even if she wasn't mentioned in the piece.

There must've been well over a hundred articles in her scrapbook for *The Pleasure of His Company.* Many were about the production, and the cast in general, along with some featuring Cornelia.

But she had also saved dozens of articles about her fellow cast members.

Dolores in particular, it seemed.

And Cornelia had given those articles about Dolores pride of place in the pages, to the point where, at first glance, one would assume the scrapbook had been put together for the young starlet by a doting mother. Which, in a sense, is precisely what it was.

A clear testament to how much Dolores had meant to Cornelia.

Part 2

A State Of Elation

Crossing the Atlantic

Chapter 5

"Next morning we woke up in a state of elation… June [2nd] had really rolled around and the happy expectancy of the brides-to-be of that year had nothing on us."

Just as it had finally come for the girls, the day arrived for me to board a ship bound for Southampton. I considered this to be one of the great gifts Cornelia and Emily inadvertently gave me.

In 1922, when the girls traveled to Europe, the only means of getting there was by ship. Yet even for budget travelers like them, the transatlantic voyage was a dazzling adventure.

If I was to properly follow the girls' journey – I had reasoned to myself – it would be necessary to trade the efficiency of an airline flight for the glamour of a transatlantic crossing.

Fortunately, this was something I was immoderately happy to do. Wednesday, May 31. I wrote in my journal about the start of my *grand voyage* with Cornelia and Emily.

"My last morning in New York: I wouldn't go so far as to call it a 'state of elation,' but I woke up in a giddy mood, bubbling with some of that happy expectancy, and finished "packing", i.e. blithely stuffing every last item into my bags…"

The ride to the terminal proved to be very interesting. My Uber driver was a charming, nice-looking man with a Mediterranean accent. He asked me how things had been for me in New York, and I told him about the pleasure of smelling the delicious aromas that wafted into the streets from all of the restaurants. We talked about food, and he spoke of making stews and cooking veggies, and he said if we were married, he would cook for me.

The flirting progressed from there, with him proceeding to explain to me how he was passionate and romantic, and how good we would be together.

I suppose it could have been creepy, but I found it flattering, and a most gratifying way to begin my journey with the girls. It certainly didn't matter in the slightest to me that a lot of what he said was most likely driven by the fact that he was working for tips.

By the time we arrived at the drop-off spot for the *QM2*, he had given me his phone number. When we got out, he handed off my bags to a nearby porter, then hugged me and kissed me on the cheek and asked me to please call him.

As the Mediterranean drove off, the porter who was checking in my bags said, "Your Uber driver was very friendly. Did you know him?"

"No, um, I just met him."

"Really?" The porter seemed dubious.

"It was kind of a long ride from midtown to Brooklyn," I added, as if this clarified everything.

With that, I handed the porter a tip. Giving me a bemused smile, he wished me a wonderful journey. This was not exactly the first impression I had hoped to make with the crew of the *QM2*.

Oh, well.

I breezed through check-in, and was whisked through to a large passenger lounge... where I sat for an hour and a half, along with the last few hundred other travelers to board the ship. This lengthy wait was unusual, we were told, and had something to do with the Coast Guard not allowing anyone on or off the ship. Finally, as the scheduled departure time of 5PM neared, we were allowed to board.

For months I had been ruminating over the *QM2*'s deck plan, so I had no trouble locating my stateroom. I hurried straight there, barely taking in the refined, elegant surroundings.

I had booked one of the recently-added single staterooms. There are two types of single cabins on the *QM2*, and I had managed to score one of six staterooms which featured not one, but two huge round windows. From the moment I stepped inside my cabin, I was in love with it.

I had just begun to unpack when I was summoned to a special muster drill for latecomers. After the drill, I hurried back to the cabin to continue unpacking, then realized it was already time for dinner, so I threw on my Mother Dolores dress (not exactly appropriate – it is a *day* dress, after all – but it was handy and not too terribly wrinkled) and raced to the dining room.

Most passengers on the *Queen Mary 2* share dinner tables in the Britannia dining room. This element of the voyage can greatly enhance one's time on the ship – or not – depending on the atmosphere of the table where one is placed. I knew this going in, thanks to Cornelia and Emily:

> "... we ought perhaps to go locate our places in the dining room... I [Cornelia] went below trying to create an impression of being a seasoned, cultivated traveler. The impression apparently didn't take with the Chief Steward because after one look at me, he allotted us two cards for the First Service (Second was the chic meal) at the table of an obscure officer, the sort who, on a three-class ship, would head a table in student-steerage... it was off to one side near the swing-door where stewards in order to get past had to graze our heads with their trays."

Back in 2003, when I had seized a chance to cross on the *Queen Elizabeth 2* during her final transatlantic season, I had trusted in the girls' wisdom, and selected the later dining option, for which I was rewarded: I was placed at a table full of marvelous people, some of whom I am still friends with, and we had the added bonus of hosting a different officer at our table each night. That was a pleasure in itself, but made more special because each officer brought his own selection of wines for our table to enjoy.

But this time around, I felt I had to be true to the girls' journey, so I opted for the early dinner service. I was shown to my table, only to find, remarkably, that it was the one closest to the kitchen, complete with swinging doors and stewards coming in and out (although happily we didn't have an issue with trays grazing our heads).

Not a chance I would've requested a better situation. Others at the table weren't pleased about our placement, but I was immensely satisfied. Plus, I was just happy to no longer be rushing about.

My fellow tablemates included a middle-aged adventure cyclist from Estonia who had just come from riding across Canada, a retired businessman headed to Europe for the summer, and a pleasant English woman about my age who was just re-starting her life after a painful divorce. But it was the trio of women traveling together who I would come to spend most of my time conversing with during our dinners.

The daughter, a woman in her late fifties, had been a ballerina in her youth. She shared with me how, at the age of twenty, she had taken off to live alone in Paris. She was smart, witty and self-possessed, and I enjoyed talking with her. She was traveling with her mother – also a sharp, savvy, engaging woman – who used to work at the Library of Congress, who took an interest in my book and gave me some great suggestions and research leads for some of my project's more pressing mysteries and questions.

They were traveling with their niece/cousin, a vivacious, mirthful woman who was great fun to be around. What I remember most about her was her lustrous black hair and her wonderfully fancy attire every evening. This lady felt that dinner on the *QM2* called for frills and sparkles, beautiful satins and silks, and always some bling. Though I couldn't hope to match her in style, I certainly agreed with her sense of occasion.

Just as we were being served our entrees, the ship's captain made an announcement that we would pull up anchor shortly after 7PM, and then explained the cause of the delay. It was not the Coast Guard who had been on board all afternoon, but the FBI.

Hmm…

It seemed they were there to investigate a missing passenger from the last crossing, a woman who had embarked in Southampton, but hadn't disembarked in New York.

It's probably best to mention here that the transatlantic crossing between America and England is a direct route, and generally speaking, there are no ports of call along the way. On occasion, the ship will make a stop in Halifax or LeHavre, but there had been no stops on this last crossing, and therefore no other port where she could have disembarked.

The FBI had conducted an exhaustive search of the entire ship and reviewed the closed-circuit footage, concluding that the passenger was not to be found on the ship, which meant at some point during the voyage she went overboard.

The captain didn't elaborate, so we were left to surmise that the woman had gone overboard by choice. Certainly, if foul play was suspected, or even if it had been an accident, the FBI would have stayed on board and we wouldn't have sailed that evening. Still, the implication that this passenger died by her own hand offered very little comfort.

Eerily enough, Emily had her own experience with a jumper on her first night aboard the *Montcalm,* while the ship was stuck on a sandbar. This, Cornelia believed was,

> "… just one more manifestation of the fact that things happen to Emily which never happen to anyone else. On the same instant in which she emerged… onto the upper deck there came from down over the side the sound of a heavy splash, and a moment later the voice of the watch calling out the colorful words 'Man overboard!' Then a second voice, less colorful but more practical, shouted, 'Throw him a deck chair'."

Which is precisely what Emily did. It took all of her strength to hoist one of the heavy teak deck chairs overboard, but she managed it… and dropped the chair smack on top of the man in the water. This caused a commotion which brought a number of passengers, including Cornelia, up onto the deck.

> "We were told that a wretched immigrant who was being deported had seized the opportunity, while the ship was stopped, to jump overboard and make for shore and freedom, but that some crazed passenger had hit him with a deck chair and sunk him. Steeling myself, I asked if he were dead… The reply was no, only unconscious, probably a case of concussion."

As we listened to the captain's announcement, I recalled Cornelia's and Emily's man overboard story, and thought it was extremely odd – not to mention unfortunate – that this strange bit of symmetry should exist between their journey and mine. This was one moment in their travels I hadn't anticipated or wished to recreate.

The upside to our delayed departure was that it lasted long enough for me to hurry through dinner and get on deck before we pulled out of the harbor. Regrettably, though, there was no time for me to change clothes first. I say this because, being attired in my Mother Dolores dress with its full skirt, I knew I was in imminent danger of repeating my less-than-auspicious departure from New York on the *QE2* fourteen years earlier.

It had been a lamentable moment, back in 2003. I had been wearing a blouse and full skirt as we sailed out of New York harbor, and as I was coming down the gangway steps, the wind caught my skirt and sent it up over my head in front of roughly three hundred people.

It had been my own fault, really. I had chosen to wear that skirt, knowing perfectly well that exactly the same thing had happened to Emily when the girls were aboard the *Empress of France*. They had been invited to have tea with the captain one afternoon.

> "We fixed ourselves up to look as much as we could like the sweethearts of the crew and on the stroke of four-thirty went where I called 'aloft' and Emily, who said I was just showing off, called 'upstairs.' Not realizing there might be an inner companionway, we climbed the outside ladder on the windy side. I grabbed my skirt in time to wedge it elegantly between my knees, but Emily arrived with hers well over her head like an inside-out umbrella from which she emerged quite flustered and saying 'Oh, mercy me!'"

It took a concerted effort, but this time around I managed to ward off any flying skirt issues, mostly by employing Cornelia's stuffed-between-the-knees technique.

The *QM2* pulled out of the harbor right at sunset. The sky took on a beguiling pink tone, and the sun eluded the clouds forming on the horizon, which seemed to be placed there merely for decorative purposes. We passed the Statue of Liberty, and barely slipped under the Verrazano bridge – gliding beneath with only about sixteen feet to spare – so close it felt like we could touch its girders. Sunbeams gleamed off of the Freedom Tower, and the first twinkles of evening lights started appearing in the city. The skyline began to shimmer as it grew smaller. And then just as we were pulling out of view of New York, the sun finally succumbed to the clouds, and we had evening. Simply put, it was breathtaking.

Sometimes life is perfect.

At one point, someone handed me a glass of champagne, and I felt very glamorous and cosmopolitan.

Which was a novel sensation. In my normal life, I'm not fashionable. As much as I try to appear tidy, and not go around looking like an unmade bed (as my mother calls it), I rarely achieve "put together" status, and I just don't have it in me to ever be chic. What I can do, though, is be prissy. It's where I shine.

And for me, crossing to Europe on an ocean liner spelled an opportunity to spend eight glorious days being "prissy as you please". As it always pleases me to be prissy, I intended to take every opportunity to do so, to the point of being unbearable.

And in this moment, I was feeling blissfully prissy.

My reverie was short-lived, though, when I made the imprudent decision to take in the view from a higher, less crowded deck.

Even though I knew better, from Emily's experience and my own, I started up the steps of the gangway.

With one hand on the railing and the other holding my glass of champagne, I had no way of controlling my skirt, which caught a draft and blew up to my shoulders as I went up the stairs. At least this time, there was a stiff crinoline under my skirt, which held my underskirt down so, mercifully, I didn't flash my underpants at the crowd of passengers above and below me.

Thank heaven for that crinoline. Sometimes it pays to be prissy.

A while later, after the "sail away" party thinned out and I'd finished my champagne, I went back down to the promenade deck, and found a quiet spot where I stopped and whispered to my 1922 traveling companions, "This is it, Cornelia and Emily. Our journey has begun."

I had made it to the beginning of *Our Hearts Were Young and Gay* – the proper start of the girls' adventures, and my own. Here we were, sailing together, and I was ending the day in a state of elation, as giddy as Cornelia and Emily had been, brimming over with rapturous plans and lyric anticipation.

Chapter 6

June 1: Day 2 and the first full day of the voyage. I awoke on this day with the happy thought of it being the fourteenth anniversary of when I sailed to England on the *QE2*.

Like the *Elizabeth*, the *Mary* is not a cruise ship, but a true and proper ocean liner – the only one sailing today. Many of today's cruise ships cross oceans, but it is not what they are designed for, and the voyages can be rough. Whereas, when an ocean liner hits choppy waters, the captain simply "gives it the spurs", increasing the ship's speed so it slices through the waves, for a smooth, easy ride. And as anyone who has ever sailed from New York to Southampton or vice versa will tell you, a transatlantic crossing is not a cruise. It is a voyage, or a crossing, but it is not a cruise.

*The **Queen Mary 2** docked in New York harbor.*
*Inset: vintage postcard of the ill-fated **Montcalm**.*

The *QM2* has the same nimble lines as the *QE2*, but is sizably larger, being one hundred and seventy feet longer and sixty-five feet taller, hence those anxious moments under the Verrazano Bridge. The *QE2* used to cross the Atlantic in six days. The *QM2* takes eight. Both ships could do it in four, if pressed.

The *QM2* retains the timeless charm of the *QE2*, but is modern and up-to-date. It boasts a planetarium, an extensive, exquisite library, a Canyon Ranch Spa worthy of its namesake, and kennels large enough to carry twenty furry family members on each voyage. The public rooms are beautifully appointed, and even the economy staterooms feel luxurious. A far cry from Cornelia's and Emily's quarters.

> "Our cabin, at minimum fare, was an inside cubicle, so far below decks it appeared to be resting just above the keel… Our luggage, piled in hopeless confusion, covered the only three square feet of floor space…so what time we remained in the place we moved about amid and on top of our luggage in the manner of hikers crossing a boulder-field."

My single stateroom on the *QE2* had been of a similar size to the girls', with roughly five feet of floor space. Lacking a steamer trunk of my own, though, I happily had plenty of room to move around the cabin.

On that crossing back in 2003, my inside, windowless stateroom was not only pitch-dark, but quiet as a tomb. Added to that, the *QE2* wasn't fitted with the modern stabilizers of today, so the ship had more sway to it.

Which meant that when I turned in every night between midnight and 1AM, I was rocked to sleep in total, silent darkness.

Not once did I wake before noon.

I never saw breakfast and nearly missed lunch almost every day.

Thanks to those glorious round windows in my *QM2* stateroom, I would suffer no such fate on this voyage, as long as I kept the curtains open. Easy to do on the high seas, for there is nothing but an endless horizon of ocean on the other side of the glass.

Though I was never invited to have tea with the captain, as Cornelia and Emily had done, our captain did host a series of cocktail parties, which afforded every passenger an opportunity to meet and speak with him at least once during the voyage.

The party I was to attend took place on the second evening of the crossing, and right before it was scheduled to start, a heavy fog began to roll in and envelop the ship, just like it had for Cornelia and Emily, after they had been at sea for two days. And for the next two days, the *QM2*'s foghorn sounded repeatedly while the ship traveled in a cloud, just as it had done on the *Empress of France* ninety-five years before.

"The foghorn started its mournful reiterant barking and kept it up at two minute intervals for three mortal days and nights. Everyone became jittery… Chunks of field ice occasionally scraped the sides of the ship. Shadows in the fog rift took on fantastical shapes and most terrifying of all, one could plainly hear… an echo reverberating from a nearby iceberg."

According to the U.S. Coast Guard Navigational Center, "Icebergs are found in many parts of the world's oceans. Perhaps the best-known location is the western North Atlantic Ocean, which is where the *RMS Titanic* struck an iceberg and sank in 1912. This is the only place where a large iceberg population intersects major transoceanic shipping lanes."

Known as the "ice line", these icebergs float towards warmer waters during the spring thaw, drifting as far as eight and a half miles per day. Which is why, a hundred and five years after the *Titanic* tragedy, the International Ice Patrol issues regular reports on the locations of icebergs. Even with all of the latest, astounding technology aboard today's ocean-going vessels, the danger from ice remains.

(Ice hadn't been the only concern for Cornelia and Emily during their crossing. They had noted that, "Stray mines from the last war… were still menacing the shipping lanes…" One could hardly blame poor Emily for being fearful during their voyage.)

For the moment, I would just have to leave the fog (and potentially a bit of ice) to the captain and his crew. My thoughts, instead, were focused on what I would be wearing to the cocktail party that evening.

In keeping with the historic feel of the journey, my formal attire on this voyage consisted of a number of "vintage" evening gowns – i.e. I had owned them for at least twenty years, including a couple which I wore on the *QE2* back in 2003. For the captain's cocktail party, I elected to wear a white satin gown which I'd always thought looked Old Hollywood – very Norma Shearer and Carole Lombard.

Unfortunately, it didn't fit the way it had when I'd bought it twenty-five years before, and I felt like a sausage stuffed into a casing. Not exactly the look I was going for, but I went ahead with it anyway.

The man at the helm on this transatlantic crossing was Captain Christopher Wells, a seasoned and skilled naval officer with an affable nature and brilliant, quick wit. By the time I arrived in the ballroom and made it to the front of the receiving line, I could see Captain Wells had already greeted hundreds of passengers, and still had many more to go. Clearly this was no time to pick his brain about fog and the ice zone.

(On my first evening aboard, I had sent a note to the bridge, asking if anyone in the crew could enlighten me about possible ice along the sailing route, but I hadn't heard a peep back. Perhaps this was simply too dull a topic for anyone but me to discuss.)

During the captain's announcements earlier in the day, he had informed us that around 2AM the next morning, we would pass over the resting place of the *Titanic*.

It was a sobering idea.

It has always struck me as odd that, for all of Emily's fears (and to a certain extent, Cornelia's, too) about an ocean crossing, and their harrowing experience passing through the ice zone in near-zero visibility, the girls never mention the *Titanic*, even though it had been only ten years since that catastrophe unfolded here in these very waters.

Though I was certain the ice posed no threat to the *Queen Mary 2*, I went to bed that night with the *Titanic* and the *Empress of France* in my thoughts. No wonder, then, I awoke shortly before 2AM.

Climbing out of my warm bed, I perched myself on the sill of one of my enormous round windows and looked out at the ocean for a while. I didn't allow myself to see the heart-wrenching sight of the *Titanic* or the poor souls in the lifeboats and water, but said a prayer for all of those who had been aboard, the survivors as well as victims. And I went back to bed, thankful for the warmth and safety of it.

The next day during the captain's noon announcements, one of the officers informed us that they were adjusting the ship's route so we would now be sailing just below the ice line. He also explained that, while the ship's technology had rendered the foghorn obsolete, maritime law dating back to the 1800s required the *QM2* to sound the foghorn. And so she did, every few minutes for the next forty-eight hours.

Once in a while, I overheard other passengers complaining about the neverending blasts of the horn, but to me they were confirmation that the girls and I were on this journey together.

The *Empress of France* departed Quebec City on June 13, 1922, and it took nine days for the ship to cross the Atlantic. Cornelia and Emily filled those days mostly by mingling with other (primarily young, unattached male) passengers, taking strolls along the promenade deck, gazing at the ocean from their deck chairs, and occasionally punctuating their journey with an unfortunate incident.

I had no trouble keeping busy on the *QM2*. The ship's daily bulletin is loaded with scores of lectures, group get-togethers, demonstrations, ballroom dance lessons, activities and entertainment. On my crossing, they even had a troupe from the Royal Academy of Dramatic Arts in London performing Shakespeare and Oscar Wilde in the ship's theatre. Rarely did I take the opportunity to simply lounge in a deck chair and watch the ocean, or read a book, or fall into a nap. In fact, by the time we would dock in Southampton, I was run off my feet.

Aboard ship, I quickly settled into a routine – two miles of early morning laps around the promenade deck to start the day, followed by a lecture or activity, then a bit of lunch. Afternoons varied, between theatre performances, tea in the ballroom or a few hours enjoying the spa, whenever I felt I was running out of steam, and needed to be quiet and keep to myself.

I would normally awake early enough to go to morning stretch class before heading up for my promenade. The 7:30am class can be a touch too early for vacationers, but it's a nice way to start the day. And there is something wonderful about lying on a yoga mat under the chandelier in the ballroom of the *QM2* which feels quite special.

Out on deck, there was usually a healthy number of people taking morning walks. A lot of them I would see every day, and we would exchange friendly hellos. It was during my daily laps that I developed the habit of stopping in one particular spot on the promenade deck, where I would lean over the rail so other passengers hopefully couldn't see or hear, and I would talk to Cornelia and Emily. I would relate what was on for the day, recall parts of their story, and hope that they really were there with me in spirit.

Arguably the most popular pastime on the *QM2* is afternoon tea, which is served daily in the Queen's Room. Though I did my best not to make a habit of it, often I found myself seated at 3:30pm, downing little salmon and coronation chicken sandwiches, pastries which were almost too pretty to eat, and scones mounded with heavenly clotted cream and jam.

It was always the best part of my day, because it was the prissiest.

One of my chief activities aboard ship was changing clothes. A typical day involved donning exercise wear for the sunrise stretch class and laps around the ship, then swimwear for the spa or pool (the weather having turned sunny about halfway through the voyage), followed by casual daywear for lectures. After that, a day dress for afternoon tea – then back into active wear for more laps around the deck, to burn off the afternoon tea – and concluding with a gown or cocktail dress for the evening.

(For this last wardrobe change, I always made a point of being in conversation with someone – anyone – in the late afternoon, so I could end it by saying, "Excuse me, but I must go dress for dinner." I was really quite insufferable.)

I don't think my fellow passengers had this same experience, but in my zeal to immerse myself in that glamorous Golden Age of Travel, I found it a delightful chore to be continually changing my attire. It appealed to my sense of history, of "how things used to be done".

And it very much satisfied that need of mine to be prissy.

My record for one day was eight times.

(Full disclosure: some of the outfits were repeats – the same blouse and skirt to attend a morning lecture and an afternoon theatre performance, with a swim in between – but it amounted to eight changes. That's a number which would have garnered respect from even the most fastidious Edwardian society maven).

One of the first activities I took on was definitely a step out of my comfort zone: I would go to the get-together of the "Solo Travelers". My fears about having to play "Pass the Orange" or games where you have to pair up with someone were quickly assuaged. Led by Tommy, the assistant entertainment director, the group was designed to give us single travelers our own posse, friends we knew we could hang out with. It had nothing to do with matchmaking.

Still, I couldn't help but be a tad disappointed. Nary a nice doctor in sight. Where were my Paul White and Joe Aub? Symmetry with the girls had failed me on this point.

The ship's dance hosts were all in attendance at Solo Travelers. These are folks, mostly men, who in exchange for sailing for free, are on board to dance with passengers who don't have dance partners, or have partners who don't dance. They were all quite nice, and I would end up hanging out with them from time to time, especially when I would be walking the promenade deck. But I never danced with them – or anyone – on my crossing to Southampton. At least not in the ballroom. I didn't have the faintest clue how to rumba or foxtrot, and wasn't inclined to attempt the ship's daily dance lessons.

Working up a sweat on the disco dance floor a time or two was the most I could manage. No skill required there.

Later I would regret not trying those dance lessons. It was one thing I felt shy about doing, and looking back now, I can't think why that was. But for some reason, I didn't feel up for taking on the ballroom challenge.

Chapter 7

Friday, June 2, 2017, ninety-five years to the day that the girls sailed from Montreal on the ill-fated *Montcalm*.

It seemed only right that on this day, I happened upon the ship's "deck tennis tournament". I was thrilled at the prospect of it, but then discovered that the "tennis" was actually more of a shuffleboard game. The good news was that this game was being played with the same style of rope rings, or "quoits", with which Emily played deck tennis on the *Empress of France* all those years ago.

This turned out to be one of the funniest – and most embarrassing – things that happened to the girls during their crossing.

Out of their desire to rub elbows with fellow voyager Sir Michael Nairn, a peer of the British realm "who had been pointed out to us as the distinguished note on the passenger list", Cornelia and Emily signed up to participate in a deck tennis tournament which he was officiating.

Unfortunately, neither of the girls knew the first thing about deck tennis, which was a sort of hybrid sport which passengers on ocean crossings often played.

Then Emily had the bad luck of drawing first play.

At the start, it looked as if she might get away with it, owing to the fact that her partner for the match was a "champion" deck tennis player. But things deteriorated when it was Emily's turn to serve, i.e. fling the rope ring across the net. No matter what technique she tried, Emily only managed to send the quoit hurtling off to the side of the court, and straight into the face of Sir Michael Nairn.

As a large crowd of passengers watched this spectacle in morbid fascination, Emily made a last, desperate attempt to get the rope ring to cross the net, throwing it as if it were a baseball.

> "Swift as an arrow that rope doughnut shot at a tangent from the court, over the heads of the rapturous audience, down to the second-class promenade and spun the cap off an officer who was just coming out on deck. Cap and missile went overboard… That formed a sort of climax."

Fearing somehow the symmetry I seemed to be having with the girls might rear its ugly head here, and I might manage an equally embarrassing incident of my own, I flatly refused to join the tournament. It looked harmless enough, as these rope rings seemed to stay close to the ground. But after the countless times I had laughed at Emily's misfortune, I definitely had some of my own bad luck coming in these circumstances. Karma demanded it.

As for the girls, they never did get to formally meet Sir Michael and his family.

"Instead we went around with a male assortment which ranged from our two nice doctors to a Princeton lad who throughout the entire voyage remained conscientiously intoxicated. There was also a merchant from Brussels whose English was not his strong point ... and an English lecturer on New Thought or some such thing..."

These days, ships don't publish passenger lists like they had in the girls' time, so I had no way of telling whether any members of the British peerage were along on my voyage. The closest I came to a "distinguished note" was my encounter with an actor who many people would know from the "Star Trek" franchise, though I knew him from another series, where I had become a fan of his.

I had recognized the man's voice when I overheard him speaking to one of the waiters in the Commodore Club. A little while later, I ran into him and his wife at the elevators just outside the bar, and I couldn't resist striking up a conversation with them. It was nothing more than chit chat about the loveliness of the voyage, and I felt it best not to let on that I knew who he was.

Let him enjoy his holiday with his wife in peace.

They were just two of the twenty-seven hundred passengers from over thirty countries aboard the QM2. And from the moment we set sail, it seemed like I was meeting all sorts of fascinating folks, from all over the world.

There was Carmel, an Irish writer with an authentic bohemian flair which could only have come from growing up in the 1960s. She was writing a book on Irish lore and goddess mythology, and had a young Russian lover who adored her.

Two of the most popular passengers on the ship were Seth and Simeon, a pair of darling teenage twins from Kansas City, who were traveling with their uncle. They struck me as very poised and wonderfully polite young men. It was their first trip to Europe – their extremely cool uncle was taking them there as a high school graduation present. I feared that if there weren't other teens on the ship, it could get rather boring for these young men quite fast. But they were old souls, mature beyond their years, and they seemed to enjoy and appreciate the experience immensely.

One evening in the Chart Room bar, I shared a table with a very gentlemanly Australian man whose son is a musician in Los Angeles, and practically a former neighbor of mine. The world felt so big and so small all at once, and every bit of it was here, existing within the graceful confines of the ship.

One unusual activity which the QM2 offers is fencing, something I had never tried. But I had seen pictures of passengers in the 1920s giving it a go (it's probably a mercy that Cornelia and Emily missed this one!), so I felt it was only right for me to have a try.

Fencing turned out to be a very popular activity, with three times as many people wanting to learn as there were masks and jackets to wear. So for our first lesson, we practiced without gear, pointing our fingers to represent our lances.

I had the misfortune of getting partnered with a middle-aged man who took the activity way too seriously. He didn't seem to be having fun with it, and became quite aggressive in his attacks. This would have been forgivable on its own, but he also felt the need to criticize my form and point out to me everything I was doing wrong.

He was right – I was pretty bad at it.

But so was he. Yet I had better manners than to tell him so.

Not sure why he was such a jerk about it all, but I will say he was fervent in his finger waving to an unsettling degree, and leave it at that.

The instructor passed around a mask and a jacket so we could all get a feel for them both. I'd never given any thought to the kit one wears for fencing until that moment. The jacket reminded me of a straight-jacket, and then when I put the mask to my face, it struck me as being rather "Man in the Iron Mask". The thought of putting on both those bits of gear together made me feel quite panicky, and I knew then I wouldn't be coming back for any more lessons.

The finger-waver would just have to find a new opponent to overcompensate with.

One morning as I nosed around some of the less populated parts of the ship, I found myself in the celebrity portrait gallery – a pair of hallways lined with jumbo-sized black and white prints of famous faces who had sailed with Cunard in the past. From Buster Keaton to the Kennedys to H.G. Wells himself (I was gratified to find), I was surrounded by glittering souls from the past. I studied the photos, wishing so much that I could have been a part of their world.

Just to amuse myself, I pulled out my phone, set my camera to black and white, and took some selfies with the portraits, doing my best to insert myself into the action of each photo. I wasn't able to nail one with Mr. Wells, because he was too high on the wall for me to get a good shot. Still, I did manage pretty good pictures with Noel Coward and Bob Hope, but my best was with Joan Crawford, cutting in on her as she dances with Douglas Fairbanks, Jr.

I came away quite chuffed with my efforts. It was some darn good camera work which I managed all on my own, *sans* selfie stick.

About halfway through the voyage, I took the opportunity one evening after dinner to visit Churchill's, the ship's cigar lounge. Cornelia and Emily didn't smoke cigars, but they did smoke cigarettes. This was as close as I would be able or willing to match them.

Stepping inside the glass-enclosed lounge, I settled myself into one of the handsome leather club chairs. After a brief discussion with Sheldon, the well-known, well-liked sentinel of the lounge, I was presented with a cigar hand-selected for me by him, which he had paired with a drink he thought I would like.

Sheldon knows his stuff. Both were sublime.

The only other occupants of the cigar lounge were a middle-aged Russian couple. The husband spoke next to no English, but his wife spoke a little. I was able to learn from her that they had just traveled across the U.S., driving Route 66 and loving it.

How wonderful is that?

For this couple to have heard of Route 66, the epitome of Americana, and enjoy it as they did, even with limited English – fantastic!

We chatted for a while, and then I was off to the disco – another out-of-the-ordinary activity for me – to meet up with my buddy Andrea of the Solo Travelers posse, who hailed from the Czech Republic, and with whom I had promised to go dancing.

From what I could gather from my few visits to the disco, the dance floor seemed to fill sporadically. Sometimes it would be packed, and at other times it would be empty, while groups of men would stand in between the tables and chairs which lined the perimeter, with no one ever daring to actually sit down.

On this night, there was a handful of people dancing and drinking, so Andrea and I had the dance floor pretty much to ourselves. We twirled and gyrated and sang along as the DJ played "oldies" i.e. songs from my high school and college years.

Ouch!

Andrea and I were soon joined by John, an energetic eighty-four-year-old English widower who was known for staying in the disco every night until closing time.

In his earlier years, John had been a doctor and professor, focusing on immunology. He had been a don at Oriel College when Hugh

Trevor-Roper was there. Hugh Trevor-Roper was part of one of the myths surrounding *Our Hearts* which I planned to investigate once I reached England, so I was intrigued by this, and one afternoon I asked John if he ever bumped into the man. He did have a vague recollection of Trevor-Roper, but said they didn't ever really interact.

John and I also spoke about his memories of D-Day and of London being bombed.

"It wasn't the doodlebugs that were so frightening," he said. "It was the stick bombs. When we heard them, we could anticipate where they were going to land by counting one, two, three. I remember those bombs. And I remember being frightened by the propaganda that came in on the radio, telling us we were going to lose the war."

"You remember listening to Axis Sally?" I asked.

"No, this was a man called Lord Hee-Haw," John replied. "His real name was William Joyce. He was a traitor who had acted as a propaganda puppet for the Nazis in the same way Axis Sally did. He just wasn't as famous as her."

"I've never heard of him," I concurred. "I wonder if he has been forgotten to history because he is male. Is that because it seems like a more sinister, notorious crime for a woman to broadcast enemy propaganda?"

"Could be. Or perhaps it's that the women like the 'Axis Sallys' and 'Tokyo Roses' are remembered more simply because their programs were more 'popular', meaning more GIs listened to them," John offered. "In any case, William Joyce was hanged after the war."

Chapter 8

Whenever I'd had it with "trying" for a while, I would treat myself to a few hours in the Canyon Ranch Spa. Though I never indulged in any of the massages or facials they offer, the atmosphere of the place alone was enough to send me into a Zen-like state. The sauna, steam room, pool and hot tub, with a waterfall producing the most sublime white noise... it was pure bliss.

But not, it turned out, without incident.

On one particular afternoon, it was getting late and most spa-goers had long since cleared off to have tea or play trivia in the pub. I was making the most of having the pool to myself when I happened to glance up and notice an elderly man, completely nude, walking from the men's locker room towards the sauna. He crossed paths with a woman coming from the sauna, who looked back at him, aghast. She noticed me in the pool, with my wide-eyed stare, and we exchanged bewildered looks.

Strangely, though, the man seemed unfazed about being nude in a co-ed spa.

Even more strange, this occurrence seemed to harken back to Cornelia's and Emily's story. It had happened in Montreal, right at the beginning of *Our Hearts*, when the girls were staying at "whatever hotel it is that isn't the Ritz" the night before they were to leave for Europe.

After Cornelia pointed out that Emily had under-tipped the bellboy, Emily had chased the lad down the corridor, while Cornelia waited in their room.

"It was some time before she returned. Knowing Emily and knowing that she attracts incident as blue serge attracts lint, I grew apprehensive. When finally she returned her face was the color of borscht before they add sour cream. It seems that after making good with the bellboy, she had wandered back counting her change, opened a door she for some vague reason thought was ours, and had acidly remarked, 'Well, I hope you feel better now' to what, when she looked up, proved to be

an elderly gentleman completely nude. The experience
had subdued her considerably…"

I hadn't stayed in Montreal long enough to give symmetry a chance
to kick in, but it had caught up to me here on the ship.

I was beginning to suspect – and worry—that symmetry wasn't
planning to miss a trick. Was every last plot point in *Our Hearts* going
to manifest for me somewhere in my journey?

Talk about a double-edged sword.

Though I was having a good time on the ship, I was feeling a bit
underwhelmed by the experience. I also had the first of what would be
a number of meltdowns I would experience during my travels. At one
point, I wrote in my journal:

*The voyage is almost over and while it has been lovely, it isn't
the dazzling adventure I had imagined for myself. Is it because this isn't
my first time traveling to Europe? Or even my first transatlantic
crossing? Have I put too many expectations on this voyage?*

*Had a slow-speed-come-apart mid-afternoon, with lots of
wretched thoughts – this whole trip, this whole idea is stupid, nothing is
going to happen to me, there is no story here, I'm trying too hard, I'm
not trying hard enough.*

*Went for a walk and talked to the girls, but I realize now that it
was actually the women who were with me. We had a quiet word at the
railing and it helped pull me out of my nosedive.*

One shipboard tradition which has survived from Cornelia's and
Emily's day to now is the passenger talent show. The magic of this
event is that it has all the potential to be a complete disaster, but almost
always proves to be remarkably entertaining.

On her voyage, Cornelia, being a budding actress with a famous
name, was invited to perform some monologues in the *Empress of
France*'s passenger talent show.

"The next evening, two days before we were to land, was
the night of the ship's concert [talent show]. I had been
asked to participate and had agreed with alacrity. Those

were the happy days when with that confidence of a Bernhardt which is vouchsafed only to the amateur I would recite at the drop of a hat and if nobody dropped a hat I'd recite anyway."

On the morning of the concert, Cornelia awoke to discover that she was coming down with a wicked cold. But she wasn't about to let it interfere with her performance.

"Somebody gave me some aspirin and somebody else gave me pyramidon and somebody else gave me something else and I swallowed it all quite indiscriminately, muttering brave remarks to the effect that 'The show must go on'... Just before I went on, that conscientious drinker from Princeton brought me a hooker of straight brandy and that did the trick."

Just as it was on the *Empress of France*, the *QM2* had a passenger talent show scheduled two evenings before we were to dock. Like Cornelia, I woke up that morning with what felt like the start of a cold.

And that was where the symmetry left off.

I had elected not to take part in the show due to the fact that I had no talent. But I was most eager to attend and learn what hidden skills my fellow passengers possessed.

I wasn't disappointed – it was a panoply of assorted talents, and the whole concert was delightfully entertaining. A man from Taiwan sang an Italian folk song, a man from Cheshire read some original poetry (humorous as well as earnest), an American teenage Guinness-record-holding cup stacker demonstrated his skills, and a Japanese couple did a sultry Rumba to "Lady in Red".

Back in 1922, after the talent show on the *Empress of France*, the ship then had a party, which the girls described as,

"... a gala dance with confetti and favors and those paper hats middle-aged people, if they're drunk, think are funny."

Following our talent show was the *QM2*'s masquerade ball, where folks put on masks and danced to the orchestra. Which was close enough to paralleling the girls' journey to satisfy me. But whereas Cornelia and Emily were never off the dance floor (even in her feverish state, Cornelia danced on into the night), I stuck around for a little while, but made an early night of it. For this I was rewarded – by the next morning, all symptoms of my cold had disappeared.

Cornelia was not to fare as well.

The morning after her performance, she was much too ill to move, and her breathing made the "sound of a threshing machine". Emily brought their young doctor friends, first Joe Aub and then Paul White, to the cabin where they delivered the same diagnosis: Cornelia had measles. After a few moments of bewildered, "How on earth could I have…?", Cornelia remembered an afternoon in Les Eboulements the week before, when she and Emily had visited a couple of cottages and purchased some of the homespun that the women there were weaving.

"The air inside was stifling. All doors and windows were closed. That, they explained, was because some of the little ones had a cold. Some of them even had a slight rash, but the Seigneur didn't think it was anything."

Having a contagious illness as serious as this was something for Cornelia to be genuinely frightened about, and not just health-wise.

"If it became known I had measles they'd never let me land. The ship, after a day or two in Southampton, was to go on to Hamburg and I'd be sent in all probability to a German quarantine hospital."

At the risk of losing their medical licenses, those young doctors stuck by the girls, swearing to keep their secret. Joe and Paul even managed to acquire some pills from the ship's medic without raising suspicion (what a wonderful, easier era they lived in), which helped keep Cornelia's illness in check.

(In Emily's version of the story, she wrote about having sent the homespun fabric she bought to her mother in Indiana, only to learn later in a letter she received from back home, that both her mother and little brother Charlie had come down with measles shortly after receiving her package. Those were some powerhouse germs.)

Luckily for me, I was spared from recreating in some fashion this part of the story, and would be landing in Southampton fit as a fiddle. My only concern with our impending arrival in England was segregating my luggage – a mind-bending task. I needed to make certain I had everything I required for the next eight weeks, because whatever I didn't take with me would be packed in my Really Big Suitcase and stored in Southampton where I would have no access to it.

On the last full day of the voyage, I was in my stateroom, just setting to work on my packing when there was a knock at my door. I opened it to find a dashing, polite young officer holding a thick envelope in his hand. He introduced himself as Third Officer Bissell and presented me with the envelope, which he informed me was in answer to the question I had sent to the bridge regarding our route, along with some charts showing the path the ship had taken. He apologized for having taken so long to get back to me with a reply, and I thanked him for going to all that trouble to answer my question. With that, he wished me a pleasant rest of my voyage and headed off down the corridor.

Diving into the envelope, I found that Officer Bissell had written a two-page explanation about the course the *QM2* was traversing, which included background geography, the presence and ever-shifting position of the ice line, and how we were sailing just below it, with the crew continually correcting our course to stay out of harm's way.

There were also two printed charts, one containing our proposed route and the other showing where the ice line was running, and the course we had taken for the crossing. It had been a lot of work, and I was quite touched that Officer Bissell had gone to such lengths to answer my question.

This happy surprise set me up for a good afternoon, and I spent a couple of hours on deck, installed in a teak wood deck chair reminiscent of the one Emily had dropped onto the fleeing refugee's head. It wasn't long before I went full-on blue mind – that calming, meditative state we fall into when we look at large bodies of water, the ocean in particular. It was a blissful time in that deck chair, as I reflected on the voyage and tried to envisage what might be in store for me once I reached England.

I decided I should get to bed early, because I planned to be up and on deck when we arrived in Southampton the next morning. Aboard the *QE2* in 2003, I had slept through the docking, and I didn't want to miss this event again.

But before I turned in, I went out on deck to enjoy the last moments of sunset. Though the light from the ship made it challenging to see any stars, I could see lights twinkling along the shoreline.

For almost a week, aside from an occasional freighter, we had been alone on the ocean, with nothing but open water to look at. Seeing the coastline of England filled me with sadness that the voyage was in its last few hours, while at the same time, I was euphoric to be stepping foot back on English soil.

In her version of the girls' story, Emily talks about their last evening on the ship, when the fog had finally lifted, and catching her first glimpses of Europe as they passed along the coastline:

> *"That night I went up on the boat deck with Joe, and suddenly those thick, clammy, terrifying clouds were gone. The moon was out, there were stars – and there was a winking light ahead, that was land. Little fishing boats were all around us in the water, and you could see them all. I cried and cried because you could see, and 'what you could see was Europe' I kept saying."*

Later, in those same papers, Emily would mention something about her and Cornelia having "a 'tiff' one morning about someone annexing the other's beau, or trying to, the night before. Could Emily be referring to this night, when she was out on deck with Joe, while Cornelia was in her sickbed with the measles? Possibly.

Chapter 9

Wednesday, June 7, 2017. Packed and ready, I was up early and on deck by the time the ship had come around the Isle of Wight and was making the turn north into the estuary which would take us to Southampton.

Braving the strong, chilling winds, I joined a handful of others who had positioned themselves at the front of the ship, as close to the bow as passengers were allowed to go. At times, depending on the direction of the wind, I was able to use the giant fish sculptures (a.k.a. the spare propellers which are mounted on the deck) to shield myself from the gusts, and at length Southampton drew near as we found ourselves pulling alongside the dock of the Ocean Terminal.

When the *Empress of France* docked in Southampton on June 21, 1922, Emily and Cornelia were in a real bind. By the time they reached the English shore, Cornelia was extremely ill and the tell-tale measles spots were starting to form on her skin. This was a very precarious situation for her, because if the health inspectors got wind of her illness, she would be on her way to that German quarantine hospital/camp.

Joe had gotten off the ship in Cherbourg, France, the first port-of-call, but Paul continued with the girls to England. He and Emily succeeded in slipping Cornelia through customs, immigration and the health inspection, and into the care of her parents, who had arrived in England the week before, and had come down to meet the girls' ship.

After their initial shock at Cornelia's condition, Otis and Maud took her, along with Emily and Paul, to a hotel a few blocks away, where they stayed for ten days while Cornelia was sick.

In keeping with the girls' experience, I had decided to stop off in Southampton, if only for a night, before heading to London. It would give me a chance to properly explore this historically significant port town, and also give me the opportunity to hopefully retrace the path of my 1922 traveling companions.

I had already booked a room at the White Star Tavern, which was right in the heart of Old Town, close to the piers. This was a new experience for me – in all of my visits to the UK over the years, I had never stayed in a pub. It had been a surprise to me on my first sojourn to the UK just how few of these true pubs with lodgings still existed. I thought those charming old tavern inns like the one at the beginning of "Four Weddings and a Funeral" were to be found everywhere. It's a true shame that they aren't.

At the White Star Tavern, I was thrilled to find that I had been given the Titanic Room, one of the inn's finest, with a bay window which overlooked the street. The furnishings had a timeless charm, and the spacious bathroom had been updated with cool twenty-first century amenities and style. It was every bit as good as The Jolly Boatman in "Four Weddings".

After I got settled in, I went for a walk around town.

My first stop was a stone's throw away from the White Star: South Western House, a splendid Victorian building adorned with ornately-carved white stone flourishes which resemble cake frosting.

These days it houses condominiums, but this six-story edifice began life as the South Western Hotel, and it is here where the Skinners and Emily stayed during Cornelia's measles outbreak.

At least I was pretty certain it was. The girls had given a specific enough description of the hotel that, even with the passage of ninety-five years, I was fairly sure I had the right place.

> "The hotel was one of those British terminal ones, part caravansary, part ticket office, right on the tracks, the sort that gives the impression of having engines running in and out of the potted palms."

Opened in 1872, the South Western remained a hotel through the first half of the twentieth century, playing host to a multitude of celebrities and royalty, including Queen Elizabeth. The hotel is also famous for welcoming many of the *Titanic*'s first-class passengers – including Bruce Ismay, chairman of the White Star Line – on the night before the ill-fated vessel sailed from Southampton.

During World War II, South Western was requisitioned by the military because of its close proximity to the docks. It became the headquarters for Combined Operations during the planning for D-Day, which in large part would be launched from Southampton. Churchill and Eisenhower supposedly met here at least once to discuss plans for the invasion on June 6, 1944.

Southampton was an important port city, vital to the Allied efforts during World War II, which made it a prime target for air raids. During the war, the city was ravaged by fifty-seven aerial attacks, with approximately twenty-three hundred bombs and over thirty thousand incendiary devices dropped on it, with nearly forty-five thousand buildings damaged or destroyed, including most of the High Street. Mercifully, the South Western Hotel had been spared any damage from the air raids.

Walking around to the far side of this hotel-turned-residence, I found railroad tracks still inset in the ground, unkempt from lack of use since 1966, when a new central station was opened about a mile away.

Circling back to the entrance of South Western House, I stepped through the doors which had at one time led to the hotel's restaurant, and was reassured to find that today it continues as a café. Though it was clear that things had been altered in the decades between when the girls were here and my visit now, one could still make out the remnants of an elegant showpiece of a dining room. On the walls, there were enlargements of vintage photos of the building, some circa 1920s, and I fervently studied them all.

Moving over to the host desk, I engaged the woman who was working there and explained my interest in the place. In the next moment, she was graciously ushering me through a set of discreet double doors into what had been the lobby of the hotel.

Its furnishings were sparse, but the lobby had retained its sumptuous marble paneled walls and columns, and high, elaborately carved ceiling mouldings. It wasn't clear how the space would have been set up when it was a hotel, but I was thrilled to have gotten a glimpse of it.

I felt certain Cornelia and Emily had clicked their heels on these floors. It was highly pleasing to find that I was starting my travels abroad squarely in their footsteps.

Once outside again, I turned back the other direction and followed along the perimeter of the ancient Roman wall which runs through the oldest part of the city, walking on paving stones which were occasionally inset with brass placards inscribed with bits of Southampton's history.

While the city's main tourist draw seemed to be the *Titanic* connection, I was far more intrigued and moved by the placards noting the *Mayflower* pilgrims had sailed from here, and how it was from these docks that many thousands of the D-Day invasion troops had been deployed.

Afterwards, I drifted along the shoreline to the ocean terminal where the *QM2* was preparing to depart. It made me think of Emily, eager to plunge into the riches of England, but stuck in Southampton waiting for Cornelia to recover from the measles.

> "She'd wander down to the docks and gaze at the ocean liners, but even Cunarders can pall in interest after a while."

From my vantage point, I watched my Cunarder pull away from her pier and turn into the estuary, heading towards open water, where she soon vanished into the horizon. Already sensing how quickly this enchanted summer would pass, I felt heavyhearted knowing the next time I saw the *Queen Mary 2*, my journey would be over.

My days in Quebec and Southampton had been all about finding the places the girls had visited, and putting myself in their footsteps. Now it was time to travel to London and start living the adventures of *Our Hearts*... and hopefully create a few of my own.

Part 3

Having A Whirl

England

Chapter 10

"We were, in our simple fashion, having a whirl…"

Arriving from Southampton into the always-buzzing Waterloo station, I headed for my London residence, as described in my blog:

… I was settling into my home base, a studio flat in the newly-renovated Imperial Wharf area of Chelsea (which, according to an English friend of mine, is very "swish").

When I was first shopping for a place to live on the vacation rental sites, I tried to find something near where the girls had stayed in 1922, which they referred to as "digs" in Tavistock Square. Nothing came up for that exact area, so I opted for cha-cha Chelsea.

Perhaps I should have gone in for something more traditional, or Art Deco – basically something more in keeping with Cornelia's and Emily's world.

*But I think that maybe, subconsciously, I knew I needed for part of this journey to be exclusively my own, and in no way linked to **Our Hearts Were Young and Gay**. Even after the most fun-filled and remarkable days spent with the girls, finding their old haunts and stomping grounds, it's nice to come home to an apartment which didn't exist when they were here.*

Just as it would be with any friends I travel with, at some point I need time and space to myself.

At Imperial Wharf, I was immediately pleased by the look and feel of the place, especially its location on the Thames. I collected the keys to the flat from the concierge office, and my bags and I headed up to the seventh floor.

The cozy space had floor-to-ceiling windows, a beautiful modern kitchen (complete with an American full-size fridge), comfortable, stylish furnishings and a chic, sleek bathroom. Best of all, there were sliding panels of frosted glass which allowed me to close off the bedroom from the living room, for when I wasn't tidy.

It was ideal.

I was definitely feeling spoiled, especially when I thought about the girls over there in Tavistock Square. Opting not to stay near Cornelia's parents, who would be taking up residence in an elegant hotel in the West End,

> "... Emily and I set forth for the more bohemian atmosphere of 'lodgings'. Through some colorful flight of fancy we had made arrangements to take over the rooms of a former Bryn Mawr student who had spent the previous winter working for a Ph.D at the University of London."

(It wasn't until I was re-reading *Our Hearts* in the spring before I made this journey that the full weight of that sentence – "working for a Ph.D" – sunk in. Hardly worth batting an eye in this day and age, but Cornelia and Emily were speaking of a female classmate in 1922 going for her doctorate, which was next to unheard of in those days. Jean Flexner was her name, as I later discovered in Emily's papers. Bryn Mawr was clearly turning out some remarkable, early feminists.)

> "She was one of those brilliant scholars far too intellectual to be concerned with creature comforts, and after we saw the way she lived we came to the conclusion that we weren't intellectual types after all... One toiled up four flights of extremely audible stairs and collapsed into our quarters consisting of two dreary, barren rooms."

Luckily for Cornelia and Emily, they didn't end up staying in their dismal lodgings for too long before Otis and Maud offered to get the girls a room in their nicely-appointed hotel.

My first task in the Chelsea flat was to set up shop on one the barstools, where I would spend numerous hours over the next few weeks pounding away on my laptop, working on blog posts and rambling on in my journal.

The rest of the unpacking I left for the late hours, and went down to explore my neighborhood.

The Imperial Wharf complex boasted four restaurants – well, three restaurants and a riverside pub serving eats. There was a picturesque river walk past some other complexes which ended at the biggest Sainsbury's (grocery store) I've ever been in.

On the way back, I walked through an expansive green space containing a fitness trail and gardens, with a lawn large enough for residents to toss a Frisbee around, and a big fountain surrounded by benches.

At the entrance to the garden, I stopped to say hello to a pillow-soft black standard poodle named Tigger, and made friends with his mom, Sabrina, a Bostonian now living in London with her husband – also American but of Irish descent.

We spoke for a while and she told me about some nice shops and restaurants in the area. She invited me to go on walks with her and Tigger, and we also talked about attractions we were both interested in seeing.

I was quite happy to have made such a cool new friend on my first night in town.

It was getting late enough for the sun to start going down, which in England at this time of year was around 10PM. Before turning in, I wrote a lengthy email to the H.G. Wells Society, something I had been planning to do ever since my snoop through Margaret Sanger's papers back at Smith College.

If I was ever to learn the identity of the Great Educationalist, I would need to call in the big guns. Between them, this group of scholars knows just about everything there is to know about Mr. Wells – including, presumably, who his friends were.

Hoping to enlist the help of the Wells Society in my investigation (and escape the mammoth undertaking of sifting through Mr. Wells' numerous colossal collections of papers myself), I sent them the information I had, along with a copy of the Sanger photo, explaining as briefly as I could about this mystery man, and asking if they might come up with any possible contenders.

Hopefully my question would interest them, and they would take up my cause.

The next morning, I moseyed over to the funky, lively neighboring borough of Fulham Broadway, so I could post a letter I had written to Sir Michael Nairn. Not Cornelia's and Emily's Sir Michael Nairn from the *Empress of* France, but his grandson of the same name, whose address in Scotland I'd managed to track down.

I couldn't know if he was aware of his grandparents' mention in *Our Hearts*, but I was hoping he would find this compelling enough to meet with me. That way I could "finish the job" for the girls by officially making the acquaintance of Sir Michael Nairn.

In the afternoon, I heard from my former neighbors in the States, Amy and Caity, who were staying nearby in Earl's Court with a group of their college music students.

It was their last night in London before heading on to Vienna. Then Amy and Caity would be traveling to Prague and Budapest as a belated honeymoon. Our visit would be quick, but I was tickled that our paths were crossing. They would come by before going to see a show in the West End.

I also heard from Alistair, that former boyfriend and longtime friend from my study abroad days, checking to see if I had made it to London. We talked about when we might be able to get together, but he had a lot of travel and activities already booked, so his schedule was tight. With any luck, we would find some time to meet, as it had been almost three years since we had last seen each other, and I was eager to hear about the plans he and his wife, Sue, had made for their upcoming adventure of climbing Mount Kilimanjaro.

Amy and Caity arrived in time for happy hour, and after a ninety-second tour of my place, we went down for beverages at the riverside pub.

We had appetizers and drinks at an outdoor table overlooking the Thames. Seated next to us was a cute young couple who had brought along their dog, a Pomeranian named Lola, who spent most of her time mingling with guests at the other tables. It turned out that Lola is a regular there. Everyone appeared to know her and she seemed to relish the attention.

Amy and Caity and I had some hearty laughs getting caught up on each other's adventures as the time raced by, and soon they had to leave for the theatre.

Before they left, Amy pointed out that the Thames riverbus stopped practically at my doorstep, mentioning that it was a great way to get to central London quickly. This turned out to be brilliant advice.

Over the next few weeks, I would pounce on numerous opportunities to see friends – old and new, residents and visitors, from both sides of the pond. But I was also very much focused on book-stuff.

Fortunately for me, one of the Cornelia's and Emily's main London activities was something I liked to do as well: go to the theatre. So for my first *Our Hearts*-related outing, I merrily headed up to the theatre district via the riverbus from the Imperial Wharf pier to the Embankment pier. Twenty-two minutes on the boat, then a five-minute stroll up to the West End to my first stop: the half-price theatre ticket booth in Leicester Square.

On my way there, without even intending to, I stumbled into Cornelia's and Emily's footsteps.

My chosen route into Leicester Square took me along Northumberland Avenue, which I remembered as the street where the Victoria Hotel had once been (this was where Otis and Maud Skinner stayed whenever they came to London, including in the summer of 1922).

I had already done research on the Victoria, and knew that it had been at 8 Northumberland Avenue, which was now home to The Grand Hotel.

Like most things, the hotel had changed some since the Skinners were guests there, but the building had withstood the Blitz, and is still a fashionable place to stay.

I had a quick look in at the lobby and bar, with their sublime marble floors, walls and columns, and it didn't take much imagination to picture Otis and Maud, along with the girls, coming down the stairs on their way to an evening at the theatre.

This thought put me back on task, and so it was onward to Leicester Square. At the half-price ticket booth, I chose a musical called "Half a Sixpence", mainly because the script (known as "the book") had been written by Julian Fellowes. Being a longtime fan of his, particularly of his "Downton Abbey", I knew I had to see "Half a Sixpence".

What I didn't know about the musical until I sat down that evening in the theatre is that it is based on a semi-autobiographical novel by H.G. Wells.

Everything is connected.

With any luck, there would be a character in the play who was a Great Educationalist, and my big mystery would be solved.

Once I had scored the ticket to the show, I meandered over to Charing Cross Road, which has nothing to do with *Our Hearts* and everything to do with another of my favorite books, the appropriately titled, *84, Charing Cross Road*. This true story from Helene Hanff unfolds through a twenty-year exchange of letters between her and Frank Doel, the chief buyer at Marks & Co booksellers, which at one time was located at 84, Charing Cross Rd.

This famous street was once lined with booksellers of all sorts, and some of those shops still exist today. But, sad to say – in fact, very sad to say – the alluring antiquarian bookshop where Frank Doel, Cecily Farr, Megan Wells, Bill Humphries and George Martin worked is no longer there.

In its place is a McDonald's.

For lovers of *84, Charing Cross Road* – and all books for that matter – the transformation could not be more crushing. All that remains of Marks and Co is a small brass plaque embedded in the wall, commemorating the bookshop.

At least it's something.

I spent a little time browsing through the other bookstores in and around Charing Cross Road, then had a pre-show drink and dinner at the pub across the street from where "Half a Sixpence" was playing.

The show was highly entertaining, and I also thoroughly enjoyed the conversation I had with two college girls who were sitting next to me in the theatre. They were over from the States, visiting Europe for the first time, on a study abroad course in London.

Kindred spirits.

Still, the best part of my day had been those moments of leaving the present and venturing into the past – Cornelia's and Emily's, Helene Hanff's, and even my own, as I walked through Trafalgar Square after the show, past where a twenty-something me had once stood by one of the fountains and been kissed as the sun set.

I wrote of this in my blog:

It's important to keep moving forward, to keep making memories, to have each new moment count for something. And I hope to come away from this summer with adventures to rival Cornelia's and Emily's, and even my own past.

But one of my initial reasons for wanting to go on this journey was my desire to bring **Our Hearts Were Young and Gay** *to life for myself. To step inside the book, and feel as if I were part of a story that I have long wished was mine.*

Many modern physicists subscribe to the theory that time is just an illusion. That everything which we differentiate as the past, present and future is, in fact, all happening at precisely the same moment.

So it hardly seems far-fetched of me to let the boundaries of time and space blur once in a while. To look for shadows and outlines of those who are standing in the same spot as myself, only at a different moment in history.

Please, indulge me a little in this. After all, aside from the Butterfly Effect, what harm can a little time traveling do?

After my stimulating day in the West End, as I headed back to Chelsea on the Tube, I spotted a headline on a newspaper another passenger was reading, about how the QM2 had performed a rescue at sea. Gracious!

As soon I got back to my flat, I Googled the story and learned how the QM2 had come to the aid of a yachtsman who was taking part in a race across the North Atlantic. Storms had made the ocean treacherous and his yacht was one of three which had to send out distress signals.

While the folks on the other two boats were picked up by freighter ships, the *Queen Mary 2* had been the closest vessel to this man, so her crew performed the rescue, much to the delight and admiration of the *QM2* passengers.

And it had been Third Officer Bissell, the wonderful gentleman who had taken all that trouble to answer my question about the ice line, who had led the rescue effort. A couple of news sources quoted him, and ran a photo of him with the rescued yachtsman.

It was a job well done for Officer Bissell, Captain Wells and all of the crew.

I just wish I could have been there.

Chapter 11

In addition to my efforts to retrace Cornelia's and Emily's footsteps, occasionally I spent a few hours here and there looking for pieces of Otis Skinner's world.

Over the course of my research, I had developed something of a crush on Otis. Dubbed "America's foremost romantic actor", he was handsome, robust, witty and charismatic – an all-around larger-than-life personality.

But it was his lifelong practice of writing to his wife every day when his job took him on the road, which won my heart. No matter the length of the theatre tour nor the abysmal hours nor the remote locations, Otis Skinner wrote each day to his wife the thoughtful, loving letters of an adoring husband, which were invariably filled with swoon-worthy sentiments towards Maud:

"Dear Heart, My thoughts and love have been with you ever since I left Cambridge."

"... I have your letter and that's balm for all my hurts."

"... my heart kept sending you messages that you would understand."

"I have thought of you all day long. Your presence has been constantly with me."

"Your sweet eyes have been haunting me all day, my wife. And you thought I'd be so busy that I'd not miss you. My love, I don't think the time will ever be when business will crowd you from my heart or steal from me the memory of your sweet lips."

"All my heart... all my love is yours."

He also wrote occasional letters to his young daughter, whom he called, "Maiden mine" and "a small and important person". Sometimes Otis referred to Cornelia by her nickname, "Bobs", which he had bestowed upon his daughter as a baby because of the way her head bobbled.

My favorite photos of Otis Skinner and Maud Durbin, taken in different eras.

(Unfortunately, the nickname was to stick throughout Cornelia's life, and though she avoids making any reference to it in *Our Hearts*, Emily refers to her as "Bobs" multiple times in her draft of the story, even revealing that Cornelia's beau, Joe Aub, called her Bobs as well.)

I had become intrigued enough by Otis that at times I would ditch the girls completely and fancy myself sporting around London with him. I compiled my outings with him into a blog post entitled "On the Town with Otis Skinner":

Although most of the journey this summer is about following Cornelia's and Emily's story, I've also taken some time to search out the London of Otis Skinner, Cornelia's father.

Born in Cambridge, Massachusetts in 1858, Otis knew early on that he wanted to be an actor, and he became one of the finest and most popular performers on the stage – and later in films – for more than sixty years.

In his early days, Otis was a dashing matinee idol (he had a sort of George Clooney thing going). But it was his talent and range that made Skinner stand out as an actor. He toured with theatre luminaries Augustin Daly, Helene Modjeska and Edwin Booth (yes, brother of John Wilkes Booth, but Edwin Booth is also considered by some to be America's greatest actor).

By the mid-1890s, Otis had become a full-fledged star, and in 1895 he married his co-star, Maud Adams, an actress born and raised in Moberly, Missouri. In 1899, their only child, Cornelia was born.

In **Our Hearts Were Young and Gay**, Emily and Cornelia recount going to dinners and plays with Otis and Maud, and also write,

> "Father took us on a few tours about town, showing us places he'd known and loved when he'd played there thirty years before with the Daly Company."

I decided that I would like some time on my own with Otis Skinner, touring about town – just the two of us.

My first stop was 3, Cranbourn St, once the site of Daly's Theatre. Sadly, the beautiful Victorian building is gone, torn down in 1937 by Warner Bros, who put in a movie theatre with a marble, sculpted Art Deco façade. Still, it was nice to see where Daly's had stood, and I could picture a young, carefree, Clooney-esque Otis Skinner being met by adoring females as he left from the stage door and stepped into Leicester Square.

Our next stop was the Trocadero restaurant in Shaftesbury Ave. Opened in 1896, the Trocadero had taken over the space formerly occupied by the notorious Argyle Subscription Rooms, a "performance hall" where rich men picked up prostitutes.

Hmmm… of course, young, upstanding Otis would never have ventured into such a place when he was with the Daly Company. But it's almost a certainty that he would at least have known of the Argyle Rooms' reputation, and I wondered if he had reflected on the place's notorious past while he was standing at the restaurant's entrance in 1922, waiting for Cornelia and Emily to arrive.

I would later discern from Emily's papers that Otis had indeed known the tawdry history of the building, and was in no doubt looking forward to enlightening the girls of its past. Emily had written:

> "That very day your father asked us to have dinner with your mother and him at a particular place which he wanted us to see."

In her papers Emily didn't elaborate further, so it seems safe to assume Otis never shared any tales of the Argyle Rooms with the girls. Most likely, any thoughts of that nature went completely out of his head the moment he saw the girls emerge from a cab at the restaurant, as I explained in my blog:

This is one of my favorite passages in the book, involving the purchase by the girls of matching rabbit fur capes.

"... fashioned along the lines of a tent... they were perfectly enormous and we could wrap them about us twice with a d'Artagnan flourish which we thought was chic and gave us a worldly air."

Cornelia and Emily had decided to debut them at dinner with Cornelia's parents at the oh-so-fashionable Trocadero (those Argyle Rooms had come up in the world).

The girls pull up in a taxi, buried under their mountains of fur, and see Otis collapsed against the building in tears.

"He looked to be hysterical. I couldn't imagine what was the matter. Emily, who didn't know him so well, thought he must be in the throes of some unfathomable mood inherent in a great actor... It never remotely entered our vaguest suspicions that we might have something to do with it."

Needless to say, Otis's tears were of "wild, uncontrollable laughter".

I was delighted to find that the marble columns at the restaurant entrance were still there, although the grand palace of a restaurant that had been there is virtually gone –it's now a cinema and coffee house. But no matter. I could still picture the girls arriving at this spot, and I could see Otis leaning against the column, supporting himself through his fit of laughter. To be almost there with them for that wonderfully funny moment was a joy.

There was one more place I wanted to find, but I didn't have exact information to go on, like I had for the first two locations. All I had was this passage from the book:

"[Otis] was especially fond of an old cemetery for actors. It was in a shoddy out-of-the-way district and the ground was unhallowed. Even in death, members of the profession were ostracized, because until well after the Restoration they were legally considered "Rogues and Vagabonds", not fit to lie with gentle folk. That pleased him highly. It was evident that he felt it a sorry day when players turned respectable."

After a lengthy tour around the internet, involving some creative search terms, I managed to narrow the possibilities down to one really strong contender: Bunhill Fields in Islington. It was a burial ground from the 1660s to the 1850s, and was where many "Nonconformists" were laid to rest. There are artists, writers, and poets there, including William Blake and Daniel Defoe, and the ground was never consecrated by the church. It was definitely worth checking out, even if I was wrong.

The district wasn't shoddy, but it was somewhat out of the way, which matched the girls' description. I spent an hour or so walking along the cobblestone paths, doing my best to make out names on headstones worn down by centuries of rain and wind. There were quite a few visitors to the cemetery that day – or should I say park, as it is now managed as a public garden? One person told me about how a large part of the cemetery had been hit in World War II, and someone else mentioned that many of the dead were under the cobblestones we were walking on. And another person and I pondered whether the unmarked mounds surrounded by low fences were the mass graves of those who died in the 1665 plague. Even if I was in the wrong cemetery, I certainly was in an interesting place. But I was pretty certain I'd gotten it right.

All in all, my time with Otis Skinner had been sweet, though I felt I never really got close to his world. At best, I could only just barely touch it. Which is a shame, because I would like to have known more about this intriguing man. It's the Clooney thing, I suspect.

Chapter 12

Wednesday, June 14 was the day of the first *Our Hearts*-related appointment I had scheduled for this side of the Atlantic, when I would be going to Bletchley Park.

Most everyone knows Bletchley Park is the famous site where women and men worked tirelessly during World War II to crack the codes and decipher the messages from Axis intelligence. It is estimated that their success in breaking the enemies' codes shortened the war by two to four years, and that without Bletchley Park's intelligence work, the outcome of the war would have been uncertain. That is how important the efforts of these mathematicians, linguists, chess champions and crosswords experts had been.

But what could this place possibly have to do with Cornelia's and Emily's story?

It all revolves around a notation on Wikipedia about a Bletchley codebreaker named Hugh Trevor-Roper, who supposedly discovered the Nazis were using *Our Hearts* as a codebook for their Enigma machine.

Huh?

Naturally, German spies couldn't carry around their own bulky, top-secret Enigma machines in order to decipher the codes being transmitted to them, so a codebook was needed. The theory was that if a spy was captured, his having on him a book which was popular, innocuous reading, would raise no suspicions.

And Cornelia's and Emily's frothy tale fit that bill.

Then again, could this book, which mentions numerous specific locations in England and France, have proved useful for more serious underlying reasons?

I had searched the internet to see if I could find information about this astonishing declaration, and managed to locate an online copy of the book from which the Wikipedia reference had come. There was nothing in the index or endnotes pertaining to the exact source of the reference, so I started researching Hugh Trevor-Roper, hoping this anecdote would be mentioned in his papers somewhere.

The first thing I learned about Mr. Trevor-Roper was his claim to fame, or should I say infamy? I remembered the news story from when I was a kid, about the discovery of some diaries reporting to be those of Adolf Hitler. The well-known expert and historian Hugh Trevor-Roper had authenticated the diaries shortly before they were proven to be forgeries.

Tough break, one might say, though that would probably be the most sympathy this man got. From what others wrote about Trevor-Roper, it seems he was widely looked upon as, well, an arrogant jerk, who could be quite vicious in his critiques of others' works. So when his assertion about the diaries turned out to be wrong, many of his acquaintances and peers openly derived some *Schadenfreude* from his humiliation.

(This was why I had so fervently pressed John, the dancer/professor on the *QM2,* for details about his former colleague at Oriel – I had been nosing around for gossip.)

I spent a couple of weeks emailing back and forth with a nice young man named Guy at Bletchley Park. While he did mention that a large portion of British Intelligence records from the war, including Trevor-Roper's contribution, was housed in the National Archives at Kew, Guy was able to turn up a few things related to Trevor-Roper and codebreaking which I might be interested in, and we made the appointment for my visit.

He also recommended I investigate Trevor-Roper's collection of papers at Christ Church College in Oxford. I was not enthusiastic to do this, as I wasn't sure about visiting the college. The last time I had been there was as the maid of honor in my dear friend Jennifer's wedding, which had taken place in the college chapel. The autumn of 2017 would mark the tenth anniversary of her death from cancer at the age of 40. So when the Christ Church archivist in charge of Trevor-Roper's papers informed me that there didn't seem to be anything in them related to *Our Hearts*, I was actually relieved.

The plan for Bletchley Park was that on the morning of June 14, I was to report to their Porter's Lodge, where Guy would "collect" me. A very good, very English, way to begin my day for sure.

Guy had given me excellent directions, and I made it to Bletchley Park right on time to be collected. The porter who greeted me was standing outside at a security gate entrance adorned with a bunker of sandbags – a working barrier which was pleasingly authentic to the period.

Guy arrived and we exchanged greetings, then he took me on a brief tour, giving me the lay of the land before taking me to their office area. At Bletchley, there isn't a dedicated research room for visitors, so I was allowed to use a table in the staff area. Guy brought me the items we had emailed about in the spring, and I settled in to look through them.

The first item was a paper/speech which Trevor-Roper had written about how he came to be involved with the Intelligence Office and Bletchley Park (codenamed "Ultra" in World War II). It was an extremely interesting tale, but didn't contain the info I was looking for.

The other items turned out to be books of Nazi transmissions which had been taken down by the codebreakers. There was something unnerving about them. I could easily imagine a tired, overworked woman (or man) sitting at a desk, headphones on, transcribing German jargon onto small sheets of paper, noting the date, time, radio coordinates and other pertinent information, then adding them to these books, to be deciphered by someone down the line.

It must have been frightening to listen in on voices who were plotting to do harm to your soldiers and your country. And there was no way for those taking down the messages to know if what was being said was innocuous or deadly.

The transmissions books hadn't offered any enlightening intel on my subject, but I was thankful for the chance to handle them. I was holding history in my hands.

One thing was for certain: if I was going to get an answer to my question about *Our Hearts* and the Enigma connection, my best bet would be to pay a visit to the National Archives.

Once I was finished, my host invited me to stay the day and tour the place, and I jumped at the chance.

As Guy walked me down to the welcome center so I could pick up an audio tour set, I asked, "When did the Germans finally find out that the British had gotten ahold of an Enigma machine and broken the code?

"Actually, the entire Bletchley Park operation remained a secret until the mid-1970s," Guy replied.

"The 1970s?" I was astounded. "How is that possible?"

"No one ever revealed the secret. It was that important to national security, even after the war ended."

"How did it come to be known about in the '70s?"

"It was the government who decided to let the world in on the secret," Guy answered. "It was during the height of the Cold War, and the powers that be felt it was important to let their adversaries know just how effective British Intelligence was."

Unfathomable! For thirty years, Bletchley Park's work and its vital contribution to the war effort were kept under wraps, a closely-guarded secret by the countless civilians and military members alike who had worked there.

In all that time, there had never been a leak.

In this day and age where there are no secrets, keeping a confidence of this magnitude is an unimaginable feat.

Perhaps the greatest part of the long-kept secret revolved around the German Enigma machine.

Looking somewhat like an oversized typewriter, this ingenious device utilized a plugboard (forerunner of a computer circuit panel) and a series of rotors to generate encoded messages which were virtually impossible for the Allies to break. The key to Enigma's infallibility was that the settings for the rotors were changed daily to a new sequence, with over seventeen thousand possible combinations. Essentially, this meant the same pattern would never be used twice.

The only way for the Allies to decipher German messages was to obtain an Enigma machine. And in 1939, a copy of the device was smuggled into England and brought to Bletchley Park, where cryptanalysts began the work which changed the course of the entire war.

I also asked Guy if there are people alive today who know how to operate and decipher the Enigma, as it would be a tragic waste if that hard-earned knowledge had been lost to history. He informed me that in the 1990s, a group of mathematicians and engineers built a replica of Alan Turing's Bombe machine, the early computer-like apparatus which had been designed to "wrangle" the Enigma. The Bombe was able to quickly determine the code sequence being used by Enigma each day, and decipher the messages being sent.

Hopefully, there will always be those who know how these devices work.

The infamous Enigma, top secret documents and the manor house at handsome Bletchley Park.

It was sunny and warm, a perfect day to explore Bletchley Park. My tour began in a modern building which houses some cool interactive exhibits, such as trying one's hand at listening for and deciphering radio transmissions. Visitors are surrounded by photos, films and recordings which place them squarely into the dark, early days of the war, before they venture out to the grounds.

Armed with an audio tour headset, I wove in and out of multiple buildings and huts (with a stop in Hut 4, the former offices of the Naval Intelligence Codebreaking unit, which now serves tasty lunchtime fare) before ambling along the lakeside to Bletchley's sublime manor house, then over to the stables.

There had been roughly ten thousand people working in this place during the war, seventy-five percent of them being women. The job had to have been grueling, the stress enormous. Yet these remarkable people kept going, unflinchingly facing each new day and every new challenge. They were ordinary people doing extraordinary work. Heroes.

I was able to take in a great deal of the place before losing steam and coming down with what Cornelia and Emily call "museum legs". I finished my tour with a restorative ice cream and a stop in the gift shop before starting my trek back to London.

On the short walk along the road between Bletchley and the train station, something quite unexpected happened. I had sudden memory recall, and not a happy one.

I had been on this road before, twelve years ago.

It had escaped my notice in the morning, when I had been coming from the other direction. But walking towards the station now, I recognized it in an instant.

I had been in a cab, coming from a nearby hotel on my way to Milton Keynes to shoot some B-roll for a documentary program I was hoping to sell to the Discovery Channel. It was my first time as a director, and I was terrified of blowing my chance, to the point where I had made myself physically ill that morning.

The ride along this road had come at the end of three sleepless nights and stress-filled days, but I still vividly remember the taxi driver pointing out Bletchley Park to me as we drove by.

The flashback made me shudder. That feeling of panic swept over me, and I stopped dead in my tracks in order to catch my breath and shake off the bad energy.

If I had ever questioned the notion of everything happening at once, and being able to tap into what was occurring in the same spot, only at a different moment... well, this had left me in no doubt. I had just run into the younger, unhinged me.

Funny, coming down the road that day in 2005, I hadn't the faintest notion I would ever be back in the same spot, let alone that Cornelia and Emily would be the ones to bring me here, and I would be visiting Bletchley Park in order to do research for my first book.

I lamented to myself, "If only I could tell that poor, scared me it was going to be okay".

But all I could think to do was go catch the train and travel back to 2017 London.

Chapter 13

Just fifteen or so miles outside of London is Hampton Court Palace, once owned by Cardinal Wolsey, Henry VIII's trusted advisor, before being commandeered by the king himself.

During their time in London, Cornelia and Emily, along with Otis and Maud Skinner, visited Hampton Court – a daytrip both colorful and eventful from start to finish.

Thanks to Maud's savvy perusing of *Muirhead's Guide Book* (the *Frommer's* of its day), the foursome traveled from London to Hampton Court by coach – as in stage coach (or more correctly, mail coach), not coach as in the Anglican word for "bus".

> "One rode on the swaying top of a tally-ho behind four spanking greys, while Lord Somebody drove. This opportunity for displaying four-in-hand skill was, we learned, a pastime of the peerage and a few horsey American millionaires who, in the interests of tradition, kept up the old mail-coach service between London and Hampton Court."

What sounded like a jolly adventure proved to be rather more harrowing than what the group had bargained for, as the coach raced through the streets of London at breakneck speed, while the Skinners and Emily clung to little handrails to keep themselves from being hurtled off that swaying top.

Add to which, the weather decided to pile on a touch more misery, and they got rained on along the way. In the end, though, Emily, Cornelia, Maud and Otis made it to the palace unscathed.

The sunny, warm weather was holding nicely on the morning I made my own journey to Hampton Court. For better or worse (probably better), the mail coach tourist experience is no longer offered these days, so I opted for the quick and painless train from London's Waterloo station, and was standing at the entrance to the palace by mid-morning.

Cornelia and Emily don't go into too much detail about their tour through Hampton Court, but they are effusive in the impression it made on them, from the magnificent public rooms to the kitchens with "the forests of chimney pots", which are all still there, possibly in the exact arrangement the girls saw them.

On my expedition through the conflagration of buildings and architectural styles which make up the palace, I took my time snooping around, poking my head into every nook and cranny – everywhere which wasn't marked "Private" or "Staff Only" – and lingering in the multiple, excellent gift shops.

(The kitchen gift shop proved to be my favorite, and it took a tremendous amount of restraint for me to not purchase the enticing set of measuring spoons they had for sale.)

Grand halls and reception rooms to stool closets, I toured it all.

I particularly liked the cardroom inhabited by an art installation of headless, ghostly seventeenth century courtiers fashioned from Tyvek. This electric-white, fabric-like material normally used in building construction gave the sculptures an ethereal glow, and a haunting, floaty appearance that I found bewitching.

In the long corridor leading to the Chapel Royal, I said a doleful prayer for Catherine Howard, Henry VIII's fifth wife, who is said to haunt the hall. It was here, according to legend, that Catherine, having been placed under arrest (by order of her husband), broke free of her guards and ran towards the chapel where Henry was at mass, calling to him, begging him for mercy. Her pleas fell on deaf ears, and soon after the girl-queen was beheaded.

I didn't stay long in the corridor. I didn't wish to feel the presence of Henry VIII, nor imagine Queen Catherine forever reliving such a horrific moment. That poor young woman deserves to rest in peace.

I took pictures of paintings and furniture, and stone passageways where lords, ladies, pages and chambermaids had for centuries skulked about. Later I discovered that a selfie I took in one of the hallways appeared to have a couple of green orbs floating in it, right around my neck. Skeptics can call them dust or whatever they like. I recognized those orbs as the spirits of long-departed beings who were making their ongoing presence known in my photo, even going so far as to coordinate with my blouse, which was most pleasing.

All of the palace and its grounds are a treat, from the perfectly manicured formal gardens to the luscious flower beds, to the indoor tennis court, where the sport known as "real tennis" is still played today by those belonging to what must be a pretty exclusive club.

Just like Cornelia and Emily, I managed to explore every part of Hampton Court without museum legs setting in. Throughout the day, I thought of them (and Maud and Otis, too), knowing their eyes had fallen on all of these same, remarkable things.

> "And then we came to the maze, or labyrinth. It was [Cornelia's] idea to go into it."

Being made of guts and sand as they were, Cornelia and Emily traipsed into the famous hedge maze which had been at Hampton Court for hundreds of years... and quickly proceeded to get lost. No one was around to help them escape – only Maud and Otis, who were waiting for them on a bench outside the maze, but couldn't offer them any guidance.

Emily and Cornelia were lost in the labyrinth for forty-five minutes (during which there was a torrential rainstorm), before a member of staff appeared, climbing onto a platform and shouting instructions to lead them out.

Arriving at the maze, I decided it was my duty to make up for the girls' dreadful experience here. I whispered to Cornelia and Emily that they were coming with me, and everything would be all right. I would get us out.

I certainly didn't want a repeat of the girls' misfortune, which was entirely possible because the weather by that time was beginning to change and match theirs: some occasional fast moving rain showers were starting to mix with the sunshine. As a precaution, I had the good sense to take a snapshot of the diagram of the maze, which was displayed on the sign outside the entry.

Yes, very wise of me to take a picture. What would have really been clever was if I had checked to make sure the picture had actually taken and was in my phone (turns out it hadn't, which I discovered only after I was well into the bowels of the maze). My healthy faith in my navigational ability had already been wiped out in just a few short turns along the hedges, and I quickly began to fear that I was about to recreate Cornelia's and Emily's experience.

Then in a stroke of good old dumb luck, I found myself at the exit, which was strangely only a few turns from the center of the maze. With extreme satisfaction in having reached both, I put on an air of nonchalance as I breezed out of the labyrinth, in case anyone happened to be nearby to witness my getaway.

As I was high-tailing it out of the maze, I noticed right near the exit, tucked away in a small dead end of hedges, was a set of ladder-like steps with a small platform atop them, where staff members could stand and call out instructions to lost tourists, just as someone had done for Cornelia and Emily.

Then just outside the exit was a long hedge with an inset carved into it, where sat a lone bench, probably in precisely the same spot Otis and Maud had sat waiting for the girls.

Everything seemed to match perfectly.

In 1922, after the girls had emerged from the labyrinth, they and Cornelia's parents left Hampton Court Palace.

> "Drenched and soaked, we scuttled across to a quaint-looking inn which hung precariously over the green bank of the Thames."

I took my exit from the maze as my cue to leave the Palace as well, and go in search of Cornelia's and Emily's riverside inn. It was pretty easy to spot. Directly across the street from Hampton Court Palace is The Mitre Hotel, which (according to vintage photos of the place) has the same name and roughly the same appearance as it did in 1922.

When I arrived, I found a sign stating that the restaurant, now called the "Riverside Brasserie", was closed for lunch, but that the bar downstairs was open. I ventured down the stairs to a nice, airy space with a large patio right on the river. Here I took the opportunity, after hours of walking, to stick my feet in the bracing current of the Thames. And just like it had been in Chicago's Lake Michigan, ten minutes in the chilly water was all it took to revive my tired tootsies and put a spring back in my step.

Though I was disappointed I wasn't in the exact location where my 1922 traveling companions had gone for tea, I decided to stay and have a drink. This led to a conversation with a couple of members of the staff, and I asked them if there was a big fireplace in the restaurant upstairs. I didn't know if they looked surprised because I knew this, or because I was asking such a random, oddball question, but the manager said, yes, there was. After I explained the reason for my question, she offered to take me upstairs to see the restaurant, and off we went.

Everything had been laid out for the dinner service, identical to how Cornelia and Emily had described it. Like it was waiting for me.

The configuration of the entrance had been changed, but other than that, it could have been 1922 in that room.

> "Tables were set, but there was nobody to wait on them.
> A fire was laid in a vast fireplace but it wasn't going."

Exactly. Again, a match I would call perfect.

Tyvek lords and ladies, and a fire laid in a vast fireplace.

It had been an exceptional day. I was overawed by how much I had been able to not just replicate, but connect to, Cornelia's and Emily's experience. It hadn't been moments, but hours I had spent with the Skinners and Emily. Those time boundaries had blurred a great deal.

Which is no doubt why I ended up with orbs in my photos.

Chapter 14

The next day was a lazy one for me, which I spent wholly in the twenty-first century. My big outing was a walk with Sabrina and Tigger to one of their favorite parks. This was the first time we had hung out since we met, and we had a marvelous stroll around the area and then back along the riverfront.

As we were arriving at the front door of her building and discussing when we might meet up again, Sabrina shared that she and her husband had plans to go to Ascot on Friday the following week with some friends. She mentioned which "enclosure" they were in and thought there could still be tickets available, in case I might wish to join them.

It is an embarrassment to admit, but in all the times I had visited England, the idea had never once occurred to me to attend Ascot. I had no notion it was even an option for me – it seemed so exclusive. Then again, I'd never really given it much thought because I have absolutely no interest in horseracing.

But I am a big fan of the movie "My Fair Lady" and, in particular, the scene where Audrey Hepburn attends Ascot Opening Day in that liquid silver gown and wearing an enormous, simply delectable confection of a hat.

That alone had me sold. I was going to Ascot.

Saying my goodbyes to Sabrina and Tigger, I hustled back to my abode, got online and, sure enough, though there were no tickets left for Friday, there were still tickets to be had on other days, and I could just buy them. No highfalutin invitation nor secret handshake required.

How had I missed this?

There was an array of ticket choices, ranging in price and level of fanciness. I selected a ticket in the Queen Anne enclosure, which appeared to be geared towards a younger, livelier crowd. And I opted to attend on Ladies Day because it sounded like fun.

At the check-out webpage, the first item I needed to select was my title. But this was no regular "Title" drop down menu, offering just the standard choices of "Mr, Mrs, Ms" and "Miss". This menu encompassed every rank in the upper crust, from "Dame" to "The Duchess of", from "Sir" to "Prince" and every peer in between. There were also other tantalizing options – everything from "Brigadier" to "Wing Commander", "The Right Honourable" to "The Reverend", to the intriguing "Captain The Jonkheer".

For a wild moment, I considered listing myself as "Viscountess". Lady Adrienne, Viscountess of Something-Posh-Sounding. But then I got panicky – what if Ascot had "poser police" who would bust me for falsely claiming to be a member of the peerage. In the end, I went with my well-earned American "Ms", and booked myself a day at the races.

Now all I needed was a really good hat.

Ladies always wear hats to Ascot.

Audrey Hepburn had worn a hat.

A resplendent hat.

I needed a hat like that.

A fascinator would also do.

Saturday, June 17, was to be a big day for me. First, I was going to meet my distant English cousin, Sean, with whom I had become acquainted through the Ancestry.com DNA database, and then friends with through Facebook. We had made plans for him to come up from his home in Brighton on this day for Queen Elizabeth's official birthday celebration.

We met at Victoria train station, and instantly took a liking to each other. Sean was warm and kind, and we gave each other the abridged version of our lives as we proceeded to St. James Park to watch the Queen's birthday parade.

It was hot and sunny, so the shade in the park was most welcome, and we were able to find a clear view of the cavalcade about halfway down the Mall. The whole of the grand boulevard was looking shipshape and Bristol fashion, sporting large Union Jacks on its light poles, while the street itself was lined with the Queen's Guard soldiers.

Soon the parade started. There was a band and horse guards, and carriages filled with members of the royal family. In all of my visits to the United Kingdom over the last thirty years, this was the first time I'd ever seen a member of the royal family in person. And now it appeared I was getting all of the immediate family in one go.

Ninety-five years ago, give or take a few days, Cornelia and Emily had come to Buckingham Palace for their own royals sighting, as they explained:

> "One day Mother, who had read in the Times that the Royal Family was to leave for the country at eleven, scuttled us off to Buckingham Palace to watch the departure. We stood along with a handful of governesses and casual passers-by – nobody else seemed to have made an occasion of it – when the gates opened and the Family appeared, rather crowded into one car like any other family starting for the station. The few men around us took off their hats, the nannies pointed out the car to their children, and Emily and I just looked. But not Mother. Not for nothing had she assisted on the stage the entrance of Kings and Queens. She fluttered to the ground in a deep, 18th Century curtsey, spreading as wide as possible the skirt of her tailored suit. We looked down at her in amazement. We weren't the only ones amazed – Queen Mary nearly fell out of the car."

With thirty-plus of my great-grandfathers having fought for the Patriots in the American Revolutionary War, I didn't think it right for me to curtsey as Queen Elizabeth's carriage passed by. But I joined in the waving and cheering with sincere enthusiasm.

After the parade, the guards opened the barriers along the Mall, allowing the large crowds to follow the royals to Buckingham Palace.

We didn't end up near the gates like Cornelia and Emily had done, but Sean and I were able to find a decent vantage point near the Queen Victoria Memorial, and waited for the royals to appear on the iconic long balcony.

When Queen Elizabeth and her family stepped out and waved to the ebullient throngs, I held my breath and took it all in. Only a few weeks before, attackers had plowed through a crowd of people here in London who were just going about their day. But the thousands of folks who had come out to the Queen's birthday hadn't let that incident break their stride.

And they never will.

A nineteen-year-old Princess Elizabeth had stood on this same balcony on May 8, 1945, with her father, King George VI, and their family, along with Winston Churchill, celebrating Germany's surrender and the end of World War II in Europe. Elizabeth had waved to the grandparents and great-grandparents of the people who were celebrating her birthday today. Those were the people who withstood the Blitz, took their civilian boats to Dunkirk to save their soldiers and, in the words of Prime Minister Churchill, never gave in. Now that unflinching spirit of theirs lives on today in their descendants.

A low rumble started to build in the distance, and we all turned our eyes towards the heavens as vintage planes and the current pride of the British skies did flyovers of the Palace, including the heart-pounding Red Arrows, leaving red, white and blue smoke trails behind them.

It was all spectacular and perfect. Long live The Queen.

Ascot was fast approaching, which meant I would have to hustle if I was going to find a hat which would coordinate with my chosen dress for the big day. Not having the foresight to know I would need my Mother Dolores dress for Ascot, I had packed it away with my evening gowns in the Really Big Suitcase down there in Southampton. So I decided to go with my white "garden party" dress with its large, vibrant floral print.

My search for a hat began at the Westfield Shopping Centre in Shepherd's Bush, which seemed to have every British store I had ever heard of and then some.

At Debenham's, I joined about half a dozen other women trying on all sorts of creative headpieces.

It became a communal shopping experience, where we each described the dresses we were trying to match, and offered thoughts and opinions on each other's contenders. Every woman there was shopping for Ascot, and it was clearly a novelty for all of us. Together we reveled in the sense of occasion and the experience. It certainly wasn't "old hat" for anyone, so to speak.

I had found a few candidates that might work, the frontrunner being an electric orange fascinator, which is basically a headband adorned with frills, feathers and frippery, melded together into a wonderfully sculptural bit of nonsense. My orange delight was less Audrey Hepburn/Eliza Doolittle and more Aunt Eller in the musical "Oklahoma" (which was where I had first heard of a fascinator), but I was pretty smitten with it.

Still, I decided that, as this was a really special occasion, I should make every effort to get my headwear choice right. I would go to Oxford Street, Europe's busiest shopping district, and hit a few flagship stores there, particularly my longtime favorite, Selfridge's. Opened in 1909, this was London's first department store, the brainchild of the charismatic American, Harry Gordon Selfridge. I like to think Cornelia and Emily bought their rabbit capes in Selfridge's.

I spent a healthy part of a day traversing Oxford Street before realizing there is a serious dearth of fancy hats in the London shops. This seems like a gross oversight, considering how summer is not just Ascot season, but also the season for weddings, graduations, garden parties and the Henley Regatta. So many occasions for wearing big, gaudy, froufrou hats. Why aren't there more to choose from?

In the end, I purchased from the Oxford Street Debenham's the same electric orange fascinator I had tried on at the Westgate, and was chuffed with my decision.

And things only got better when the saleslady wrapped it up in a gigantic hatbox.

Ever since my arrival in London two weeks earlier, I had seen numerous women walking around carrying enormous hatboxes, and I thought it awfully glamorous of them. Now I was joining their ranks. I felt transported to a different time, when ladies routinely wore hats and gloves and pretty dresses.

It was quite a haul from Oxford Street to Chelsea, and toting my oversized hatbox through the Tube stations and crowded sidewalks should have proven to be a hassle, but I was utterly enthralled with the situation.

It even reminded me of Cornelia and Emily, when they had lugged huge boxes filled with their newly-purchased fur capes across town to their lodgings. This sense of kinsmanship with them made me all the more detestably prissy as I merrily made my way home, swinging my hatbox gleefully from its long, luscious satin ribbon handle.

Back at the flat, there was an email waiting for me from the H.G. Wells Society. It had been less than a week since I contacted them about the Great Educationalist, and those marvelous folks had come up with a name for me: F.W. Sanderson.

Sanderson had been a longtime headmaster at the Oundle School in Northamptonshire, and Mr. Wells had thought so highly of him that he had written a book about Mr. Sanderson entitled, *The Story of a Great Schoolmaster*.

A schoolmaster was certainly an educationalist.

And a portrait of Sanderson which I located on the internet seemed to resemble the small, blurry image of the man in the Sanger photograph.

Jackpot!

Sanderson simply had to be The Great Educationalist.

There was just one problem.

In Googling around for a photo of the man, I discovered F. W. Sanderson had died six days before Cornelia and Emily arrived in England.

It seems that on the evening of June 15, 1922, Mr. Sanderson had just delivered an address to the National Union of Scientific Workers at University College, London. Suddenly, right there at the podium, he dropped dead of a heart attack just as H.G. Wells himself, who was moderating the event, asked him his first question.

But how could the Great Educationalist *not* be F.W. Sanderson? Something had to be off.

That evening I went back into town via the riverbus to Embankment. It was always a pleasure to cruise along the Thames, which for over two thousand years had been navigated by Romans, Saxons, Vikings, and other marauding hordes. A lot of history had unfolded along these banks.

The sun's light was beginning to soften, and as we motored past the Houses of Parliament and Big Ben, I took in their majesty and felt an overwhelming sense of gratitude and joy to be where I was in that moment. A minute later we arrived at Embankment Pier.

Proceeding into the West End, I headed over to St. Martin's Theatre, and attended performance number 26,932 of "The Mousetrap".

For a long time the play has been perceived as being a real "tourist" thing to do, because the show has been running for a gazillion years. I had never seen it, but I had read the play, and felt it was high time I saw it performed, especially with the tidy fact that it had been running since 1952, making it sixty-five years since it opened. A nice addition to the ninety-five years and seventy-five years thing I had going with *Our Hearts*.

Before the show began, I conversed in the lobby bar with a couple who had come down from the north for a few days to celebrate an anniversary. We were joined by a good-looking young man in his mid-twenties, who had just that morning come over from Norway on a lark, and hadn't even figured out where he was staying for the night. I seriously considered offering to let him stay with me in Chelsea, and if I had been about twenty years younger, I probably would have done so.

Cards on the table, this guy was the perfect "backpacking-through-Europe-hook-up" that every young woman in her twenties should encounter at least once in her travels.

But, reality check.

I had to keep in mind that as much as I had been immersing myself in Cornelia's and Emily's twenty-something journey, I was not that age anymore (not even in hailing distance, truth be told). So no matter how young I might feel at heart, I had to be honest with myself and accept that I was simply too old for this adorable guy.

Way too old.

No matter how much flirting he was doing with me.

He had been the one to approach me and start the conversation. Maybe he liked older women. Or he couldn't tell just how much older than him I was (a happy notion!). Then again, he might have just been trying to charm his way into a free place to stay, and I looked like a safe, harmless elderly lady to him.

Whatever the truth, I knew that I didn't want to be the creepy old woman.

It's always best not to be the creepy old woman.

Instead, I suggested he try Bayswater, a funky area just north of Kensington Gardens where all the hunky young Aussies hang out, which I happened to know from personal experience.

During the 1950s and 60s, a large number of backpackers from the Land Down Under had settled in the Earl's Court area, earning that neighborhood the nickname "Kangaroo Court". But by the time I arrived in the late 1980s, the London hub for Aussies and Kiwis had relocated to Bayswater.

And from what I could tell from passing through that area in the last few years, this was still the go-to place for cool young travelers.

I figured this guy could score a place to stay, or at the very least have some fun with people his own age.

"The Mousetrap" has more humor in it than I remembered – well, at least until someone is murdered. This was an entertaining production, and I was glad I had chosen to see it. And it wasn't until very close to the end that I remembered the surprising solution to the mystery.

Agatha Christie is an icon and a legend for a reason.

Leaving the theatre, as I stepped onto the pavement, I was caught off-guard by an otherworldly sensation – a giddy excitement, like anything could happen. I recognized it as the feeling I used to get in my twenties, whenever I came to London. Was it something about the twilight, or the reverie of the bar and theatre patrons all around me? Could it be linked to the encounter with the handsome young Norwegian? Or had Ms. Christie and "The Mousetrap" somehow dropped me into the past?

Whatever it was, it was lovely.

As much as I had been enjoying my time in London, it had been in a comfortable, familiar way. But out of the blue, this evening I inexplicably felt as though I were that twenty-something girl again, the one who was just on the brink of starting her life. And I'm certain it is she who I would've seen, had I stopped and studied my reflection in one of the store windows.

Blurred edges of space and time once again, only now it was me on both sides of the equation.

I held my breath as I walked, afraid of breaking the spell, and relished that delirious sensation until it evaporated. And then I got on the Underground and went home.

Chapter 15

Ascot Thursday dawned, and I awoke feeling bubbly and expectant about the day. A lot of it had to do with the fascinator, I suspect. Here is what I later wrote in my blog about my day at the races:

I took the train to Ascot, which was a treat in itself. Almost everyone on board was decked out in the requisite finery. The female passengers looked like a beautiful garden of flowers, with madcap, vibrant creations blooming from their heads, while the men were dressed either in suits or morning dress, a.k.a. top hat and tails, a must for all gentleman entering the Royal Enclosure. The champagne and various beverages were flowing, and there were high spirits and laughter throughout the train car, even with a standing room only crowd.

In no time we arrived at Ascot, and I toodled over to the Queen Anne enclosure in the center of the racetrack oval, which I found teeming with food and cocktails and music of all kinds. Milling around amongst the crowd was like being in the center of an enormous, incredible fashion show. It was all quite splendid.

I managed to maneuver into a spot on the front line in time to see the royal family arrive in a procession of carriages. It had taken me almost thirty years to see a royal in person, and now within just the span of a week, I had seen a whole pack of them - twice! I was struck especially by the notion that I was seeing not only the reigning monarch, the only one most everyone alive today has ever known, but two future kings - Prince Charles and Prince William - as well. But from what I could see, their turns would have to wait for a good while - Queen Elizabeth II was looking bright as a penny.

From there, I proceeded to a large tent, where I mingled and chatted with a number of fellow attendees, sampled the dainty sandwiches and pastries, had a couple of glasses of champagne, and never again made it close to the track to see the races. Occasionally there would be the sound of horses' hooves building momentum, and some cheers, and I might glance at a TV monitor to see the finish. But that was pretty much the extent of my experience with the races themselves. As I mentioned earlier, horse racing really isn't my thing.

By mid-afternoon, I was ready to pack it in and head home to London. I left before the races ended and the after-parties began, but I needed to get out of my shoes.

I had seen the fashions. I had worn my fascinator. That is what Ascot had been about for me – the pomp and pageantry of it all. And I had not been disappointed. My day had been perfect and complete.

Another, less official Ascot tradition I discovered on the day is Ladies Day brings a number of male-to-female cross-dressers to the races. While some are the dazzling divas known as drag queens, many are simply men who enjoy dressing up as women. I found it wonderfully endearing that these gentlemen should so wholly embrace the opportunity to glam up and join the fashion show that is Ascot.

Of course, as it is with all of us women, some are better than others with the hair, make-up and styling. I encountered one stunningly gorgeous soul in the powder room. She was statuesque and chic, and I wanted to tell her so, but she passed by too quickly, and then I never saw her again anywhere.

Later in the day, on the station platform waiting for the London train, I found myself next to another cross-dressing Ascot attendee. Unlike the breathtaking beauty in the ladies' room, my traveling companion was a guy in a dress, bless his heart.

Despite his efforts with the make-up and the luscious synthetic locks, he just wasn't ever going to pass for female. I wondered if he knew this. Hopefully if he did, it didn't matter to him.

While we waited for the train to arrive, we began a conversation about shoes. He was holding some fierce red stilettos in his hand and wearing flip flops which, he informed me, he had picked up for a few quid from one of the vendors lining the walk from the station to the racecourse. He said it was the only way to do Ascot in heels.

Throughout the day, I had seen women pulling flip flops out of enormous shoulder bags and making the switch, while I suffered in my heels. I had been foolhardy enough to be snooty about those big handbags, priding myself on having the standards to carry only an appropriate-looking clutch.

But now, at the end of the day, I realized that I had paid the price for my vanity. Those women with their large purses filled with water bottles, sunscreen and flip-flops were wise and absolutely right, and I was resoundingly clueless.

Soon our train arrived, and my new friend I sat across from each other, where he began opening up to me.

I could see, under the make-up, he was a nice-looking man. We introduced ourselves and he gave a female name, but informed me he was a man – and a heterosexual one at that, he troubled to add – who just likes to dress as a woman.

"It's how I best feel comfortable," he explained. "I am at my happiest this way. And at this point in my life, I could even see sacrificing my career in order to live this way."

"You would really have to give up your career?" I asked.

My friend leaned in, almost whispering, "I'm an actor. I've won a Bafta. It would be hard for people to understand. But I prefer to live this way than continue working."

I hadn't been expecting that answer.

I guess my new friend trusted that, as an American, I wouldn't be able to work out who he was. He revealed to me that he is attracted to women, and had been married before, but that the marriage had ended after a few years because they were completely incompatible.

And one other thing: he let his first name slip.

I may not have remembered the female name he had introduced himself with, but I latched onto this bit of information.

I did wonder just how much of what he was telling me was the truth. Was he really an actor? Had he really won a Bafta? Or was this all just a big made-up story to amuse himself on the train ride home, hoodwinking the gullible, nosey tourist? Might he be "taking the piss" (an expression which is always surprising to hear used by the famously polite English)?

I did my best to study and memorize his face so I could do a hardcore internet search for him when I got back to the flat. I trusted the male name he had said was genuine, because that had come out accidentally – in fact, I wasn't sure he had even realized he'd said it. Or, if he did, he glossed over it, hoping I wouldn't catch it.

Perhaps my friend was telling the truth, and felt like he could confide in me because I was a foreigner who probably wouldn't have any idea who he was. But still, why would he disclose such specific details about himself, and divulge that he was famous? It seemed dangerous.

Then again, was it all truth or lies? It was hard to read him, and the make-up and hair helped camouflage what was real in what he was saying.

We talked some about me, and he began moving closer, speaking more intimately with me, winking and flirting, and I wasn't certain where to go with it. After all, I had struck up a conversation with this person thinking I was making a new girlfriend, with nary a thought of potential romance.

Our tete-a-tete was then interrupted, when the train stopped at a station somewhere on the way to London and two young Frenchmen who got on sat down beside us. The four of us made polite conversation, and the Frenchman next to me began to pull focus from my Ascot friend.

At Clapham Junction, I got off the train, while my girlfriend/boyfriend continued on to Waterloo. He looked slightly disappointed that this was the end of our time together, and he kissed my hand as we said goodbye.

Back at the flat, once I was out of my Ascot-wear, I hopped on the laptop and Googled the first name of my friend along with "Bafta". Numerous names popped up, and I was able to narrow the field down to one strong contender. His features were similar to those of the man on the train, possibly. He was about the right age, and his height and build matched that of my friend's. And from what I could remember of the actor's voice from the shows I had seen him in, he sounded like my friend, sort of.

If this was the man, well rats! I wish I had exchanged info with him. Because I remembered this actor from a number of films and TV shows, and I had certainly found him likeable, attractive, even sexy at times.

But really, I couldn't be sure.

There were discrepancies. For one, the contender was still married to his wife. So that was a conflict.

Then there were the names of colleagues he should have remembered but didn't. Another red flag.

There was just no way to be certain of this man's identity.

Perhaps one day the actor whom I believe I met that day will share this part of his life to the world. I certainly won't be naming any names, because there's every chance I have it wrong.

In the meantime, I carry the hope of someday crossing paths with my Ascot buddy, and he gives me a nod or a wink to let me know we've met before.

Until that happens, he will just have to remain my journey's Great Educationalist.

Chapter 16

The day after Ascot Thursday, as I was walking to Sainsbury's, I ran into Sabrina and Tigger. He had just gotten a haircut, which made him look and feel like crushed velvet. Utterly adorable.

Sabrina and I gabbed for a time, and I told her about my plans to visit Hever Castle the next day. Being as much of a culture nerd as I am, she eagerly said yes when I invited her to go with me.

Dating back to 1270, Hever Castle is most famous for being the home of Ann Boleyn, Henry VIII's ill-fated second wife and mother of Queen Elizabeth I. Being one with a fascination for Tudor history, I'd had Hever Castle on my to-do list for a couple of decades.

I was pleased I had run into Sabrina, though it had been a surprise.

"Weren't you all going to Ascot today?" I asked.

"Yes, but it fell through. Our friends were getting the tickets from their friends, but then they didn't. It was a whole thing," Sabrina replied.

"That's lousy."

"Yeah, I was looking forward to it."

"I wish I'd known. You could have come with me yesterday," I said, then added, "It was Ladies Day."

I would fill her in on all those details later.

"Darn it, that would have been fun," Sabrina lamented. "The worst part is that I'm not getting to wear my really great fascinator. I was pretty excited about that."

So it ain't just me, I thought.

Offering a sympathetic smile, I nodded, "I understand."

Ascot really is all about the hats.

Shortly after I returned to the flat, I got an email from Sabrina saying she had looked up Hever Castle's website and saw they were having a big weekend of World War II-themed attractions and events in honor of Armed Services Day. This sounded like an exciting prospect to both of us. And I could only smile at having yet another tie-in to WWII.

Again it was an excursion which didn't include Cornelia and Emily. I would end up addressing the question of these side trips in my blog (not that anyone was asking):

It would seem like from my latest posts that I must've lost interest in following Cornelia's and Emily's story, but that is hardly the case. Every day I read a bit of **Our Hearts**, *and continue my research on the girls and their travels. And any time I am in the West End, especially when I'm going to the theatre, I think of them and imagine them strolling through those same streets (sometimes in their nutty rabbit fur capes). The girls are very much with me.*

Because of the mishap with the Montcalm, and the eight days waiting in Canada for another ship, compounded with Cornelia being bedridden in Southampton with the measles for ten days, the girls were severely delayed in getting to London, so their time in the city was cut rather short. Whereas I'm spending nearly five weeks here, the girls barely got more than two.

So aside from a few passing references to places they visited, and their stories from Hampton Court and Easton Glebe (more on that in a later post), there is very little for me to search out in London. Which I don't mind, as it gives me some free time to have a few new experiences of my own, while also allowing me to revisit parts of my own past travels.

Sunday, June 25, started out with questionable skies, but the forecast hadn't called for rain, just clouds.

Then again, this was England, so anything could happen.

Sabrina and I took a casual approach to getting to Hever Castle, just catching whatever the first train was without minding about exact times.

As we waited on the platform, I told her about my day at Ascot, including my very interesting train ride back.

"So I don't suppose this particular situation has ever come up for you, has it?" I asked.

"Dating a transvestite?" Sabrina thought for a moment, then, "No."

"What would you have done, if it had been you? Would you have gone out with him?"

Sabrina thought for the briefest moment, less than a nanosecond. "Yes, sure, why not?"

"I don't know. I've never really given it any thought," I replied. "Do you think it would alter your physical attraction to a man?"

"No, I can't see having a problem with it," Sabrina replied without any hesitation or judgment in her voice.

I kept going. "What about being intimate? What if he was in drag – could you still do it?"

This gave Sabrina pause, then, "Yeah, I think so. It wouldn't be any big deal. It would still be him under the make-up."

"I suppose…"

"Probably no different than being with a guy in a Halloween costume," she reasoned.

I began to wonder if I had missed an opportunity with my Ascot friend. Had I let that Puritan DNA of mine spoil what could have been a budding romance?

Possibly.

The next train rolled in, putting an end to our discussion, and as we climbed aboard, Sabrina filled me in on the various events scheduled at Hever during the day.

The train ride through the countryside of Kent couldn't have been prettier or more pleasant. At one of those picturesque little stations festooned with hanging baskets, we changed from the big Southeastern Railway train to a smaller, regional one which took us to Hever Station.

It was then just a brief walk through some fields and country lanes, and up past an ancient half-timbered pub and the village church to reach the castle.

Immediately we were struck with the beauty and the layout of the grounds. Whereas some of the great estates have elaborate, ostentatious grounds, Hever Castle and its surroundings were beautiful in an understated, natural way.

The estate was buzzing with all sorts of interesting sights. In the center of everything was a WWII Spitfire, being watched over by gentlemen representing the Home Guard.

Further on, in front of the castle was parked a vintage double-decker bus, which had been turned into an interactive experience called "London During the Blitz". Nearby, under a large canopy, there were activities for kids, such as the sobering craft project "Make Your Own Gas Mask". Across from the canopy, I was proud to see a trio of left-hand drive jeeps representing the American troops who had flooded into England once the US entered the war.

But first we wanted to step a little further back into history and tour the castle. Sabrina and I viewed a lot of the rooms together, but soon got separated as we went at our own paces. Our friendship was still new, and I was glad she was spared my lengthy conversation with one of the docents about Henry VIII, the Boleyns, and who murdered the Princes in the Tower (had it been Henry's father, Henry Tudor, or his great-uncle, Richard III?).

After being on Henry VIII's turf at Hampton Court, it felt good to be here in Boleyn territory, where the king had been just the lovesick suitor of Anne. Of course, later he would have her beheaded, seizing Hever Castle from her family and then giving it to his fourth wife, Anne of Cleves, who, of all of Henry's wives, on balance, probably fared the best of the lot.

I rejoined Sabrina at the gift shop and cafe, and after a satisfying bite of lunch, we headed over to the gardens and a series of tents. The largest tent served as the grandstand, where a trio of female singers decked out in 1940s garb were performing big band hits of the war years.

Next to the tents, a pick-up game of what appeared to be half-cricket and half-baseball was being played by folks dressed in G.I. uniforms – soldiers and sailors both – as well as a few women who were sporting "A League of Their Own" baseball uniforms. There were also a few "civilians", again in period dress, who had joined the game, while a large group of men and women, vintage WWII from head to toe, merrily cheered them on.

There was something mesmerizing about that game, with everyone laughing and delighting in the spectacle – the mood was ebullient and infectious, and Sabrina and I were swept up in the joy and spirit of it all. The uniforms, the clothes, even the hairstyles, with "Chattanooga Choo Choo" being sung in the background – it all looked and felt so utterly authentic, that it began to feel as if it was indeed 1942, with everyone taking a brief respite from the worry of the war for an afternoon of fun and laughter.

It was as if we had all passed completely through the time and space portal, and it was the most wondrous sensation.

After enjoying the game for a while, Sabrina and I checked out the tents and were particularly struck by the one selling handmade reproductions of 1940s hats. Oh, there were some heavenly creations! It made me wish to come back next year in vintage apparel. I very much wanted to be part of that homefront ballgame crowd, and slip into their 1940s world for just a moment or two.

We then explored the extensive flower gardens and prodigious man-made lake, all of which had been installed by the American tycoon William Astor when he purchased Hever in 1903.

On the lake, visitors paddled around in boats, while a mother swan sat at the water's edge with her offspring – though larger than babies, the juvenile swans retained their sweet, soft-looking grey fluff and inspired lots of gushing and cooing from the tourists.

Museum legs were coming on for both Sabrina and me, so we made our way back to the train station, then on to London and the twenty-first century.

Along the way, we looked through our photos, and talked about the centuries of history we had just taken in, all in a matter of a few short hours. Sabrina revealed how she had experienced the sensation of being transported to the past during the ballgame, and we agreed that it had been the best part of an all-around terrific day.

Sometimes you travel to a destination or take in a sight, and it's good. You're glad you got to see it, to be there. It's what you expected, and it didn't disappoint.

And then sometimes, when you're really lucky, it turns out to be spectacular, a glorious surprise, a memory you will cherish forever.

The day at Hever Castle had been one of those times.

Nothing less than magic.

Chapter 17

The next day started off on a great note, when I received a very kind email from Sir Michael Nairn. He wrote that hadn't been aware of his grandparents and aunt being in *Our Hearts*, but he believed there might be photographs of his family's travels which would include that voyage. He also invited me to come up to Scotland and visit with him and his wife Sally, our schedules permitting. They were leaving soon for Italy for a few weeks, but hopefully we could work something out.

I was elated! Could I pull off what the girls hadn't managed, and become friendly with Sir Michael Nairn... and perhaps score some photos from their voyage on the *Empress of France* as well? The idea of it all was intoxicating.

Outside, it was a perfect summer day, so I took the opportunity to indulge in a long walk from Chelsea to the Victoria & Albert Museum in South Kensington.

A few days earlier, I had searched through the online archives of the museum's textiles and fashion collection, because I believed they might have a piece of the *Our Hearts* puzzle – an unusual article of underclothing which I wrote about in my blog:

*An incident which I consider to be one of the funniest in **Our Hearts Were Young and Gay** involves an item known as a "safety-pocket". A forerunner to today's money belts, this Victorian accessory served the same purpose for female travelers in the late nineteenth century, safeguarding their passports, money and important papers.*

At the very beginning of the Our Hearts, Cornelia explains that her mother has coerced her into wearing one for her journey abroad, describing it as, "a large chamois purse that dangled at the knees in the manner of a sporran and was attached... to an adjustable belt around the waist. It was worn, supposedly inconspicuously, under skirt and slip..." But Cornelia's slinky, skin-tight 1920s wardrobe is no match for this bulky object, which not only protrudes from the outline of her dresses, but also tends to swing out of control at the slightest movement.

Her only consolation comes when she discovers Emily has been forced by her mother to wear a safety-pocket as well.

Not surprisingly, it doesn't take long for these items to become a terrible embarrassment to the girls. It happens right at the start of their travels, aboard the "Montcalm", when they try to make the best of the fact that their ship is stuck on a sandbar and listing to one side. They attempt to dance on a slippery, tilted floor with some nice young men whom they had met earlier in the day. Cornelia explains:

> "Gradually I became aware that something soft and strange was bumping against my knees... [My partner] began glancing downward uneasily and I realized that something was, in all probability, hitting him, too. Then with a wave of horror, it dawned upon me what was happening. That mortifying safety-pocket of mine had got swaying and was rhythmically and indiscriminately thudding first against my limbs then against those of the mystified young man."

At that same moment, Cornelia sees Emily, her face beet red, walk off the dance floor with her partner. Clearly the same thing has just happened to her. That pretty much spells the end of the safety-pockets.

On my first sojourn abroad, my mother sent me off with a twentieth century version of the safety-pocket, which was a pouch suspended by a cord worn around my neck, that hung down to my waist. So instead of flapping beneath my skirt, my pouch bounced beneath my shirts and tended to give me the appearance of being roughly five months pregnant. So I related well to the girls' embarrassment.

I had yet to find a photo of a safety pocket anywhere on the internet, so my best bet was the V&A, which has an extensive collection of garments and accessories throughout the centuries. Somewhere in their archives, there's even a whole book about the evolution of pockets. Not what the general public might consider electrifying reading, but it might just help me in my quest.

The Victoria & Albert was buzzing with large crowds when I arrived. Many were there to take in the Pink Floyd exhibition, while others queued to view one hundred-plus garments from designer Balenciaga – just two of many marvelous, focus-pulling attractions the V&A had on offer.

My plan was to knock out the safety-pocket question first, then spend some time looking at the pretty fashions before having tea in the Gamble Room.

It was going to be the most lovely, girly, prissy day.

I went to the V&A's general information desk to ask one of the nice ladies behind the counter where I would go to inquire about a vintage clothing item. She asked for specifics, and I explained how I was doing research on a safety-pocket.

Ever-so-helpfully I stated, "It's sort of a nineteenth-century version of a fanny pack."

The woman blinked at what I said and then hastily pointed me in the direction of the textiles hall, saying, "They might be able to help you better."

Another woman passing nearby with a group of school kids in tow looked at me somewhat disapprovingly, which I found curious, but reasoned that she was just worn out from being on a class field trip.

There wasn't any sort of research desk in the textiles and fashion area, so I stepped up to the reception counter where a couple of staff members were collecting tickets from the steady stream of visitors to the Balenciaga collection. The young woman noticed me and came over to help. Once again, I explained what I was looking for, again cheerfully making the fanny pack reference.

She hesitated, then got the young man's attention and she took tickets while he came to my assistance.

I was beginning to grow somewhat frustrated by everyone's reluctance in helping me, but I persisted, delivering my same spiel yet again, at which the young man drew in his breath before breaking into a wry smile.

In a flash, it hit me why everyone seemed so perplexed and rather put off by my request, and I felt my cheeks go hot with embarrassment.

Had it really been so long since I lived in England that I had forgotten about the word "fanny"? How that gentle American word for backside – as innocuous as "tushy" or "derriere" – to the English is a vulgar slang term for lady parts. Though not as bad as the c-word, it's still quite crass, pretty much on par with the kitty-cat word.

I was being a potty-mouth in the Victoria & Albert Museum.

Basically, I had been telling everyone I encountered that I was looking for a "pussy pack". On realizing this, I apologized profusely to the two people at the counter and then explained again, using the proper English term "bum bag". At this, they suggested I speak with one of the curators (who didn't seem to be anywhere in sight) and gave me the names of a couple of books they had on display which might contain what I was looking for. The history-of-pockets tome I'd read about online was stored away somewhere in the bowels of the museum. A curator would be able to help me with that.

I checked out the two books, but couldn't find anything. Still stinging from mortification, I decided not to seek out a curator. Suddenly I found I didn't really care about safety-pockets, and just wanted to be back outside enjoying the sunshine.

I even skipped tea in the Gamble Room.

I wasn't feeling very prissy anymore.

Illustration of Cornelia and Emily from **Our Hearts Were Young and Gay**; *the closest I ever got to a safety pocket, or even a photo of one.*

Cornelia and Emily had been humiliated by safety-pockets, so in keeping in sync with the girls' journey, it was probably only fitting that I should be humiliated by the wretched objects as well. There seems to be no end to the trouble those irksome safety-pockets can cause.

When I returned to the flat from my disturbing day at the museum, I was pleased to find I had another email from Sir Michael. Before I left on my trek to the V&A, I had sent him my available dates, but they weren't going to jive with their schedule, so it meant I wouldn't get to meet up with him and his wife. But he did say that he would have a look for photos, and email me scans of anything he came up with, which I thought extraordinarily kind of him.

Still, I was disappointed about not getting to meet the man himself. Sir Michael would have been the "passenger of note" in my book, just as his grandfather had been for Cornelia and Emily on their transatlantic crossing. But, for better or worse, that symmetry with the girls had kicked in once again. Which was probably just as well.

After the day's fanny pack incident, perhaps it was best that my manners and etiquette not be put to any tests at present.

Chapter 18

Happily it was cloudy and cool with chances of rain on the day I traveled to the National Archives at Kew. Had it been a sunny day, I would've been tempted to veer off to Kew Gardens instead. But the gloomy weather was sure to keep me indoors and focused on the growing pile of research topics I needed to investigate.

The Kew archives are housed in a nice-looking modern building which thankfully doesn't give the appearance of being too overwhelming. Perhaps that is due to the pretty fountains and the pond encircled by wildflowers and a walking path, which greet you as you arrive at the building.

After following the check-in protocol (which involved stashing everything in a locker except for my phone, notepad and a pencil, then placing those remaining items in a see-through bag and passing through a check point where it was all inspected by a guard), I spent a little time reviewing a book written in the early 1900s about the mail route which ran through southern England.

I had hoped it might be a starting point for enlightening me on who was at the reins the day the Skinners and Emily rode on top of the old mail coach to Hampton Court.

All that I had to go on was that the man looked like Rudyard Kipling, and was a member of the British peerage. But the book offered no information about the Royal Mail route to Hampton Court, or the four-in-hand club members who drove the coaches.

It was a bust. Not a promising start to the day.

Just as I finished skimming the book, a staff member came over and informed me that the other items I requested would have to be viewed inside a special room with stricter access, and it would take twenty minutes or so for someone to bring the materials to that room.

Classified info! I felt like a badass.

I used that wait time to hop on a computer and access the online archives, where I'd been told I could view scans of British immigration log books, including those from 1922.

With just a few clicks, I was looking at the logbook which confirmed my earlier research, that the *Empress of France* had docked in Southampton on June 21, 1922. Below this header, the list of the ship's passengers included the names Emily Kimbrough, Cornelia Otis Skinner and Paul Dudley White.

It was a victory tinged with defeat. I was thrilled to have proof positive that I had worked out the correct year of the girls' journey, but this information simultaneously deepened the biggest mystery for me.

The Great Educationalist.

For weeks after I had learned about F.W. Sanderson, I had clung to a crazy, desperate hope that either I had gotten the date of the girls' arrival in England wrong, or there had been a misprint or an incorrect transcription of Mr. Sanderson's death date.

It was time to settle the Sanderson question once and for all. While I was here at Kew and had access to the periodical records, I pulled up Sanderson's obituary. It seems all of the London newspapers had carried the story of his speech at University College and his shocking heart attack at the podium.

June 15, 1922.

Six days before Cornelia and Emily docked in Southampton.

Nothing had been recorded wrong, there was no mistake, and no question about it now.

F. W. Sanderson couldn't have been the man Cornelia and Emily met.

Unfortunately, he had been the one and only name proposed by the experts who know H.G. Wells the best. There were no other viable candidates. If H.G. Wells scholars couldn't sort out this mystery, then there was no chance I would.

For a good while, I was disheartened by the fact that I would never know the identity of The Great Educationalist. But then again, Cornelia and Emily never knew the answer, so it was only right that I shouldn't either. It was in keeping with the symmetry between their journey and mine.

After the partial win with the immigration record, I was ready to enter the inner sanctum of the special reading room. A staff member let me into the small, locked room where a few other researchers were inspecting photos, ancient-looking papers, and other fragments of history. I sat down to a set of large log books labeled "Secret" and

"Most Secret", which contained the correspondence of Hugh Trevor-Roper to his superiors in the British intelligence office during World War II.

It was time to follow up on the question which had taken me to Bletchley Park: that odd reference I had come across on Wikipedia, claiming Mr. Trevor-Roper had discovered that *Our Hearts* had been used as a Nazi codebook.

After my lack of success at Bletchley, I had made another run at the source of the reference, and contacted the editor of the book in which the assertion had been made. The editor had referred me to a college history professor who was the author of the article itself. I got in touch with the professor, who couldn't recall – let alone physically locate in his records – the origin of this information.

All we could conclude was that the story had to be true, only because it was a very precise statement, about a specific person and a specific book (the latter of which the professor had never heard of). It was highly implausible that the professor could have invented the story himself, given that it included the title of a book he didn't know existed.

This proved nothing, though. And I wanted to be certain of the truth. The answer, the proof, had to be somewhere in Hugh Trevor-Roper's papers. So I scoured the top-secret logbooks, but came up empty-handed.

Somehow that professor had stumbled upon information which I – who had spent months actively searching for it – couldn't locate. It was wildly frustrating.

But that wasn't the worst of it.

I came away from those logbooks feeling more unsettled by something I hadn't known to prepare myself for: my first experience reading about World War II in the present tense.

This wasn't history I was viewing, propped up in a glass display case in a museum. The words I was reading weren't being cited with quotation marks around them and a corresponding footnote number at the end of the passage, inside the safety of a textbook written well after the fact.

In these collected letters, World War II was now.

I felt shaky as I read Hugh's missives about upcoming Nazi military campaigns which, he noted, were being financed with assets stolen from the Jewish community, while they themselves were presently being rounded up and sent to work camps.

Presently? Work camps?

A passing reference to an unspeakable horror. And it was happening right there in that moment, as those words were being typed onto the page.

There were notes on spy operations involving Agents ZigZag and Snow, two names I knew from the history books. But here in these pages, those men were alive, darting in and out of intelligence reports which were tracking their *current* movements.

In one passage, Trevor-Roper reported his discovery that the Nazis were moving stolen artwork to the city of Siegen. This rang a bell for me, having just re-watched the film, "The Monuments Men" a few nights before on television.

Based on real life events, and directed by and starring George Clooney (who has a sort of Otis Skinner thing going), the movie tells the story of a group of civilian museum curators, art historians and professors whose mission it was to search for, recover and return the millions of art and cultural pieces which had been stolen and hidden by the Nazis.

Siegen is where Clooney's character, Frank Stokes, and his team realize the Nazis are storing stolen artwork not within the city, but in a copper mine just outside of town. This is a breakthrough moment for the men, giving them the key to finding vast stores of pilfered treasures in numerous mining towns.

Trevor-Roper's words concerning Siegen are sparse, but it's safe to assume, at the time of this transmission, British Intelligence would have been unaware of these secret hiding places. It made for strange reading, knowing I had intel which Hugh Trevor-Roper didn't.

Page after page, there were details of events I had only ever studied in the past tense, with the reassuring knowledge that the Allies had triumphed in the end. But within these logbooks, those uncertain, frightening days in 1943 were happening in the here and now.

Once again, I found the edges of time and space were blurring, but this time it was not a welcome experience. I hurried through the books as quickly as I could, just wanting to be done with them.

It had been a roller coaster of a day, my first foray into serious research. I was wrung out by the time I left Kew, thankful to have the strain on my brain over and done with.

It was time to get back to the spirit of *Our Hearts Were Young and Gay*, to the lighthearted pleasure of being in London and seeing the sights with the girls.

The sun was back with a vengeance the next morning. It was now July and things had turned hot. Being a seventh-floor apartment with no a/c or cross ventilation, it could get toasty in the flat.

Fortunately, those large modern windows of mine had a release latch, so I could pivot them on their hinges like the top of Dutch doors into the room, which helped draw in a breeze.

In addition to this, on hot nights I had taken to sleeping *au naturale* with an ice pack pressed up against my back, and was able to cope with the heat.

After the gray, misty skies and being inside the day before, I was determined to make the most of the dry weather. I had the whole day with nothing scheduled, so I decided I would just roam around, spending the day with London itself, and see where I ended up.

But things hadn't started off well.

I had awoken early that morning to the sound of a man's voice calling out "Hello?" from what I thought was the hallway.

No one answered.

After a couple more unanswered "Hellos?", I thought I should investigate. Perhaps the hello was directed at me. Strange that they wouldn't knock, I thought.

Easing out of bed with a careless leisure, I ambled over to the armoire, and after a few moments' searching, I pulled out a sundress and slipped it over my head.

Turning around, I found myself staring at a nice-looking young man who was hanging from a rappelling rope outside my open window, not more than fifteen feet away from me.

It was his voice that had been calling out to me.

There was no pretending that I hadn't exposed myself to him, but, gentleman that he was, he covered as best he could.

"Oh, I didn't see you there," he lied. "I'm washing the windows, and if you could just push these windows closed, that would be great."

I managed to eke out a, "Sure," and, stepping over to the windows, I swung them shut. Turning on my heels, I scurried into the bathroom and remained there until I was fairly certain the washer was gone.

For his part, my new friend made quick work of the cleaning job before swinging away from my flat as rapidly as he could manage.

Mortifying.

And then I remembered Cornelia's and Emily's window washer.

It was in Dieppe, the morning of their first full day in France. Remarkably the girls had also awakened to a man outside their open window (come to think of it, he was washing not the windows, but the roof of the portico). For over an hour, Cornelia and Emily spoke in French with the man while he worked and they ate breakfast in bed.

Cold comfort.

This seemed like a needless bit of symmetry, I thought to myself as I got dressed for real. Must I recreate every last detail of the girls' journey?

At least the naked part seemed needless.

The blush in my cheeks had finally begun to recede as I headed downstairs and out towards the park, where I ran into Sabrina and Tigger. After giving Tigger a few kisses and scratches on the head, I turned to Sabrina and fessed up about exposing myself to the window washer.

She brushed it off with a wave of her hand, "Oh, don't worry about it. I've done that so many times, the guys are used to it. Now we pretty much just wish each other a good morning and carry on like normal."

Once again, Sabrina had shown herself to be unfazed by life's twists and turns.

She is a star.

I thanked her for the reassuring words, then headed off on my walk. Crossing over from Imperial Wharf to lovely, rambling Battersea Park,

I wandered at a leisurely pace along the tree-lined paths, and spent a good while at the fountains where a number of dog owners were watching their pups play in the fountains. In a deeper pool, a couple of dogs were swimming after tennis balls, while others were bounding in and out of the water. Nearby, two other, less excitable dogs were wading in a small, shallow fountain. It was a joyful sight to behold, those beautiful pups with their happy spirits, and I was wishing Sabrina and Tigger had come with me.

I walked through to the end of Battersea Park, then crossed back over the Thames at the Albert Bridge. It may not be the grandest bridge in London, but I do so like it. Painted in Neapolitan colors, it always makes me think of candy and ice cream.

From there I strode along the north side of the river all the way to Westminster and the Houses of Parliament. It was the first time since my arrival in London that I had stood in front of them, and I spent a good while staring and gasping as I took in all the changes I was seeing.

There were multiple layers of thick concrete barriers protecting the iron gates which encircled the building, those gates having at one time been enough security on their own. There were the standard uniformed police officers, and then a number of officers wearing bulletproof vests who were carrying machine guns.

It wasn't just strikingly different from when Cornelia and Emily had been here, but also from when I had last visited as well.

Though I understood it – this was just a sign of the times – it made me sad, because I was pretty certain all of this would remain in place from here on out. It was never going to get better, more lax. If anything, the barriers and fearsome appearance would only get worse over time.

I was ready to escape back to the happiness of Chelsea. The walk to Westminster had taken some steam out of me, so I opted to return home by way of the Waterloo train station.

To get to Waterloo, I would need to walk across Parliament Bridge. It had not been that long ago that a man in a van had mowed down pedestrians on the bridge before hopping out and killing a police officer who stopped him as he charged towards the Parliament building.

I was keenly aware of this fact as I started across the bridge, noting the newly installed barriers between the pavement and the sidewalks.

There were scores of people on the bridge taking photographs, seemingly carefree and unaware of what had transpired on this very spot just recently.

I wondered how many of them knew, and had thought about where they were now standing. Whether they did or they didn't, there was a strange comfort in seeing crowds of people enjoying themselves, without a worry in the world.

Those new barriers were a sign of the times, but the mirthful tourists on the bridge were a testament to the resilience of the human spirit.

Chapter 19

The study abroad course which had brought me to England when I was twenty-two had begun in the summer, in the pleasing university town of Cambridge. The program consisted of three weeks attending lectures and writing a paper, followed by two weeks up in Scotland taking in the mind-blowing array of theatre productions, stand-up comedy and other live performances which make up the famous Edinburgh Fringe Festival.

After that, we students had a five-week break to spend traveling around the UK and the continent. Armed with a Eurail youth pass and an international hostel card tucked into that fanny pack – excuse me, bum bag – of mine, I would perform the rite of passage that was backpacking through Europe, before heading to Oxford for the fall term.

I had known from the beginning of my journey with the girls that at some point during my time in England, I would visit Cambridge. So many of my best memories came from there, and I was enamored by the idea of returning to Cambridge after almost thirty years.

For a twenty-two-year-old girl from Missouri, it had been daunting, traveling abroad for the first time, but it didn't take me long to get my bearings, thanks to eight of my fellow classmates from Stephens College who were on the course with me. We had a glorious time during those weeks in Cambridge, embracing our new world, meeting other students, flirting with English boys, and generally having a whirl, as Cornelia and Emily would say.

My 1942 copy of *Our Hearts* had come with me then, along with a brand-new travel journal, in which I had inscribed on the front flyleaf a few of Cornelia's and Emily's closing lines:

> "We would come back again, but it would never be the same… There would never again be a 'first time'".

It was essential, then, that the girls travel with me now. With that same 1942 *Our Hearts* in hand, I headed to King's Cross Station and in just a little over an hour, we were once again in Cambridge. I took my time on the walk from the train station into town, to really absorb where I was, and hopefully connect to this place which held so many joyful recollections for me.

As I got close to the city centre, I unexpectedly came upon a massive twenty-first century shopping mall called the Grand Arcade. There was no identifying what centuries-old buildings had been swallowed up when that behemoth was wedged into the cozy streets of Cambridge. Yes, yes, time marches on and you can't stop progress and all that, but this was not a welcome discovery for me, nor an encouraging beginning to my stroll down memory lane.

I walked from there over to the entrance to King's College, one of Cambridge University's finest schools. It had been here that I had stood almost three decades ago, frozen in wonder as a young man with dark hair and glasses came through the college's gate in his wheelchair, followed by a small entourage.

It was the summer of 1988, when *A Brief History of Time* was taking the scientific world and the bestseller lists by storm.

And there I was, coming face to face with its author, Stephen Hawking.

He and his posse were past me within an instant, and I could only stand and stare after them, marveling in disbelief that I had just crossed paths with the most brilliant mind on Earth.

But had it been right here? Or had this happened at the other entrance to the college, the one facing the Queen's Road? It had been such a profound moment, a treasured memory, and yet it had slipped a little from my grasp. How could I have let my recall become fuzzy like that?

From there I wove through a small, winding street to the tucked-away entrance to Clare College, and passed through the main quad, where all those years ago, we Stephens women had come for classes, and eaten our meals in the buttery (the college cafeteria).

Just past the quad was the Clare College bridge, arguably the prettiest bridge along the Backs (the name given to the area along the River Cam where a number of colleges back up to the water). The view from the bridge is the stuff of picture postcards – the exquisite gardens, punters on the river, the sublime King's College Chapel overlooking a meadow filled with languorous grazing cows.

For a while I watched the flat-bottom boats known as punts pass beneath the bridge, as their occupants navigated the river with varying degrees of success. Some of my happiest memories of Cambridge were of punting alongside the colleges with my fellow Stephens women, and I was enthralled watching the nervous, intrepid souls attempt to steer their little boats.

But not all of the punts were small. Outnumbering the traditional punts were supersized variations of the boats which seated four across. They were filled with as many tourists as they could hold, and these "puntoons" took up most of the space on the crowded waterway.

Disheartened by this sight, I directed my attention to seeing if I could still locate a secret I knew about the bridge. I found it to be as I remembered, and this confirmation buoyed my faltering spirits. I then took a moment to stand in the spot where I had been kissed by a cricket player named Andrew on a beguiling summer evening in 1988.

(Speaking as a rabid anglophile, I feel compelled to say, it is very satisfying to have been kissed by a cricket player on the Clare College bridge.)

From this vantage point, I studied the college's sublime gardens, and noticed that the nimble weeping willow which had stood at the water's edge, where we would sometimes retreat to after class, was no longer there. About thirty feet from where it had stood, a smaller weeping willow grew, which would one day block the idyllic view of the gardens.

The changes were starting to take their toll on my spirit.

I continued on across the Queen's Road and walked down the drive to Thirkell Court, the residence hall where our group had stayed that summer.

There had been some changes here, too.

The Henry Moore sculpture that had resided in the courtyard was nowhere to be seen. Inside, the hallways which were once lit only by the light coming through the windows and an occasional single shaded bulb now appeared to be perpetually under interrogation, almost glowing from the white glare of oversized fluorescents in the ceiling.

Upstairs in the bathroom, the subway tiles and swimming pool-sized cast iron tub had been replaced by a pair of pre-fab shower units with an unfortunate design which never had been or ever would be fashionable.

And I had been so fond of that tub.

It had been the centerpiece of the residence hall's classic Edwardian-looking bathroom – crisp white with a black floor. The tub was long enough to stretch out in completely, and deep enough to where I could submerge myself entirely under the water. In the US, I had grown up with tubs where either one's torso stuck out of the water, or one had to bend at the knees in order to get one's shoulders wet. And American tubs always had that overflow drain which wouldn't allow the water to get deeper than four inches, six if you were lucky.

In England they have no such scruples about preventing bathtub drowning, and this tub could hold water a good eighteen inches deep. There were two faucets, one for hot water and the other for cold. When it came to rinsing our hair, we either had to go with soaking it in the tub water, or contort ourselves under the taps, going back and forth between ice cold and scalding hot streams. In time, we were clued in by a British student, who instructed us to use a pan from the kitchen to mix the hot and cold streams, then dump it over our heads. We were college-educated women, yet we hadn't been clever or resourceful enough to figure this out on our own.

Despite the inconvenience with washing our hair, to us that tub was a luxury and a treat. I have a marvelous memory of leisurely soaking one morning in an almost-too-hot bath. It was early and everything was quiet, and I was in almost a Zen-like state, marveling at the extraordinary fact that I was soaking in a tub in Cambridge, England, watching the steam rise off my skin when I lifted my arms from the water.

Sometimes life is perfect.

These changes to my residence hall were insignificant, really, but they made me feel strangely disconnected and a bit glum, and I was ready to get out of there.

Adding insult to injury, I had wanted to leave via the building's "secret passageway" – i.e. the after-hours entrance students used once the gates were locked for the night by the porter – but I couldn't remember how to get to it. Frustrated by this, I left through the front door and headed back across the Queen's Road to the footpath which ran along the Backs.

My spirit rebounded a bit, as I saw that at least this hadn't changed.

I strode along the path, pausing at Trinity College and Newton's Mathematical Bridge.

Spanning the River Cam, this eighteenth century wooden structure had been designed by Sir Isaac Newton, and was constructed without using nails or bolts.

Somewhere along the line – one of our professors had explained to us – a group of scholars had disassembled the bridge in order to understand Newton's design, and then found they could not put it back together, and eventually resorted to using nails and bolts to reassemble it.

What an idiotic thing for them to have done.

Such a waste and a shame.

Except none of it is true.

And here's the kicker: I didn't know the Newton story – which I had believed for thirty years – was an urban legend until I began writing a blog post that evening about my visit to Cambridge, and was double-checking the name of the college on Wikipedia.

At least this one illusion hadn't been shattered for me until after I had returned to London.

Crossing to the other side of the Silver Street bridge, I carefully maneuvered down an ancient set of steps to the riverbank where a number of proper punts floated idly next to the boarding area for the puntoons, which was crowded with tourists.

It was here that we Stephens women had docked that day, on our first outing in one of the boats. Having been given a ninety-second tutorial in how to punt by one of our professors, five in our group had taken on the challenge and quickly succeeded in learning at least the rudimentary points of punting. Figuring that the occasion called for some celebratory wine, Sally, Deborah and I had waited in the boat while Jennifer and Stephanie went up and across the bridge to score a couple of bottles at The Anchor Pub, which sits facing the landing.

Ten minutes later they returned with not only the wine, but three cute English boys as well, who then joined us in our punting. Our one-hour excursion turned into five hours going up and down the river, filled with flirting, riotous laughter, and a few of us ending up with dates for that evening.

That is how you go punting.

After grabbing a few photos of the boats, I went back up and over the bridge to The Anchor itself. This had been our go-to spot, our hangout. Mercifully, I found that the place had hardly changed at all.

This stop was to be the big finish to my day, where I would raise a glass to times past, and to all of those bright, beautiful souls with whom I had shared the once-in-a-lifetime adventures of my first time abroad.

And what better way to toast on a warm, sunny day, than with the quintessential English summer drink, Pimm's and lemonade? I had been introduced to that splendid concoction right here in this very establishment, by that cricket player from the Clare College bridge.

I took my drink out to the platform area overlooking the river and silently toasted to old friends and glorious memories, then took a sip of my Pimm's. After the discouraging morning I had just experienced, it was only fitting, really, that the drink tasted watered down and flavorless, and not as I had remembered it.

Appropriately symbolic of the day I was having.

It had been a rougher landing than I had expected, here in Cambridge. Clearly, the long stretch of time between my visits had caused small, gradual changes to appear large and drastic. Or maybe my memories had gone awry.

I left The Anchor feeling as flat as my drink had been. It was time to return to London.

Back on the train, I reflected on the day, trying to work out if I had gotten any of... well, whatever it was I had come for.

Why had it been easier to connect to Cornelia's and Emily's past than to my own?

And then in a moment of clarity, I remembered the postscript I had written in 1988 on the back flyleaf of that travel journal of mine.

I had inscribed, "I would come back again, but it would never be the same. There would never again be a first time".

Those prophetic words had circled back around to me today, and were ringing in my ears. There was no surprising revelation nor sting in them, but nevertheless I had been blindsided. I had gone to Cambridge anticipating a day of happy nostalgia, only to find myself standing precisely in the moment where that postscript of mine had become completely and astonishingly true.

When I saw Stephen Hawking there on the street that summer day in 1988, I hadn't known what to do or say.

Twenty-nine years later, there was something important I needed to ask him.

If only I had known then to quiz Professor Hawking about the illusion of time – or if there was a way for me now to step back into 1988 – I would ask him if there was any scientific basis for these sensations I was having of time blurring whenever I would stand where Cornelia and Emily had once been. Or even where I, myself, had stood.

Then again, the cold, hard truth of science might burst the bubble, and I would learn that these moments I so relished were nothing more than an illusion, a figment of my imagination.

That was an unacceptable notion. I preferred to keep believing all of this was real.

Chapter 20

Tuesday, July 4, 2017. Back in the States, my fellow Americans would be celebrating Independence Day. But the English aren't big on celebrating that particular holiday, so I opted to mark the occasion by spending the day with Jane Austen.

At least it's how I thought it would go. Instead, it became about what I would later refer to as, "Winchester and the Evolution of the English Gentleman".

Because you just never know how a day will turn out.

There were multiple reasons for me to visit the town of Winchester, and for me to be excited about it. The first was that it was where Otis had taken Emily for an afternoon of sightseeing during those ten long days they were staying in Southampton, waiting for Cornelia to recover from the measles.

The second reason was that it would give me the chance to revisit Winchester Cathedral (not to be confused with the similar-sounding Westminster Abbey in London). It had been more than a quarter-century since I was here, working as general backstage crew on a production of a play written by Francis Warner, the Oxford University professor who ran my study abroad program.

His plays are really more works of poetry, whose lyrical beauty I didn't fully appreciate in my twenties, when I was here with the production of "Byzantium", a story of the emperor Constantine.

(One of my most vivid memories of working on that play was that one of my jobs involved helping the quiet and really cute young man who was playing "Belisarius" into the Roman battle armor portion of his costume, which fit over his tunic. That young man's name was Simon Beaufoy, who just a few years later would go on to a brilliant screenwriting career, with film credits including "The Full Monty" and "Slumdog Millionaire".)

But the main reason I was eager to visit Winchester was that, in remembrance of the two-hundredth anniversary of Jane Austen's death, there was a big exhibition happening at their discovery centre, featuring her handwritten letters, some rarely seen portraits of Austen, and a silk pelisse (a Regency-era overcoat-type garment) believed to have been worn by her.

In anticipation of my visit, I had stayed up the night before to finish re-watching for the umpteenth time the last episodes of the 1995 miniseries adaptation of "Pride & Prejudice". I would be able to peek at Jane Austen's personal things, then offer remembrance and a word of thanks at her grave in Winchester Cathedral, all hot on the heels of my evening with her Mr. Darcy.

Needless to say, I was looking forward to a full day of unbridled prissiness.

It was a lovely morning with Jane. I pored over every item in the exhibit, from the astonishingly small coin purse she had made for herself, to movie posters of the myriad film productions based on her works.

But what meant the most to me was reading her letters. That writer of such gentle, endearing stories was herself fearless and unapologetic for who she was and what she was doing.

If she had self-doubt, she didn't record it anywhere.

She is my hero.

As I headed from the exhibit to the Cathedral, I passed a most welcome sight: a proper, old-school fish and chips shop. It was, surprisingly, the first of its kind I had seen since arriving in England, which seems to have been overtaken by smoothie bars, fast fusions, and generally healthy eats. This could be one of the last true chippies standing, and I salute it.

I continued on towards the Cathedral. As I entered its gardens, a tall, nice-looking guy who appeared to be in his thirties followed me in and spoke to me. I had noticed him earlier when we crossed paths on the High Street, and now he was introducing himself (let's call him James), and inviting me to go have a coffee.

It was flattering that this young man was interested in me, but I had not softened in my views about being a creepy old woman. I declined, but thanked him for the sweet invitation. He then asked if we could at least just sit in the garden and talk for a few minutes.

That I could do.

(Full disclosure: This wasn't the first time I'd been picked up when touring one of the great English houses of worship – which are apparently more of a hot spot for me than any bar or pub ever was. During my study abroad year, I had met three gorgeous Australians while I was visiting Westminster Abbey. It's how I learned about the Aussie enclave in Bayswater. I ended up dating two of the three young men. One of them was a long-haired saxophone player. Doesn't it seem we all have to go through that long-haired musician phase when we're young? Sorry, I digress...)

James and I sat down on a bench in the garden which boasted an unusual feature: a sculpture of what appeared to be either a little dog or a fox curled up asleep under it.

We conversed about his job and my book project, and I gave him my website info. He was like so many of the young men I remember from my years living in England – just very polite and very engaging.

That is something which young Englishmen have always had over young American men: they really, really know how to charm women. They go about it in such a gentlemanly way.

And yes, most of the time, it's just a line. But it's a very effective line.

Back in the present, James and I had been making small talk for maybe ten minutes when he leaned in and kissed me.

It was rather surprising, and sweet.

And then he kept kissing me. Part of me thought I probably shouldn't let this continue, especially because there were other visitors to the Cathedral gardens whom I was fairly certain had witnessed

James introducing himself to me. But the other part of me could only think of how this would make a good story for my book.

Utterly mercenary, yes, I know.

He was cute, he was charming and this was nice, so I let it go on for a bit. But then when he suggested we go somewhere a little more private, I told him I really needed to get on with touring the Cathedral. He asked if he could see me again. I informed him I would be leaving the UK soon, and he said he would keep in touch with me, with the hope that we could meet up again before I returned to the States.

We said our goodbyes, and I walked away feeling more pleased than not about the encounter.

Rejoining Jane Austen inside the magnificent, towering Gothic walls of Winchester Cathedral, I took my time visiting her grave marker. For decades, I have laughed and cried and taken comfort in her words, which I never tire of reading. There at her grave, I thanked her for everything she has given me.

Which is a lot.

As I moved in and out of the transepts and back down the nave, studying the Cathedral's breathtaking architecture, I thought back with great fondness to the people and that play, "Byzantium", from all those years ago. I could picture it so clearly, and it was wonderful to bring those memories to life again. Then all too soon, it was time to get back to London.

After an obligatory stop at the Cathedral gift shop, I headed back to the train station, but not before popping into the chippy for some scampi and chips, soaked in malt vinegar and wrapped in newsprint.

Ninety minutes later, I arrived at my flat in Chelsea and found I had received a lovely email from young James, telling me how pleased he was to have met me.

Darling.

Then there was the postscript.

James explained that he had taken a naughty picture of himself to show me *just exactly how excited he was* about our encounter, but that he was too much of a gentleman to send the photo without asking me first.

Excuse me?

It wasn't so much the thought of receiving my first unsolicited dick pic which bothered me, as it was the "gentleman" reference. Is this what distinguishes a gentleman these days, that he asks first before sending a nude selfie?!

With that, my Jane Austen day evaporated.

And poor Mr. Darcy! The quintessential English gentleman had just been run through with a sword.

When did unsolicited dick pics become a normal part of courtship? I could accept that the young man I met was no Mr. Darcy, but couldn't he at least be more like the young men I remembered from my first time abroad? Had the guys on this side of the pond lost their edge over the Americans in the way they seduced women?

I could almost feel Cornelia and Emily averting their eyes and stifling their laughs. There wasn't an inkling of symmetry to be found between their romantic adventures and mine.

Which to this point amounted to one Bafta-winning cross-dresser and one "junk mail" sender.

The next day was a hot one, which was rough because I was spending a lot of it in the flat doing laundry, packing, and finishing up the last details for the France portion of the journey, which I would begin the following Monday.

My time in England was almost over – a startling realization. For nearly six weeks, I had been living the pages of *Our Hearts Were Young and Gay*, experiencing moments of magic whenever I found myself connecting to Cornelia's and Emily's adventure. But there had been more to it than that. It was as if a wondrous spell had been cast over my entire journey, even to where the routine, uneventful days – the laundry days – were permeated with that magic as well.

I did my best to hold tight to every moment, appreciating it, being in it, but the hours and days had slipped away. France was sure to come and go in a flash. It gave me pains to know I couldn't make these enchanted days slow down, but I would do my level-best to ensure the spell wouldn't be broken.

I was getting nervous about this next leg of my travels, and not just because I was going to parts of France I'd never been to before. I simply wasn't excited about it, as I wrote in my journal,

"I think it is because I'm worried about it being isolating. Between being in a car alone for a week, and not speaking more than a few words of the language, this could easily turn into a lonely experience, even for me, who cherishes my alone time. I just need to trust that this part of the trip will bring me what I need for my book, even if I cannot know or say what that is."

That afternoon, I went over to say, not a "goodbye" but a "see you soon" to Sabrina and Tigger. I took with me the few perishables I had left in the fridge, along with some odds and ends I'd decided to jettison in England. I had already mailed a box of souvenirs to the States, which had included my fascinator. But the giant hatbox would have to remain behind with Sabrina, and she seemed most pleased to have it. Her unused fascinator from this season would be rested and ready for next year's Ascot.

There was another email from Winchester James waiting for me when I returned to my flat. Now that I had told him it was a "hard no" on the dick pic (so to speak) he had changed his tone. He dismissed it as "a silly suggestion" and had decided to try out a more subtle approach, endeavoring to romance me instead of dirty talk me.

It didn't hurt for him to try. Who knew?

Maybe I might just be able to salvage the story after all.

Chapter 21

Saturday, July 8, was to be bittersweet. It was most certainly a big deal, and I had been looking forward to it for months. But it would be my last hurrah in England, just like it had been for the girls ninety-five years ago (minus one day).

It was time to follow Cornelia and Emily to H.G. Wells' house for lunch.

In 1922, the year of the girls' trip, H.G. Wells and his family were living at Easton Glebe, a classic Georgian home on the grand Easton Lodge estate belonging to the Daisy Greville, Countess of Warwick.

A descendant of King Charles II and his mistress, the actress Nell Gwynn, Daisy Greville was a prominent supporter of education for women, and of aiding the less fortunate in housing, education and jobs (no question, she would have been acquainted with The Great Educationalist, and must've enjoyed conversing with him). A longtime friend – and possibly mistress – of randy, rambunctious King Edward VII, the Countess of Warwick was the inspiration for the song, "Daisy, Daisy".

The Countess had let Easton Glebe to Mr. Wells, and this home would serve as the setting for his novel, *Mr. Britling Sees It Through* – a novel about an American who joins a famous thinker and his family during a weekend country house party.

Emily would later recall in her writings that when she stepped from the house onto the terrace and walked through the garden, she felt as if she were walking through the pages of *Mr. Britling*.

(Thinking back on it now, could Emily have had some inkling of the affair between Mr. Wells and Margaret Sanger? After all, in *Mr. Britling* – a thinly-veiled portrait of Mr. Wells and his life with his second wife, Catherine – his fictional counterpart is very forthcoming about his numerous infidelities. Even naïve Emily couldn't have missed this. Then again, Cornelia and Emily did describe themselves in their younger years as being "not altogether bright".)

The girls' day at Mr. Wells' house is one of my favorite parts of *Our Hearts*, and I wanted to get as close to their experience as possible – minus the humiliations they both suffered while they were there.

In the spring, I had learned that in 1950 the Easton Lodge estate had been broken up into pieces, and that the Countess of Warwick's great manor house had been almost completely torn down (strangely, one wing of the house had been left standing, and had been converted into a home of its own). But blessedly, Mr. Wells' Easton Glebe still stood.

Going on the premise that it never hurts to ask, I had written a letter to the current owners of Easton Glebe, explaining my project and asking if I might imposition them with a visit to their house. Soon I received a very kind email reply from Vincent, inviting me to come for lunch one day when I was in England, stating that he and his wife Diana would be happy to show me around. I was ecstatic!

I had the exact day in mind for my visit: Sunday, July 9. The obsessed, geeky part of my brain had pretty much worked out that this was most likely the day the girls went to Mr. Wells' home, given the "clues" they offer in the book regarding their timeline.

Unfortunately, Vincent and Diana already had plans for that day, but were happy to host me on Saturday, July 8.

And now here it was.

That morning, I packed up a first edition of *Our Hearts* and a framed copy of the "Margaret Sanger photo", along with a bottle of wine, to take as thank you gifts for my hosts.

I traveled by train to Stanstead Airport, where Vincent "collected" me outside the arrivals hall. He said he had no trouble picking me out of the crowd, since I had given him a description of myself as having "Lucy-red hair".

We drove along the country lanes bordering what once had been the Countess of Warwick's estate, and Vincent pointed out the wheat field which had been an American air squadron landing area during WWII.

Exactly ninety-five years (minus that one day), almost to the hour, after Cornelia and Emily visited Easton Glebe, I was arriving in that same driveway, pulling up to the stately red brick house which H.G. Wells would recognize today as the one he'd lived in.

It was all a perfect match to what Cornelia and Emily had described – the beautiful, sunny day, the ride through the captivating countryside, turning in at the gate marking the entrance to Easton Glebe. My skin tingled.

It was easy to picture the Skinners and Emily pulling up to this handsome home and being as captivated by it as I was. As I got out of the car, I whispered to Cornelia and Emily that we were here at Mr. Wells' house again. And I couldn't help but wince at the thought of poor Emily's panicked reaction upon their arrival.

> "Emily said it had just come over her all of a heap that she was about to meet Mr. H.G. Wells and she hadn't planned what she'd say to him… and she slid down onto the floor of the car as it came to a stop and saying, 'I'll just stay out of sight until I can collect myself', she went into a curious crouching position like a praying mantis. At that moment the door behind her was flung open and she bulged out rear first into Mr. Wells himself, so the formality of a conversational introduction was side-stepped."

Vincent and I entered the house through the large, sunlit kitchen, where he introduced me to his wife Diana. I also met their dogs, Dottie and Siggy, and then Diana gave me a tour.

Their home was at once both elegant and warm. Besides the drawing room and dining room Cornelia and Emily wrote about, there was a wonderful card room which Vincent and Diana use as their main sitting room. She then showed me Mr. Wells' study, which Vincent now uses as his office.

Passing through the rooms which Cornelia and Emily had written of made my blood rush – this was the closest I would get to the girls, as well as Otis and Maud Skinner. I did my best to stay in the present, to make conversation, and cover the profound emotional reaction I was having, but I felt as if I was as much in the room with H.G. Wells and Margaret Sanger and my girls as I was with Diana.

After the tour of the house, we enjoyed lunch in the same dining room where Emily had experienced her second embarrassing turn of the day, the poor girl!

As she had stood to leave after their lunch, Emily somehow had become ensnared in a servant's bell cord which was attached underneath the table, ripping it loose from its mounting. To her bewilderment, the cord wrapped around Emily's leg, trapping her, and Mr. Wells had to crawl under the table and untangle it from her. The rest of the party had sat in silent chagrin, all except Cornelia:

> "… I smothered my face in a portière to keep Mr. Wells from hearing my maniacal yells of rapture."

As we ate, I attempted to splutter out my gratitude for my hosts' unbelievable kindness and hospitality in letting a virtual stranger barge into their home. Vincent and Diana explained that they've had a number of Wells enthusiasts come to the house over the years, including the H.G. Wells Society. I told them about enlisting the society's help in my attempt to solve the mystery of the Great Educationalist, as we dined on coronation chicken and salad made from Diana's garden, followed by strawberries and cream – again, fresh from the garden. It was all simply sublime.

After lunch, Vincent, Diana and I moved out to the terrace which had so much reminded Emily of *Mr. Britling*, and they showed me around Diana's garden, pointing out in particular a spot at the end of it where Mr. Wells' summer house had been.

Apparently there is a common practice amongst English writers, where they eschew a comfortable desk and chair in their home and do their writing in the garden shed, and Mr. Wells had used his little summer house for this purpose.

Diana then pointed out the building which had once been the barn. This is where the girls had been coerced by their host into playing "the Wells game" (a version of volleyball which Mr. Wells had invented), and Cornelia had taken her turn at embarrassing herself in spectacular style.

After making a poor showing through a few rounds of the game, Cornelia, in a determined effort to help her team, had delivered a mighty wallop to the ball as it came at her, and inadvertently smashed it directly into the face of the Great Educationalist,

> "… who was on my own side and no further from me than a couple of feet. It was the only time during the course of the day his face changed expression… I was too horrified at what I'd done even to apologize. After going over his face with his fingers and making certain his features were still there, the eminent worthy changed places with the person furthest from me, and the game continued…"

When the estate was divided up, the barn had been separated from the Easton Glebe property and was made into a home of its own. A wall with a gate now divided the two properties. Peeking through the wrought iron, I could just make out the fountain area and steps where Cornelia and Emily had been photographed with the Great Educationalist in 1922.

Of the gifts I'd brought them, Vincent and Diana had seemed especially pleased with the picture of Otis, Margaret Sanger and Mr. Wells.

Returning to the terrace now, Diana worked out that the photo was taken in front of the doors to Mr. Wells' study. She was intrigued that in the photograph, there appears to be a pergola framing the study doors, which is no longer there today. She and Vincent felt that this was a very smart idea, as the study faced west and often became intolerably hot in the afternoon.

Studying the stone walkway and the brick walls, we were able to find traces of where the pergola had been mounted, and they began to play with the idea of putting in a pergola like the one which had stood there before.

Before they took me back to the train station, Vincent and Diana wanted to drive me over to meet Paul and Paul, the current homeowners of the Countess of Warwick's remaining wing. As we pulled away from Easton Glebe, we found that their dog Dottie was following behind the car, wanting to come along. As we passed through the gates, Vincent stopped, and the "cheeky girl" was allowed to hop in and join us.

It was just a few minutes' drive through the forests and fields before we arrived at what had clearly been part of a great stately manor. We were met at the front door by one of the Pauls, who was just on his way out to look for their dog, Coco, who had run off. He apologized for not being able to invite us in and show me the house, but we said, with Dottie wagging her tail triumphantly, we understood about rambunctious dogs.

Before we said our farewells, Paul informed us they had Canadians staying with them. It seemed they, too, had been invaded by visitors from the New World. Hopefully they weren't some crazed nerds. Like me.

On our drive to the train station, Diana reiterated how interested they were in the photograph I had brought them, and how delighted they were to know Mr. Wells' solution to the afternoon sunlight issue.

This gave me a good deal of satisfaction – after all of their kindness towards me, I was able in return to give them a small piece of practical history which could prove useful to them. It was a drop in the bucket compared to what my new friends had given me on that extraordinary Saturday afternoon, but at least it was something.

Part 4

Setting Forth On Our Own

Normandy

Chapter 22

"We were now really setting forth on our own and on that territory known delectably as 'the Continent'".

Shortly after their visit to H.G. Wells' house, the girls left for France. Cornelia's parents stayed behind in England for a couple of weeks before traveling to Paris where they would meet up again with the girls.

Monday, July 10. The day had come for me to sail to France. By taking the ferry from Newhaven to Dieppe, I was following Cornelia's and Emily's itinerary.

This was my first time crossing the Channel on that route. My few other crossings had been from the more-often traveled Dover to Calais, but it had been decades since I had done that, opting instead to travel via the Chunnel once it opened in 1994.

I had been sad to learn that, though there was still regular ferry service from Dover to Calais, the hovercraft had been put out of business by the Chunnel. I had always meant to travel on it sometime because it reminded me of the crafts they rode in at the beginning of the old cartoon, "Johnny Quest".

At the crack of dawn on that Monday, I said my goodbyes to my sweet Chelsea flat and hustled over to Victoria Station, where I hopped on the first train to Brighton, then caught the train to Newhaven. It had said on the ferry website that passengers needed to be at the terminal by 8:15AM for the 9AM sailing because they closed boarding at that time.

I was cutting it close, but I managed to breeze into the passengers' waiting room at 8:20am, where, as it turned out, the staff had no imminent plans to get us on board. This gave me time to hit the café and grab some tea and toast.

At the counter, a very nice woman named Anne, who had been looking at the menu alongside me, ordered the same thing, and we chatted for a bit about our travels. She and her husband were going over to look for a second home in the Normandy countryside. In

Dieppe, they were to meet their daughter, Stacey, who was driving up from her house in Paris. I told Anne about my book project, and she was very kind, and interested in my journey.

When our food arrived, we moved to separate tables in different corners of the room. A moment later her husband joined Anne at her table, and I heard her telling him about me, explaining how I was a writer.

It took me by surprise to hear myself referred to as a writer. This certainly felt like news to me.

Up until now, whenever I had spoken to anyone about what I was doing, it was always in almost apologetic terms – this was my first attempt at writing a book, it was a new thing for me, I was giving it a try, etc.

But Anne had only heard, within all of my spluttering, that I was a writer. This is how she saw me, defined me.

It was a lovely, unexpected gift which I hadn't known I needed.

To her, I was a writer.

I needed to be that to myself as well. In that moment, I made a promise to myself to own the title of writer, to proclaim it without apology to the world, and to know it myself. It was one of the most significant moments of my journey, and I wanted desperately to tell Anne how important her words were to me, but I decided to leave her be – mostly because I didn't want to shatter her illusion of me!

After I finished eating, I went back out to the waiting room and sat down in one of the long rows of seats. Directly behind me was a darling young woman with a china doll face and funky style. Sitting with her was her boyfriend, who could have come from Central Casting – that is, if anyone had been looking for an affected, intellectual type with long scraggly hair whose clothes suggested he had just rolled out of bed wearing them.

The boyfriend was intermittently griping about having to wait so long to board. It had gone past 8:45 and there was no sign we would be getting on the ferry anytime soon. For some reason, this guy was blaming his girlfriend for his present predicament. I could hear her quietly trying to reason with him, but he just kept moaning and working himself up more about it until he finally stomped off, stating that he wasn't going. She was left sitting alone, fighting back tears.

Within moments after he disappeared, a staff member called us all to get on the bus which would shuttle us to the ferry. The young woman remained seated as the rest of us went out to the bus. Once aboard the shuttle, I sat down and watched for her, growing angrier every moment at that stupid guy, cursing him if he had ruined everything and kept her from going on her trip.

At the very end of those climbing onto the bus, I saw him first. He got on and headed towards the back. A few passengers later, she appeared and, in what I considered to be an act of divine intervention, sat down next to me.

Not for nothing had I been raised in a family of strong-minded women and attended a strong-minded women's college. I had held my tongue earlier, and had begun to regret it. Now I seized on the moment and pushed in.

The idea of a moody, mopey guy spoiling a woman's travels was a personal affront to me, and I wasn't going to let that boob in the back of the bus get away with his behavior.

After a minute or two of polite chit-chat, in which I learned her name was Katie and she was headed to France for a fun, quick (no mention of "romantic") getaway, I dove right in.

"I'm sorry to be so forward, but I'm American and have no scruples about such things. You seem like a terrific person, and right now you need a girlfriend to have your back about this situation with that guy. I overheard everything in the waiting room. He was so off-base, and I'm glad that you didn't let his tantrum stop you from coming."

Without giving Katie the chance to be taken aback, let alone respond, I continued, "But I'm telling you now, if he utters one more word of complaint at any time – about anything – for the rest of your trip, just leave him where he is. Dump him right there. He shouldn't get to wreck your holiday."

This made her laugh a bit. I pressed on, "I'm not kidding. If your girlfriends were here right now, they would be saying exactly the same thing to you."

She agreed, and told me that she was still bothered by him, but that she was going to enjoy her weekend away. This was supposed to be a happy thing for her, and she was going to make sure it was.

About this time, we got to the ferry and went our separate ways once on board. I figured that somewhere along the line, she had met up with the whiny boyfriend and he was still being enough of a brat to upset her, because a while later, as we were leaving Newhaven, I saw her standing alone on the top deck, looking wistful and rather sad. But I didn't attempt to approach her again.

Besides, I, too, was having my own issues as the boat pulled away from the shoreline.

I was struck with sadness that I was leaving a country which was like home to me. It was that same heavy feeling I got every time I stepped on a plane at Heathrow or Gatwick airport.

But it was more than that now.

I looked out at the chalk cliffs we were sailing away from, and knew that the next time I set foot on English soil, my journey with the girls would be over. *Our Hearts Were Young and Gay* concludes in Paris, so at the end of July, when I would board the Eurostar train at the Gare du Nord, I would be declaring an end to my travels with Cornelia and Emily.

At this point, they were not only my old friends, but my travel companions. And knowing full well that I would never replicate this journey, I was keenly aware that I would never again travel with the girls. The mere thought of it was extremely disheartening.

The weather had changed overnight, and it became increasingly gloomy and cold as we headed out across the Channel, so I went inside and did some refresher reading on the Dieppe portion of *Our Hearts*.

It had been a much prettier day when Cornelia and Emily had sailed. They wrote,

> "Dieppe, with its church towers, its snug, deep harbor, the line of summer hotels bordering the wide plage [beach], and the 15th Century chateau crowning its white cliff, is a charming port of entry into France. It all looked just as it should…"

A promising start for the girls but, as it always was with Cornelia and Emily, there was bound to be an incident.

After some shady dealings in the Dieppe customs hall, where the girls had bribed an official to let their bags through uninspected (a brazen move, but then these two were made of guts and sand, remember?), they had been sales-talked by a local into letting him convey their luggage to their *pension* in an ox cart, while they followed behind him on foot. He had promised it was not a long walk, but it had proved otherwise, and at the end of their exhaustive trek, he had berated them for giving him too small a tip.

It took my boat four hours to cross from Newhaven to Dieppe. There seemed to be a lot of families on board who were headed over for what was presumably a few weeks of holiday. They already looked tired. No one appeared to be teeming with enthusiasm about their upcoming plans.

At one point, I ran into Anne from the Newhaven café, and chatted some more with her and her husband Alan. But, after my hurried morning getting to the ferry (and the stupid boyfriend incident), I was content to slink into a corner and sit quietly in a chair until we reached France.

When we got close to port, I went out on deck to look for Cornelia's and Emily's Dieppe.

Happily, it was there.

The white cliffs of Newhaven and Dieppe.

One of the first things I saw was a church atop one of the cliffs, its tower rising gracefully above the town below. I saw the wide "plage" and the crescent of hotels which lined it. And there, crowning the white cliff, was the chateau, somewhat obscured by newer buildings which had sprouted up around it, but still proud.

It all looked just as it should.

I also saw Katie, standing at the rail below me, this time with her tiresome boyfriend, his arms wrapped lovingly around her. She looked a lot happier than she had been. She noticed me watching them and smiled up to me. I gave her a thumbs-up sign with a questioning face and she nodded. Her boyfriend saw the exchange between us, and if she hadn't mentioned our conversation to him before, then she was probably about to enlighten him now. Because a bit later, when we were getting off the boat, he very graciously smiled as he let me off in front of him. I gave him a wan smile in return, just to make sure he knew that I knew he was a tosser.

For my one night in Dieppe, I had booked a room at the Chambres d'hote Atypik, owned and operated by what sounded to be a very amiable couple named Isabell and Laurent. Shortly after I had booked the room, I had received a lovely email from them, with instructions for finding the hotel. Their English, though far better than my French, was still a bit cryptic:

> "Hello,
> We are touched by the confidence you give our guest room and delighted to welcome you. No problem which ferry you will be catching.
> To come our street is one way and there are 2 numbers 3 and 5 street cité de limes.
> Once in the street of not going down to the bottom the house is about 200 meters on the right. The facade is brick red and the windows are grey. There is a blue sign.
> Waiting for you soon we wish you an excellent end of the day.
> Kind regards
> Isabelle and Laurent"

I had been extremely pleased to receive their note because it was so similar in tone to one which Cornelia and Emily had received from the proprietress of their pension in St. Valery-en-Caux, a Madame Corue, who had written that,

"She was anticipating our arrival with the pleasure the most vivid, and she begged us to accept her sentiments the most distinguished."

It was good to see that this charming civility was still alive and thriving.

I had Google-mapped the pension, and it hadn't appeared to be too far from the port. But on arrival at the dock, just as Emily and Cornelia had discovered, it was actually a greater distance than it seemed. Which was no great crisis, except that I had assumed there would be taxis waiting to meet the boat. Perhaps because there simply weren't many passengers who came over *sans* car, no taxi driver bothered to cruise the dock.

There wasn't even the option of the ox cart like the girls had.

Well, I told myself, the girls had arrived at their pension on foot, so it only makes sense the same should be for me right now.

At least my pension was quite a bit closer to the port than Cornelia's and Emily's had been… and they had managed to walk to theirs in heels.

I summoned up some fortitude and started across the parking lot. I hadn't gone more than a few feet when Anne and Alan, riding in their daughter Stacey's car, pulled up next to me and offered me a lift which, after one feigned attempt at declining their offer, I accepted most heartily and gratefully.

So much better than arriving behind an ox cart.

As I had with her parents, I immediately liked Stacey, and her dog, Luna, too, who rode in the front seat with Stacey and Alan. My new friend punched the address I had for my pension into her phone, and within a few minutes they were dropping me off at the bottom of an attractive one-way cobblestone street, just below numbers 3 and 5. I thanked them heartily and we mused that maybe we might run into each other in town.

As they drove off, I walked to the doorway of number 3 Rue Cite de Limes. It appeared to lead to a private home. Same with number 5. Neither had a blue door nor a sign.

What was wrong?

I started thinking back to Isabelle's and Laurent's enigmatic instructions about 2 numbers 3 and 5, and how they were 200 meters up on the right. I hadn't gone 200 meters up the street, but I was about to now.

The road sat on a hill, with a healthy slope to it. I trudged my way up the street, pulling my bags behind me on the bumpy stone sidewalk until, mercifully, I came upon the second set of numbers 3 and 5 Rue Cite de Limes. There was that blue sign and the grey windows. I knocked at the door, smiling to myself that, in the end, I had arrived at my Dieppe pension on foot, just as Cornelia and Emily had done.

Laurent answered the door, and was as warm and kind as if he was greeting an old friend. Inside, the pension exceeded its photographs and was utterly beguiling, and I expressed this to Laurent in an enthusiastic mixture of French and English (with possibly a word or two of Spanish thrown in). Laurent showed me to my *chambre pour le nuit*, which was a large yet cozy space with a shabby chic vibe and starring a prodigious soaking tub at one end of the room. I was already wishing I could stay longer in Dieppe.

But I was following the girls, and Cornelia and Emily had stopped here for just the one night before traveling to their real destination.

"Emily had been told about a little seaside town halfway between Dieppe and Fecamp called St. Valery-en-Caux where a Buffalo suitor of hers, who, she said, was 'awfully continental,' used to spend his childhood summers."

The town of St. Valery-en-Caux lies twenty miles west of Dieppe along France's Normandy coastline. It is in this picturesque village that Cornelia and Emily spent numerous days honing their French language skills, and filling their afternoons with bike rides through the countryside and swims in the sea with their friend Therese, daughter of the local barkeeper.

It was with a lot of affection that they wrote of St. Valery and its people, and it's clear that the girls' time here was one of the best parts of their entire summer. Which made me eager for my own visit to the town, to see how much I could step into their world and share their memories.

Getting to St. Valery was no easy task for Emily and Cornelia, as there was no direct train service between there and Dieppe. They would have been required to travel seventy-plus kilometers to Rouen on the morning train, then wait all day to take the evening train the seventy-plus kilometers back to St. Valery. So Cornelia and Emily, at somewhat of an expense, hired a car and driver to take them the thirty kilometers to St. Valery along a scenic coastal road.

Riding in the back seat of this "open touring car" (read "gigantic convertible"), the girls were surrounded by their mountain of luggage, which the driver had piled in and formed "an impregnable barrier" around them.

"Occasionally we'd hear the voice of the driver asking us if it was not beautiful, the view, and we'd shout back, 'Oui, n'est-ce pas?' We had to take his word for it. All we ever saw on that brief and extravagant outing, except for a patch of blue sky, was a close-up view of a lot of labels saying *S.S. Empress of France*, 'Not wanted in stateroom' and the like."

Just as it was with the girls, I found that the train was not an option for me. But this was not due to an uncooperative train schedule, but to the fact that the station in St. Valery had been destroyed in 1945, when a train carrying American troops suffered a major brake failure. The train left the tracks, crashing through the station, killing eighty-nine soldiers and injuring another 152. Another station was constructed sometime later, but train operations between St. Valery and Rouen ceased in 1996.

So I would need to travel by car as well. My plan was to pick up a rental car in Dieppe the next morning and drive along the coastal road to St. Valery, hopefully with Cornelia and Emily in tow, so they could finally see the panoramic views they had missed in 1922.

I would stay in St. Valery for a few days, then take a week or so to explore the beautiful countryside and rich, profound history of Normandy.

It meant I would be venturing off from the girls' travels and setting forth on my own, before rejoining them in Rouen.

After tidying myself up a bit, I headed into the city center on a mission to locate the rental car office, which was supposed to be somewhere in the vicinity of the train station. There didn't seem to be a consensus between any of the maps I'd studied as to where the office was, and its address was sketchy. With this in mind, some reconnaissance work seemed like a prudent idea.

But before I reached the train station, I ran into Anne, Alan, Stacey and Luna strolling around town, and ended up spending the rest of the day and evening with them.

I would just have to figure out the rental car situation in the morning.

We started with a couple of drinks at an outdoor café, over which I got to know Stacey. A few years younger than me, she was a powerhouse fitness instructor living in Paris with her French husband and her kids, and she was an absolute riot. Everything she said was zany and funny, and she was full of energy. Her parents were an equal match for her marvelous wit, and we all laughed uproariously there at the café for a good two hours.

As the afternoon turned into evening, we went for a walk to the plage, along the crescent of hotels, where I assumed the girls had stayed, because they talked about taking a walk along this street. But almost all of those summer hotels had disappeared, the buildings having long since been converted into apartments. Perhaps Dieppe wasn't the tourist destination it had once been.

We walked on, making a loop around the Cathedral, then to dinner at a seafood restaurant back in the city center. We dined on different flavors of mussels, as the wine and laughter flowed for the next few hours.

After dinner, we bade each other farewell, and though they didn't want me walking back to my pension alone, I insisted, as it was just a few blocks away. Besides which, we were only a couple of weeks past the summer solstice and it was still practically broad daylight outside. Waving farewell to my new friends, I ambled back to Isabell's and Laurent's, reflecting on how much I'd managed to pack into one day, and what a wondrous adventure France was already proving to be.

Chapter 23

The next day started off so well. I had breakfast at the pension which consisted of fresh fruit, croissants with Isabell's homemade apricot jam, and tea drunk the French way – in a bowl, which was a first for me.

I followed that delectable experience with a long soak in the giant bathtub in my room. All of it set me up for a wonderful day.

To top it off, Laurent drove me down to the train station, which my latest map check had shown as the location for the rental car office. No wonder I hadn't been able to find it!

I went inside the station to an enclosed office area where there was a large car rental sign. There was someone ahead of me, so I waited about fifteen minutes. When it was my turn at the counter, the lady working there informed me that this was an information desk only, that the sign was merely an ad for rental cars, and that the office was outside and around the corner.

Wheeling my bags behind me, I searched for the rental office for an hour and a half, walking up and down every street within a quarter mile of the train station, looking for a building that is supposed to be a four-minute walk from the station. I couldn't find it anywhere. Finally I broke down and turned on my cellular service (with those merciless international roaming charges), and called the local office. As luck would have it, the man who answered didn't speak English, then got fed up with my French and hung up on me.

How could I not find the place? How could I not see it?

There is a phenomenon known as scotoma, where a person's mind overrules what their eyes are taking in, and doesn't allow a person to see something, even if it is right in front of them. Call it selective vision, call it a blind spot, but whatever it is, the mind is able to pull it off with considerable ease.

If this was what I was experiencing, well, it was most inconvenient.

Time was running out for me to pick up the car or forfeit the total cost of the rental for the week, so I had no choice but to cancel the car reservation. I called the 800-number and explained the situation. They apologized to me, but couldn't enlighten me as to where that stinking office was located, so they had to take the cancellation and not charge me.

This was nuts. Such an absurd defeat.

My best option at this point was to take the train to Rouen and see about renting a car there. Which would not be so bad – Rouen was where I was headed at the end of my Normandy road trip, anyway. The only downside was that I wouldn't get to drive along that coastal road from Dieppe to St. Valery. Seems that just like Cornelia and Emily, I wasn't meant to take in those panoramic views.

I found this less-than-fortunate moment of symmetry oddly comforting.

I took the next train to Rouen, arriving around noon, only to discover that the rental car offices – all of them – were closed for lunch and wouldn't reopen for another hour and a half.

This left me to cool my heels and gnaw on a giant train station baguette while I waited for the offices to reopen.

I also used that time to whip up some raging self-doubt about what I was doing, to the point where I had to remind myself that nothing bad had actually happened, and that travels don't always go smoothly – there are bound to be times when things don't work out as planned.

The strange thing was that, along with the self-doubt, I had a sense of calm about this detour. As I waited for the office to reopen, I made these notes in my journal.

"The thing is, I've been nervous for days about the rental car, feeling certain that I was going to have an accident of some sort. Now, here in Rouen, I'm not feeling that fear. I'm almost starting to wonder if I couldn't see the rental office in Dieppe because I was headed for disaster if I had gotten a car from there. We will just have to wait and see how it all goes. That is, if I'm lucky enough to actually score a rental here."

Had it indeed been scotoma back there in Dieppe? If so, perhaps it had been a blessing, some sort of subconscious self-preservation on my part. This idea was exceedingly appealing to me, and I latched onto it, telling myself that my journey was unfolding exactly as it was supposed to.

But there was definitely some sniveling going on as well.

"This is hard on my own. I feel lost. But I am very glad no one is having to go through this mess with me, and witness me being weak and whingy. I just wonder if it all would have gone wrong in Dieppe if I'd had someone with me. I'm already getting fed up with struggling with the language, and now I'm feeling stranded."

Blessedly, when the office finally reopened, I was able to obtain a rental straightaway, and in no time, my luggage and I were in the parking garage, standing in front of our car: a bright red Renault.

As in electric, screaming red, which they called "Rouge Clair".

Dubbing the car "Claire", I loaded her up with my stuff, and took my time sorting out the seat, steering wheel, lights, wipers, mirrors, all that stuff, just like a responsible adult. The owner's manual was in French, but I managed to work out – or at least make a reasonable guess at – what I needed to know.

It took a while of pressing buttons, but I got the car's built-in navigation system set to give me voice directions in English. There wasn't an American accent option for the voice, only English and Australian, the latter being a new one for me. I do love Aussies, and really liked the sound of the dude's voice, but I feared he could prove to be a distraction, so I went with the English accent which sounded the most like a butler. I figured I could always switch over to the Aussie, if I started getting lonesome on the road.

I entered the address of my hotel in St. Valery-en-Caux, and within moments my navigator Jeeves was directing me and Claire through the streets of Rouen.

An hour later, I arrived in St. Valery-en-Caux to a cool, gloomy day with occasional spit-rain. Jeeves directed me straight to my hotel, which was located within the Place du Marche (the market square). It was nice, with a friendly staff who coped with my French and spoke a little bit of English themselves. But it certainly couldn't equal Isabell's and Laurent's pension. Not many places could.

Cornelia and Emily don't mention in their book specifically how long they stayed in St. Valery, but it was probably at least two to three weeks. They wrote extensively about their time here, providing detailed descriptions of the town, so there was a lot for me to look for. And I had given myself just a few days to cover it all.

I spent a little time getting settled into my room, then went exploring, beginning with a jaunt around the *bassin*, or inner harbor. The Henry IV house was there, exactly as Cornelia and Emily described.

> "There was a 16th Century gem with leaded casements and ornately carved beams known as the Henri IV House, no one knew why, but it was a popular belief, or hope, rather, that the amorous monarch spent a night of love there."

This eye-catching, half-timbered structure sat amongst a row of more "modern" buildings, dating anywhere from the 1700s to the 1900s, any one of which could have been where the girls stayed when they came here. There was no way to know, unless I went into the public records, and tried to locate which property was owned by a Madame Corue in 1922.

This was one piece of the puzzle I was prepared to just let go.

I stopped at the Henry IV house to get info on its opening hours, and read that it was having an exhibition of photographs of the town before and after it was bombed in World War II. It hit me in that moment: while I had been able to see battle scars from the Blitz in London – wherever a modern structure resides between centuries-old buildings – this was where the war was going to really show itself.

I walked from the Henry IV to St. Valery's lighthouse, already knowing the path well from having read Cornelia's and Emily's words countless times,

> "… a long jetee terminated in the inevitable solitary lighthouse, and beyond that the shimmering sea."

The weather made for a lonely, haunting day, an ideal backdrop to this poignant moment for me, as I walked along the shore front, knowing I was seeing exactly what Cornelia and Emily had seen.

But soon my enthusiasm began to lag, as my reverie began to butt up against an unfortunate truth: it's impossible for even the most bucolic village to remain unspoiled these days.

Too many people.

Too many cars.

Too many sprawling utilitarian buildings.

And who needs a whole compound of inflatable bounce houses sitting smack in the middle of the beachfront?

That last one stung the worst. It was almost comical, that St Valery's captivating sea view, the same one which Frenchmen have looked out on for a thousand years plus, should be obscured by oversized air-filled castles and slides in garish primary colors.

I walked back and around to the other side of the *bassin*, and rambled along the promenade, peering over the sea wall onto the beach where the girls most likely went swimming. I crossed my fingers that I would get to swim at least once during my stay. It was a biggie on my checklist but – hothouse flower that I am – I would need a sunny day for it. Preferably a warm, sunny day.

By now I was pretty famished, having had nothing to eat since that gargantuan baguette in the Rouen train station, and I decided to make it easy on myself by going to dinner at a brasserie next to my hotel.

As I was being seated, I offered the friendliest smile I could manage and tried to speak French to the waitress, but she seemed impatient with my attempt (which I thought was terribly unkind, because I was getting the right words out – she appeared to just not like my accent). She spoke to me in English and handed me a menu in English and I gave up.

It had been a long day full of stresses of many kinds, and I was out of patience. I certainly didn't need any shade from some snarky waitress.

I felt deflated and I didn't try to hide it.

Perhaps it was wishful thinking, but the waitress seemed to sense that my change of mood had something to do with her rudeness, and she softened up slightly. But I wasn't going to let her off the hook. I was civil and silent, and when the meal was done, I delivered the most insulting blow an American could muster: I didn't leave her a tip.

A shocking thing to do, but I was that upset.

No doubt the waitress never felt the sting of the put-down, since no one else seemed to be leaving a tip for her, either. This was France, after all, and it wasn't their custom here.

But I knew what I had done, and it gave me a sense of vengeful satisfaction.

Chapter 24

The next day was a repeat of the first, weather-wise – cold, gloomy, blustery, with the added attraction of choppy seas, so there was no chance of having a swim. Still, I decided to make something of the day, despite the weather, and elected to start by ascending one of the hills to get pictures of some paths the girls had talked about:

> "Rising on either side of St. Valery were great chalk cliffs, twins of the Dover ones… along the edge of these cliffs went winding paths, worn by the generations of lonely women who, of an evening, after their work was finished, would pace the high promontories, sometimes knitting a sock or crocheting a bit of lace, their eyes searching the horizon for the sight of a home-coming sail."

In my walk the day before, I had noticed a long set of stairs cut into one of the hillsides flanking St. Valery, and now I set off to climb them. Taking a different route through town to the stairway, I came upon something I hadn't seen, or noticed, on my first day's outing.

There, cut into the white cliff the girls had written of, were the shell remains of a Nazi fortification – an ugly, concrete rectangular box, which would have served as a great vantage point for soldiers to scout and fire weapons from.

Suddenly I felt very much on my own. The girls had vanished. Cornelia and Emily would never have laid eyes on this atrocity.

It was then that I first began to understand what would be made painfully clear in the days which followed – the idyllic village which the girls had visited was not the place I was seeing today.

I felt as if a line had been drawn between their experience and mine: the line of World War II. And as the days went on, in spite of the nice moments I would have, and the charms which St. Valery offers today, that line would seem to widen into a chasm.

A bit demoralized, I hiked up the hill, stopping at the point along the steps which rested directly over that hideous bunker. I took a few photos from that spot, but didn't remain there long.

At the top of the hill, a solemn obelisk rose proudly into the sky. On reading its inscription, I learned it was a memorial to members of 51st Highlanders, an infantry division of the British army, who died defending St. Valery in 1940.

The 51st Highland Division had been part of the British Expeditionary Force (BEF) during the first few months of World War II, sent to defend the French and Belgian lines against advancing German troops. The 51st Division was stationed at the Maginot Line, which was south of where the German troops soon overran the Belgian and French borders. Moving swiftly, the Germans had been able to surround the BEF, causing them to retreat north to the English Channel, resulting in the famous, heroic evacuation at Dunkirk.

All except for the 51st Division, which was cut off from the rest of the BEF, and had no means of escape. Left behind in France, the soldiers fought on with other British and French troops against overpowering German forces. Eventually, the 51st Division would find themselves outnumbered and outgunned at St. Valery.

Defying orders from the War Office not to attempt another Dunkirk-like evacuation, Admiral William James gathered 207 boats in the waters off St. Valery. For two days and nights the boats remained there, even coming under fire.

But, cruelly, heavy fog rolled into St. Valery on both nights, rendering an evacuation impossible, and the 51st Division was forced to surrender to General Rommel and the Germans.

More than ten thousand soldiers were taken prisoner and were marched to Germany to POW camps. For the British, this signaled the end of the Allied resistance in France. Four days later, France surrendered to Germany.

It hadn't registered with me at first, but as I read more of the inscription on the obelisk, it dawned on me that it was written in English. The beautiful people of this village had honored those British who tried to defend them in 1940 with a memorial in those soldiers' own language.

The centuries-old animosity between England and France didn't exist here in this place. There was only admiration and gratitude.

That tragic bit of history and those fallen heroes would have some redemption when that same division, the 51st Highlanders, would send

Rommel into retreat in North Africa, then liberate St. Valery-en-Caux in August of 1944.

Reading of this in English on the placard of the memorial, I was breathless. I turned and looked down to the village of St. Valery, and its mish-mash of old and new buildings. It was still picturesque, even with its numerous battle scars.

Beyond the monument, there was a narrow, winding dirt path which ran along the edge of the cliff, well-worn as if it had been tread by those fishermen's wives the girls had written of. Cornelia's and Emily's world did exist in this place.

At least some of it did. I was just happy that this heartrending detail from the book was still intact.

On my way back down the hill, I was met on the last set of steps by a sweet but rather aromatic cat who came bounding up to say hello and be petted. It was the easiest, friendliest encounter I'd had since arriving in town, and I sat for a good while scratching his head while he rubbed against my legs and purred. It was a welcome, happy moment, but I did come away smelling of sour milk and cat pee.

Despite my odor, I went to the exhibit at the Henri IV house, which featured some compelling photos of the town during the war, along with a 3-D recreation of the village in the early 1900s. At its center was the Place du Marche (where I was currently staying), with a small, ancient-looking church in the background. It didn't seem to resemble the church which currently stood there. I had a bad feeling about it, but I wasn't ready yet to confirm my suspicions and face up to the truth.

Leaving the Henry IV house, I traipsed along the cobblestones and took pictures of the *quai* where Cornelia and Emily had joined in St. Valery's celebration of Bastille Day. Perhaps tradition would hold, and they would have the same festivities happening this Bastille Day, which was just two days away.

Whatever miscalculations I might have made with Emily's and Cornelia's journey timeline, I was in no doubt that by Thursday, July 13, they were in St. Valery. As if to reward me for my efforts in having the girls back here exactly ninety-five years later, the heavens offered up welcome sunshine on my Day 3, and it was warm enough for me to have my swim.

Just before noon, I walked along the sea wall to where steps lead down to the shoreline. The girls had prepared me for the rocky beach, but even their use of the word "agony" didn't seem strong enough for the punishment my feet took as I staggered to the sea. The tide was low and, mercifully, sand replaced the rocks as I got closer to the shoreline. I made a mental note to be back out of the water before the tide came in – I couldn't fathom trying to negotiate the rocks once they were submerged.

At first, the water was cold to the point one would call it bracing, but soon it seemed to get better and was really quite pleasant. I swam for about half an hour, and had wanted to stay in longer but the tide was coming in, fervently pushing me back to shore. I obliged its wishes, allowing the waves to deliver me to the water's edge.

I managed to get back to the lower sea wall ahead of the tide, and was beginning to gather up my things and move to higher ground before the sea swallowed up my present position. Another swimmer, a middle-aged French woman was out in the shallows about twenty feet in front of me, struggling on those rocks, now hidden beneath the water.

I set down my things and waded out to her, extending my hand. Together, we got across the rocks and to the sea wall, where a young French couple had been sitting but hadn't moved a muscle to help.

The lady thanked me, and I replied "De rien, mon plaisir" in my best accent, but she knew in an instant that I was American. Or so I thought.

She asked me, "Est-ce que vous Anglaise?"

"Non," I replied, "Je suis Americain," to which she seemed to brighten.

Suddenly it occurred to me that – the memorial to the 51st Highland Infantry notwithstanding – the problem I'd been having with some of the French folks (like that snarky waitress) might not have been because I was American.

It was probably because they thought I was British.

I would keep this in mind during my travels. For now, though, I could only hope I had scored some points for the Americans.

Enduring again the misery of the rocks, I made it up to terra firma, where I sat for a while on the ocean wall, soaking up the sun as the summer breeze dried me off. I watched the tide overtake the lower wall where I had been stationed earlier, and consume the rock beach, until there was nary a single one of those torturous stones to be seen.

I then went back to the hotel for a quick change of clothes before heading out in search of lunch. The sunshine had greatly restored my appetite as well as my spirits, and soon I found my way to an Italian seafood restaurant, where the wait staff was jovial and very kind to me, even after they discovered that I was an English speaker by birth.

There was a moment where I got tripped up trying to order, as the menu items were printed using their Italian names. I found myself placing my order in my best French (which often tends to come out with a Spanish accent), but using my best Italian for the name of the dish itself. It was odd, changing accents mid-stream. And my guess is, the pronunciation I delivered on that Italian entrée of mine probably sounded a lot more like American English.

It was a real rum mix of languages I presented, but the saintly waiter was able to make out what I was attempting to say, and brought me a delicious seafood pasta dish which I enjoyed under the radiant summer sun.

Lunch had fortified me well for a tough task I still had left on my list, the one I had been putting off ever since my visit to the exhibit in the Henry IV house.

From the restaurant, I walked around the corner to the Place du Marche and its neighbor, the Place de la Chapelle, and began putting the pieces together.

Cornelia and Emily wrote of an occasion where they visited a church in St. Valery. It is one of the most bittersweet passages in *Our Hearts*, and it meant a lot to me to find that church. Although the girls didn't recall its name or give clues to its location, I was pretty certain it would have been situated in the appropriately-named Place de la Chapelle.

Only that church didn't exist anymore.

A late 20th century church now stands in the "Chapel Square" and as soon as I entered it, I knew I had the right building, or at least the right location.

This church, like the one the girls had visited, was dedicated to la Vierge Marie. I found further confirmation of my hunch in the form of a large picture of the former church, displayed on the vestibule wall. In the corner of that picture was the shrine to the Virgin Mary, which the girls wrote about.

> "… before her altar, a touching assortment of offerings, some dating from days past, some freshly recent… Some were in payment for a vow made when a ship had been nearly lost in a tempest, some waited there in prayer for those who had set forth gaily with the fishing fleet but had not returned."

Knowing that I was standing where the girls had been, but not really, not exactly, I became a bit weepy about that chasm between our worlds, and for what had been lost.

I lit a candle for Madame Corue and Therese and all of the inhabitants of St. Valery. They were no longer just characters in a book. They were people who lived and worked in this town, traversing these same streets, and who, in 1940, would have had to endure the bombing of this village – their home – then witness its surrender to enemy forces.

What had never occurred to me in all the times I had read *Our Hearts* was all too painfully apparent now: at the time Cornelia and Emily would've been putting pen to paper about the people of St. Valery, these dear souls would've been living under Nazi rule and undoubtedly enduring hardships about which I could only speculate.

That connecting strand between the girls' world and mine now felt twisted and strained as it stretched across the widening divide between our experiences. My breathing had all but stopped and my heart was starting to ache like a mourner for a lost loved one. After a few minutes, I returned to the sunshine outside.

The day was still bright and lovely, and as it was to be my last one here, I made the most of it, taking pictures of the shoreline at high and low tides, and of fishermen bringing in their catch, which they would immediately sell right there on the dock. I then made a return climb up the hill to the monument, where I planned to undertake a rather unsettling expedition.

The night before, I had read somewhere online that near the obelisk there was an entrance to that wretched Nazi bunker. I had actually seen it the other day, not realizing what it was. To me it appeared to be just a ruin grown over with bushes. Feeling the need to investigate it properly, I steeled myself and, armed with the flashlight on my phone, I hiked down through the overgrowth and stepped through the entrance to the bunker.

Within three to six inches of the opening it turned dank and creepy, but I proceeded on as far as I dared. Which turned out to be not very far. I passed through only a couple of pitch-dark rooms before coming upon filthy sleeping bags and detritus that pointed to this being someone's home.

In that moment, I felt the full force of being a woman alone in a sketchy place. It was frustrating, but I didn't have the guts and sand, nor the recklessness, to forge ahead into the bunker's labyrinth on my own, and I beat a hasty retreat back to the safety of the sunlight.

Once I was back down the hill, I made my way to the other side of the harbor, and wended my way through narrow cobblestone streets lined in ancient buildings which had been spared from the bombs that had taken down so much of the village. I wandered aimlessly up a winding hill where I came across an old convent. As I meandered back down through a quaint medieval street, I met a lovely older lady who spoke to me as I was taking photos. I managed a brief conversation in French with her, asking about the age of her home and complimenting her on its beauty. I couldn't tell if she was able to make sense of anything I said, but she was very gracious nevertheless.

It was a happy note on which to end my days in St Valery, and I was awfully thankful to have it. For tomorrow I would be heading to what was surely to be a profound and emotional experience: Omaha Beach and the American Cemetery.

Chapter 25

Friday, July 14: Bastille Day, or French Independence Day. The day had started with a rude awakening for Cornelia and Emily, literally.

> "We were in St. Valery for the 14th of July. The expression of patriotic sentiment began at dawn when a cannon directly below our window went off with a report which almost blew us out of bed... That '75 continued saluting the Bastille at five and ten minute intervals all morning and Emily and I, who both hate explosions to a psychopathic degree, retired to a distant wheat field until the Bastille apparently considered itself sufficiently saluted."

For better or worse, I woke up in St Valery-en-Caux with no sound of a cannon firing, as the girls had done. In fact, as I took my bags out to load them in the car, there were still very few signs that any sort of celebration would be happening soon.

For Cornelia and Emily, this day seemed to be one of their happiest, most favorite memories, as they danced late into the night with the locals and, linking arms with some of their fellow guests, sang down the streets of town to their pension. The celebrations of that evening had more than made up for them being blasted out of bed that morning.

Seeing how the festivities in St. Valery-en-Caux at present appeared to be non-existent, I didn't feel any twinge of remorse for not staying in town. I was eager to spend my day on the Normandy beaches, honoring those who fought and died so that France could retain the freedom it would be celebrating on this day.

Before I left, I said a word to Cornelia and Emily, apologizing for taking them away from a highlight of their journey, and pulling them away from their fun. I invited them to come with me, even though where I was going didn't exist during their travels, or even when they penned *Our Hearts* in 1942.

I would be taking them with me to June 6, 1944 – D-Day – and the beaches of the Normandy invasion.

I hit the road early, which was a lucky thing, because it took me ages to make the drive – village roads, toll roads, and traffic all seemed to collude to make my way slow-going. And just to put a special button on the morning, I had stopped at a services area on the side of one of the main highways, only to find the restroom facilities were nothing more than holes over which one squatted. And nary a square of toilet paper to be had.

Lovely.

After a hard-fought drive which had included going over the traffic-laden Le Havre bridge, I finally made it to the American Cemetery in Colleville-sur-Mer.

I began my visit with a tour of the museum, which was a moving experience from start to finish, where one thing stood out for me above anything else.

In a display case captioned, "What They Carried With Them", along with personal items and some tins of rations, there were two copies of Armed Services Edition books.

These pocket-sized paperback books were part of the story of World War II which I never knew about, until I came across an Armed Services Edition of *Our Hearts.*

It turns out these little books were an invaluable part of the Allied war effort.

In December 1942, when Cornelia's and Emily's book was published, America had been at war for over a year, and the country was galvanized to not only supply the troops with the weaponry needed to defeat Germany, Italy and Japan, but to support the soldiers fighting on those fronts in any way they could.

A number of New York's largest publishing houses had formed the "Council on Books in War" as a response to reports coming out of Germany of state-sanctioned book burnings. The Nazi campaign to obliterate any literature they deemed "un-German" was so pervasive that it is estimated, by the end of the war, Germany had destroyed over one hundred million books.

The Council on Books came up with a plan to supply American soldiers with reading material, not only for entertainment and to boost morale, but to fight against Hitler's "war on ideas".

Working within the severe paper rationing restrictions which had been in place ever since the US entered the war, the Council designed small paperback versions of popular books.

Printed on magazine paper, the books could withstand damp weather conditions and rough handling better than traditional books. They were lightweight and cut to the exact measurements of a soldier's uniform. Larger books were designed to fit into the back pocket of a soldier's pants, while smaller books fit exactingly into the shirt's breast pocket.

Beginning in September 1943 and continuing until 1946, the government supplied over 123 million copies of 1,227 different book titles to the troops, making the Armed Services Edition program (ASE) one of the largest wide-scale distributions of free books in history. The genres of books ranged from history to humor, fiction and non-fiction, great works of literature to current bestsellers. Instantly, they became widely-popular with the troops, as Molly Guptill Manning explains in *When Books Went to War*:

> "... Armed Services Editions – portable, accessible and pervasive paperbacks ... were everywhere: servicemen read them while waiting in line for chow or a haircut, when pinned down in a foxhole... They were so ubiquitous, one sailor remarked that a man was 'out of uniform if one isn't sticking out the hip pocket'... With books in their pockets, American GIs stormed the beaches of Normandy, trekked to the Rhine and liberated Europe; they hopped from one deadly Pacific island to the next, from the shores of Australia to the backyard of Japan... Books of humor made them laugh when there was nothing funny about their circumstances. Tales of life back home transported them to the places they missed and hoped to see again. By reading, the men received the closest thing to a respite from war."

Having spent five weeks at number one on the New York Times Bestseller List at the beginning of 1943, *Our Heart Were Young and Gay* was selected as one of the titles to be printed in the second series of books to be sent to the soldiers in October 1943. Emily would write to the Council on Books to thank them for the honor, stating that she and Cornelia were prouder of the Armed Services Edition than of being chosen as a book of the month.

*Top: A first edition and an ASE of **Our Hearts**;*
Bottom: Display case at the American Cemetery.

As it would turn out, this sweet, funny story of two girls traveling to Europe in 1922 would be such a hit with the battle-hardened GIs that it would be reprinted and sent to the troops again in February 1945.

What's more, there would be not just one, but two anecdotes which would come out of the war about the ASE version of *Our Hearts*. The first was recounted by Private Robert Healey, who had taken part in the Normandy invasion. On returning to Omaha Beach the day after D-Day, he came across a fallen soldier, his arm outstretched, and just a few feet from his hand was a copy of *Our Hearts Were Young and Gay*.

On the other side of the world, a similar story would emerge from Saipan, by a Captain J.H. Magruder, who wrote to the *Saturday Evening Post* about coming across a fallen marine with an ASE sticking out of his pocket. The book was *Our Hearts Were Young and Gay*. This incident would later be taken up by Hollywood and fictionalized in the John Wayne movie, "The Sands of Iwo Jima".

It's astonishing that, with over 1,200 different books distributed to the soldiers, there should be two of these accounts involving *Our Hearts* and – as far as I could find – no similar anecdotes about any of the other ASE titles.

Especially given that, on the surface, Cornelia's and Emily's story of two young women traveling to Europe in the 1920s seems like an odd choice to send to soldiers, its bestseller status notwithstanding. But then again, in between those most-welcome, laugh-out-loud moments, the book must have also served as a reminder of better times, of what the boys were fighting for. And the lively, lovely England and France that Cornelia and Emily had captured was very much worth fighting for, very much worth saving.

In her compelling book, Guptill-Manning had written of how when the men of the 1st Division were traveling in the landing crafts to D-Day, they read on the way over, and a newsman traveling with them reported that the men were so calm it seemed more as if they were going to a drill and not a massive, pivotal battle.

She also wrote about how many men, when they were lightening their packs before they crossed to Normandy, jettisoned more practical items before giving up their ASEs – that the launching grounds in England were strewn with personal items, but very few books.

Seeing the two ASEs in the display case, I didn't make note of the books' titles. Just them being there meant so much to me – they certainly didn't have to be copies of *Our Hearts*.

Those books had been important to a couple of the young men who came ashore at Omaha Beach that day. I just prayed that the books' owners weren't beneath any of those headstones outside, but I feared it was what the books' presence in the display case signified.

Leaving the museum, I found outside that the day couldn't have been lovelier – sunshine with a light breeze and an occasional puff of a white cloud drifting across the sky. Steeling myself, I made my way down to the cemetery.

Even though I had braced myself for the hit, I wasn't prepared for the scope of what I was seeing, and I felt as if my breath had been knocked out of my body.

The cemetery is located on a gently curving hillside, so that you can't see an end to the crosses and Stars of David which mark the resting places of the soldiers. The headstones seem to go on forever. A painful forever.

It is worth noting, the grounds of the cemetery are captivatingly beautiful and immaculate. A place worthy of honoring these greatest of heroes.

For a time, I walked in and out of the rows upon rows of grave markers, stopping occasionally to read them. There were boys from every state. Some had been killed that very first day, June 6, 1944, while others had died days or weeks later from their injuries.

I felt compelled to walk the perimeter of the entire cemetery, around each of the four corners, in order to pay at least a passing visit to every grave. In the far corner, away from any nearby visitors, I broke down and cried for the young men who had died and then remained so far from home. I cried for their lost potential, and for the pain their families had to bear.

I thanked them for what they had done. They had fought for the most noble cause in human history. Those young men stood up against the greatest, most far-reaching evil the world had ever seen, and they saved us. I told them I was so sorry they had to do it. And I said a prayer and a blessing for them to rest in peace.

And then I remembered the soldier who had died on Omaha Beach with the copy of *Our Hearts Were Young and Gay* next to his hand. It hadn't occurred to me before, but I suddenly understood that he was somewhere in the cemetery, under one of the headstones. Now my visit had become personal, about one young man in particular who had lost his life on June 6, 1944. I wished that I could have known which headstone was his, and who that young man was.

But, really, he was all of them.

The day was slipping away, and there was still Omaha Beach to visit. I was keenly regretting that I hadn't allowed more time, so I could get to all of the beaches where the American, British and Canadian soldiers had landed, and see everything there was to see in this area teeming with history.

It meant I would just have to come back again. I was glad to place that on my to-do list.

It was a short drive from the cemetery to the beach, and soon I was making the turn onto the "Rue de la 1st Division". When I arrived, there were still a number of people out enjoying a day at the seaside, in the water and relaxing on the beach. I chose to park at the top of a hill near the memorial to the 1st Division, and then walked down to the obelisk honoring those heroes. Stopping there, I said a prayer of thanks to those young men who truly, literally, stared into the guns, unflinching and unrelenting.

Near their memorial stand remains of Nazi bunkers, where German soldiers mowed down those Americans as they tried, and eventually managed, to advance. Seeing those bunkers got my blood up, and without even thinking, I spit on one of them on my way down the hill to the beach.

As I took my last steps down the slope and started towards the water, I met up with a golden retriever who was sniffing a bit of bunker which protruded from the sand. I stopped and petted the sweet fellow, then walked on for a while down the beach, finally stopping to wade into a shallow pool made by the low tide.

Looking out at the channel, it didn't take much effort to see the landing crafts, and the soldiers coming towards shore. I could feel them around me, running past me in the sand, and almost hear their voices and the noise of the guns, almost smell the smoke.

They are still there. Those brave young men invested too much of their souls into this place to just dissolve into the past.

I wondered, what must the soldiers think of all these people here now, who are so carefree and unaware of their enduring presence on this sacred ground?

But then it occurred to me that perhaps this is the best way to heal the wounds of the past. We move forward in joy, in peace, and in hope, filling the beaches of D-Day with laughter again and infusing them with positive energy. Picnics, flying kites, playing in the water, soaking up the sunshine.

Hopefully it brings those soldiers some comfort. It is what they would have wanted for themselves and their families.

Maybe in its own way, it is a tribute to the soldiers' sacrifice.

After a while, I turned and looked back across the beach to the hillside, deliberately choosing to keep myself in the present moment. I wouldn't allow myself to see the young men – boys, really, so far from home – attempting to cross the beach, some of them losing their lives, with smoke and gunfire all around.

That young man with the copy of *Our Hearts* had fallen somewhere here in the sand where I now stood.

Fighting to stay in July 14, 2017, I focused on the families enjoying the beach, happy and relaxed, basking in the sparkling sunshine. And

I watched delightedly as my golden retriever buddy made the rounds, saying hello to everyone he encountered on his way back to his family.

Before I left, I wrote "Thank you" in the sand. I wanted to make sure that the soldiers knew, even by my one little gesture, that they were remembered.

I put on my shoes and made my way back along the beach and up to the memorial, taking the same hill those brave young men had scaled. It was my very humble way of honoring their courageous efforts and their fight.

Though my experience on this day was a world apart from Cornelia's and Emily's, Bastille Day had proven to be one of my favorite memories from the entire journey. Just like it had for the girls.

And I was glad I had asked Cornelia and Emily to come along. Though their travels and their book pre-date this watershed moment in history, they are tied to this place by the soldiers who read – and were hopefully uplifted by – their story.

Still, on this day, my focus wasn't on the girls or their book, and I didn't follow in their footsteps.

Instead, I walked in the footsteps of heroes.

Chapter 26

I was emotionally spent by the time I was in the car and on the road to Bayeux. God bless that navigation system – it made quick work of my journey and delivered me to my hotel for the night, which was situated in the oldest part of the city. Providence was smiling on me, and I located a space to leave Claire for the night around the corner from where I was staying.

(Parking had been one of my main concerns from the first moment after I decided to rent a car. My skills at parallel parking are limited at best, and it was an ongoing source of worry throughout my week-long road trip that I wouldn't be able to find a place to leave the car, or I would inadvertently leave her in some no-parking zone whose hieroglyphics I had misunderstood. I lived in mortal fear of waking one morning to discover Claire had been towed to who knows where, and I wouldn't be able to get her back.)

I checked in at the hotel, and instantly fell madly in love with it. Housed in an ancient building, a converted something or other, the hotel was a sublime mix of medieval architecture and swinging contemporary furnishings. My appointed room was huge, with three tall windows, a fireplace, a killer slate-tile bathroom with massive shower and showerhead, and even its own little kitchenette.
The *pièce de résistance* was the bed – modern and groovy, padded white vinyl, with some sort of colored lighting effects built into the underside of the frame, it was a sensation.

The whole place made me feel "as mondaine as all get out," as the girls would say.

(It would turn out, unfortunately, that I would never figure out how to get the colored lights going, and in the end, I would be too tired to pursue the matter. Oh, well. If I'm being totally honest, I really wasn't cool enough for the bed, anyway.)

After I had settled in, I hit the streets of Bayeux, and it was love at first sight there, too. Creamy yellow sandstone buildings, ancient, narrow cobblestone streets, a gorgeous cathedral. It was one of the prettiest cities I had ever visited.

I strolled around town for a bit, and just as it had been in St Valery, there was no sign that any great Bastille Day celebration was about to take place. This didn't concern me much because I had a more pressing dilemma on my hands: where to have dinner.

If Bayeux wasn't already wonderful enough, in walking around town, I discovered that the city was teeming with delicious-looking restaurants. It took a while to weigh my options, but finally I chose a cozy place, with outdoor tables situated quite close together, and divine aromas wafting from the kitchen into the street.

I was seated next to a French couple who were very polite and very patient with me as we exchanged a bit of small talk in their language. On my other side was a German family complete with two adorable dogs, one of whom repeatedly put her paws in my lap and gave me kisses. The family was warm and engaging, and we were able to speak a little as well, in French – a second language for both of us.

After my day at Omaha Beach – the French soil where that central battle between Americans and Germans known as D-Day had taken place – Bayeux had brought me back to a happier time: now. In this engaging little restaurant, the French, the Germans and my American self broke bread together (literally and figuratively), enjoying our food and wine and conversation. It was just what I needed to reaffirm that kindness and the human spirit can and always will prevail.

There is a phenomenon known as the "Golden Age Fallacy", which is generally defined as the erroneous idea that an earlier time period is better than the current one. But here in this moment in history, we were the ones living in a Golden Age of friendship and goodwill between our nations.

I headed back to the hotel, still searching along the way for that elusive Bastille Day party, but there was none to be had. In my swanky room, I stood at one of the massive windows which looked out towards the Bayeux Cathedral, hoping maybe there might be some fireworks, but all was quiet.

Instead, I had to settle for a good night's sleep in a bed that was way too cool for me.

Saturday, July 15. Now that the great occasion of Bastille Day had passed, I was ready for a day of balls-to-the-wall sightseeing which would make any "12-countries-in-6-days" tour company proud.

I hit the ground running, starting with a hot-footed hustle through the Bayeux Cathedral. While perhaps not as storied or famous as Notre Dame or Rouen, it is exquisite, a masterpiece of Gothic architecture, and worth every second of the eight and a half minutes I spent touring it before heading on to the next stop, which was a biggie: The Bayeux Tapestry.

I wasn't sure what to expect with this iconic piece of needlework, especially what sort of reaction I would have to it. When something is historic, world-famous, legendary, and so on, it's a real roll of the dice whether or not it can live up to one's expectations, and what sort of response it will elicit.

Take the La Brea Tar Pits, for example. One would be lead to believe, simply from Bugs Bunny's insatiable quest to see them, that they would be "all that".

Not so.

In fact, they're kind of a letdown.

Yes, the Tar Pits have great geological significance. But for me, with my limited understanding of this significance, the whole thing looked like nothing more than a pond with a cloudy black puddle in one corner. I found myself more excited over a random pool of tar which had broken through the asphalt in the parking lot.

The Bayeux Tapestry felt iffy – possibly another Tar Pits.

I prepared myself to be underwhelmed.

Happily, I found the tapestry to be both exceptionally beautiful and interesting, impressive in its scope (but who wouldn't be dazzled by 68 meters, or 230 feet, of intricate needlework), and I applauded not only its artistry, but marveled over the amount of meticulous laboring it must've taken to produce the piece.

I even learned an obscure historical fact (according to the tapestry): the people of England pretty much accepted, and didn't throw up a fuss, when in 1066, Harold Godwinson crowned himself king of England, even though William, Duke of Normandy had been named next in line to the throne by the late king, Edward the Confessor. But then Halley's Comet appeared in the sky, which the people took as a bad omen, and they switched their allegiance to William.

This would eventually lead to the Battle of Hastings, where the Duke of Normandy defeated Harold for the English crown, becoming William I, better known as William the Conqueror.

History is determined by the fortuitous timing of a comet which happens to blaze past our planet every seventy-five years – how berserk is that?

Yet it's all right there, recorded in needlework.

I was so taken with the tapestry, I even lingered over it for longer than the allotted fifteen minutes I'd given it – to the point of robbing myself of precious time in the gift shop – but it was well worth it. Still, I needed to get on the road.

On my way to rejoin Claire the Car so we could leave for Falaise, I crossed paths with a French couple, who were trying to get to the tapestry. I gave them directions in French that they were able to understand, which I found exceptionally satisfying. Perhaps I was starting to make some headway with this language stuff.

As I neared my car, I came upon a woman standing in the middle of the street whose first words to me were, "Do you speak English?" She was Dutch, didn't speak a word of French, wasn't at all bothered that I couldn't speak Dutch, and was just so happy and relieved I could speak English. She and her husband were trying to work out if they could park in a questionable spot on the side of the road, and it was causing them great distress.

Ah, kindred spirits.

I offered them my reassuring parking space and they were thrilled. I told them I completely understood.

As I steered Claire out of Bayeux, I got it into my head to switch the accent on the navigation system from British to Australian.

I was now on Day Five of my isolating Time-in-the-Car, without even Cornelia and Emily to keep me company.

This had gotten me thinking that it would be nice to have someone from the Land Down Under join me for the ride. With just a little bit of imagination, an Australian navigator could perhaps start to feel like a companion – almost-kinda-sorta like having a boyfriend in the car, riding shotgun and sharing the journey with me.

At first, it was good. But soon, I began to feel like my Aussie boyfriend wasn't so much navigating, as he was telling me how to drive. Which I really didn't care for. Whether it was something about the accent, the voice of the speaker, or just my imagination, it really seemed as if the Aussie was second-guessing my driving.

He began to irritate me, and I grew increasingly annoyed with him each time he told me to turn here or keep on in that direction. It wasn't long before I had to pull Claire over to the side of the road, and go back to my reliable British butler/navigator.

Still, we made good time to Falaise. This engaging town is famed for its statue of William the Conqueror and his predecessor Dukes of Normandy. Being a descendant of William the Conqueror – one of *many, many millions* of descendants – I looked upon this visit to my grandfathers' statue as a sort of mini-pilgrimage.

Leaving Claire at the first bona fide parking space I could locate, I made my way through town over to the square where the monument stands, and took my sweet time studying the six predecessors and then the Big Duke himself.

With the Dukes; the Porte de Cordeliers (Claire the Car can just be seen underneath the arch.)

Just a few steps away was a mammoth castle which perhaps needed exploring. Instead, I chose to blow it off and stay on my insanely frantic schedule.

"After all," I thought, "I've already done a cathedral, a tapestry and a statue today."

I can take only so much culture before those museum legs set in.

After talking myself out of touring the castle, I had an interesting chat with a man from South Africa who was waiting for his wife to emerge from a frightfully old church. It was a joy to get to speak English, and the man's colorful stories of traveling through Europe, living out of a caravan (a.k.a. recreational vehicle) were an unexpected highlight of my day.

This is why I like to travel alone. While it is possible to meet and engage with others when one is traveling with a companion, it seems a much easier proposition when one is on their own. Perhaps because it almost becomes a necessity for the solo traveler to interact with strangers, which forces them to be outgoing.

In fact, the South African man related a story to me exactly along those lines.

"We were camping in Provence and got to talking with this one young man. He was backpacking around Europe by himself, sort of like you" my South African friend explained. "He told us that for the first week or so, he had camped in fields and woods to save money."

"Oh, then, not exactly like me. I have yet to do any 'roughing it'," I laughed.

"You've probably been better off. This young man started feeling isolated and lonely very quickly. He ended up deciding it was better to spend a little money to be in a campground, just so he could have the company of other people."

I completely understood. "Yes, money well spent."

Unfortunately, I didn't have time for continued conversation, as I still had miles to go before I slept. So I hustled back to Claire the Car and got on the road to Combourg, a neighboring town to the famous Mont St. Michel, which I would be visiting the next day.

I made it to Combourg late in the afternoon. The hotel I had booked was quite nice – with a sort of New England feel to it, oddly enough – and I somehow managed with half-French, half-English to communicate with the staff.

At least I was finding that, as time went by, I wasn't including as many Spanish words in my sentences as I had been early on. I took that as a win.

That evening, I did my standard tour around town in search of some dinner. This was my third town in six hours, and I was feeling too tired for a proper meal. Instead, I went with some shortbread cookies and peanut M&Ms, which proved to be a good combination, and in keeping with the spirit of proper road trip provisions (I happen to be a staunch follower of the credo, "It doesn't matter how old you are, when buying snacks for a road trip, it should look like an unsupervised eight-year-old was given $100").

I got back to the hotel early enough to take a shower before bed, and when I finally hit the sheets, it only took moments for me to be out.

I slept like the dead until my slumber was shattered by a fire alarm sounding off right around midnight. It ran for about ten minutes before it finally got shut off somewhere by someone.

Everything seemed fine, but then I worried, what if something was wrong? No one in the hotel seemed to have a clue as to why the alarm had gone off, and as far as I could tell, no one seemed motivated to investigate the matter.

This made it rather difficult to get back to sleep, but I eventually managed it.

Chapter 27

Everyone who'd ever been there said I had to go. I had seen pictures of the place since I was a kid, and it truly is one of the world's most magical sights. But still, I wasn't all that fired up about it. A nice idea, but it wasn't something I'd been looking forward to with bated breath. This made me feel a little guilty in having the good fortune to be there.

I felt certain that once I arrived at Mont St. Michel, it would captivate me. With this in mind, the next morning I loaded up Claire and got an early start on my excursion.

A quick bit of history on the fabled island and its abbey:

Part fortress and part religious sanctuary, the Benedictine abbey dates from the eighth century, a combination of imposing Romanesque and fantastical Gothic architectural styles. The small village below the abbey has a population of fifty full-time residents (as of 2015), which hosts a staggering three million visitors a year.

For hundreds of years, the faithful have made pilgrimages to this holy place. During the Middle Ages, pilgrims would walk across the marshy quagmire of the bay at low tide, which was extremely dangerous. It was said that those who braved the quicksand and the high tides which could roll in fast, should first make out a will, because there was no guarantee they would make it there and back safely.

In the nineteenth century, France built a road to Mont St. Michel which made it possible for more pilgrims as well as tourists to visit, but there was a major flaw in the design: it blocked movement of the seawater, which caused a massive silt build-up around the island and proved unhealthy for the eco-system of the Couesnon River, which surrounds it. In 2014, thankfully, the road was removed when a new causeway was opened, which allowed the water to once again flow freely for the first time in 150 years, which in time restored the natural balance around the island.

It was still fairly early when I pulled into one of the car parks by the recently constructed bridge, but the place was already filling up quickly with tourists. My first view of this mythical place had not been what I expected, but it was hardly a disappointment. The day was gray and foggy, and when I looked out to the island, all I saw was a low, rocky shoreline. There was no abbey, no spiked tower soaring into the heavens. Nearly all of the island was lost inside a cloud, and it was wonderfully mysterious.

Not being as plucky as those pilgrims from the past, I opted out of navigating the marshes and quicksand of the bay and, joining up with a healthy crowd of other tourists, I strode across the 1.6-mile footbridge to Mont St. Michel. As I neared the island, the gauzy blanket surrounding it began to loosen its hold, and by the time I was nearing the end of the causeway, the haunting, otherworldly fortress began to emerge from the mist.

I had wanted to go on foot to the island as a sort of nod to those pilgrims of the past, and when I arrived at Mont St. Michel, I took a few moments to remove my shoes and step from the pavement onto the sand, walking out a bit between the island and the mainland, where I could connect with those centuries of faithful journeyers.

Soon it was time to join the pack of other visitors who were meandering through the utterly charming, postcard-perfect medieval streets of the village, and begin my ascent to the abbey. The narrow cobblestone streets were lined with heavenly-looking patisseries and baguette shops, souvenir shops catering to every taste level (I say this with affection, as my own personal taste tends to run to the lower end of the souvenir spectrum). There were quaint tavern-looking bars and beautiful restaurants, and occasionally there would be a doorway or a passageway leading to an inviting, winsome hotel.

All quite arresting, but the hike was rather rough-going. The incline itself was steep, and made none the more pleasant by the sheer number of people making the same climb as myself.

Moving up the winding, constricted street, shoulder to shoulder with a thick sea of other tourists, it didn't take long for me to feel agitated and slightly panicky.

I realized I was visiting Mont St. Michel in the wrong way. It would be much easier to see the island by staying overnight in one of those gorgeous hotels, enjoying unhurried meals in the lovely restaurants, and exploring the sights before and after the waves of tourists had passed through.

Aiding in this plan – according to the warning signs posted at the entrance to the footbridge – it seems that often the evening tides are high enough to cover the bridge, turning Mont St. Michel back into a proper island. This undoubtedly must empty the streets, sending the daytrippers scurrying back to the mainland, and leaving only those fifty residents and overnight visitors to savor the quiet.

It all sounded very romantic.

Another time.

Right now I had a mountain to scale and a marauding horde to overcome in my quest for the summit. The hike to the abbey stayed steep and crowded, and when the "Dungeons" attraction at the side of the cramped street caught my eye, I decided I needed a respite from the throng, and darted into the small ticket vestibule to investigate.

Immediately I regretted this decision. The man behind the counter made a full-court press at me, describing the attractions I would see on the tour, and how I needed to take it now, because I wouldn't be able to once I had visited the abbey (there was only one way up and one way down, and I wouldn't pass by here on my descent).

After all, he asked, when would I be back?

I don't react well to the hard sell – I find it off-putting – and in my hot and cranky state, I certainly was in no humor to be pressed. I did my best to be polite, but turned and walked out, offering no apologies or reason for declining.

Outside, I resolved I would check out the dungeons attraction online, and if it looked worthwhile, then great, it would give me an excuse to come back. I could save it for when I would return and do

Mont St. Michel the right way, in one of those romantic hotels, sharing a sumptuous meal with someone special as the tides swallowed the causeway.

This was my thinking as I continued my trek up the hill.

Then without warning, it came over me like I had stepped in some of that quicksand in the bay:

I will never come back here.

I will never have that lovely experience of enjoying this place with a special someone.

I only know how to be alone.

These thoughts came racing out of nowhere, hitting me hard and making me profoundly sad.

To be thinking any of this was unusual for me – what I had told my South African friend in Falaise was completely truthful: I really enjoy, and even prefer, traveling on my own.

I never could have come on this journey with a partner. And if I had a partner, I never could have come on this journey.

This journey which means the world to me.

Just me and the girls.

So many times in my travels I would come across a couple having a miserable time together, with one of the pair so excited to be in a place, and having the moment spoiled forever by their complaining partner (like Katie and her tiresome boyfriend in Newhaven).

On those occasions, I would always give thanks that I was on my own, with no one there to wreck my happy experience.

But, unbeknownst to me, a storm had been building on the horizon, and the isolation of the past few days had blown in over me.

Suddenly, I felt lonely, and something beyond it.

It was as if lead had been poured into my bloodstream. It wiped out my strength, leaving me shaky, and I slunk down onto a rock wall just below the entrance to the abbey. In that moment, I found myself being extremely grateful for the steep slope I was on. It provided camouflage for the emotional collapse which was overtaking me. Anyone passing by who might notice me would most likely assume I was just stopping to catch my breath.

But in reality, I was circling the drain. That one little non-event in the ticket office had somehow brought on an onslaught of bad memories.

I was catapulted back to when I first moved to Los Angeles in my early twenties, and the dreams I had of how my life would go. I imagined meeting a man with whom I would explore glorious California, and eventually the world. I had pictured us taking off on the clichéd, quintessential couple's weekend, driving up Pacific Coast Highway with the top down.

California dreaming, indeed.

For sixteen of those years in Los Angeles, I had, in fact, been involved with someone who owned a convertible. But we never made that drive up the coast. We barely made it out to an occasional dinner. Because what we had was barely a relationship.

This had suited me just fine. I had always been a fiercely independent person, and being on my own was what felt right and normal to me. So I didn't much mind if my relationship was... well, stunted.

And I certainly never pressed the issue of us driving up the coast together because, truth be told, I knew he would probably be like Katie's boyfriend, and ruin the experience.

Even so, when that relationship unexpectedly came to an end, along with being completely heartbroken, I couldn't help but feel that I'd been swindled out of a thousand memories that we should have made together, but didn't.

Without even noticing, I had allowed those girlhood fantasies of mine to be ground into dust, and blown into the Mojave Desert.

It was only then that simpleton me fully realized...

I hadn't ever really been part of a couple.

And I hadn't tried to be.

But this had been ages ago, ancient history. That man and that questionable relationship had long since ceased to be even a blip on my radar.

So where in the hell was all of this coming from?

There on the hillside of Mont St. Michel, I had been sucker-punched.

The worst part of this bushwhacking was that up until now, I had fully believed I was traveling light on my journey – not just physically, but in spirit as well.

It came as a tremendous shock, then, to find, not only did I still possess this particular piece of old, worn-out emotional baggage, but I had carried it all the way across the Atlantic Ocean and then the English Channel, loaded it into the rental car here in France, and had now dragged it, bumping over the cobblestones, to the top of this mountain.

I only know how to be alone. It was ringing in my ears.

Was this something I needed to work on, to change? Did I even want to change?

Was I swindling myself again?

There was only thing I knew for sure:

Being on my own was not a character flaw, or a mistake which needed to be corrected.

So, seriously, what the hell?

All of these depleting thoughts rained down on me at the base of the abbey, and no amount of deep breathing or positive thinking could protect me from the deluge.

"This is what it is," I realized, "to be Dolores Hart's Jessica."

I had so much admired that young woman from Cornelia's *The Pleasure of His Company*, who treasured her freedom and jumped at the opportunity to have an adventure.

I thought about how I had so cavalierly snorted with derision at Debbie Reynolds and her Jessica's 'dumb ending' of settling down.

Mother Dolores was right. I was her Jessica.

I was really glad of that. I couldn't have had it any other way.

But, like it does for everyone, the life I'd chosen came at a cost.

And for some reason, this was a cost which needed to be covered right here at the top of Mont St. Michel.

A moment later, as I was still working to get my head around all of this, mercy arrived in the form of a couple of nuns who appeared in my sightline, carrying a small push mower as they walked past me.

Inexplicably, this non-sequitur was somehow able to break the spell of those troublesome thoughts of mine, pulling me out of myself, and putting me back on my feet.

As I stood up, that dingy, beat-up piece of emotional baggage caught my eye. Deftly, I moved away from it and left it sitting where it was, pretending it didn't belong to me, as I finished my ascent to the abbey.

With that, the tempest which had blown over me seemed to dissipate as quickly as it had materialized.

There was no accounting for what had happened, or why.

I was just thankful it was over.

In the chapel, there was a service being conducted when I arrived. No spoken words, just music, with both monks and nuns kneeling in prayer, so calming and beautiful. I sat down on a bench and stayed there listening to the music until I was able to rid myself of the last of the lead and quicksand that was still clinging to me.

This was an extraordinary, almost mythical place I was in, I told myself, and I needed to be present for it, and appreciate the wonder which was all around me.

Just in case I never came back.

It was time to shake off that body blow and get back to enjoying the day.

Even by myself.

I took my time exploring the abbey's labyrinth of towers, cloisters and its aptly-named Crypt of the Big Pillars.

But I was most taken by the massive brass sculptures peppered throughout the abbey which appear to be glimpses of an enormous phoenix-like creature who lurks within the ancient stone walls.

It was all colossal, formidable and divine.

Happily, I was able to make my descent from the summit without any other painful recollections surfacing, and leave Mont St. Michel just as the real hordes of tourists were starting to show up.

Once I was back in the car, I plugged in the address for my hotel in Deauville, that glamorous seaside resort town and adult playground. I would spend my last night on the road there, before taking Claire back to the rental car office in Rouen.

On the way to Deauville, I made an unplanned stop along one of the country roads, at a funky antiques-salvage store. It was the Route 66 sign in the window which had caught my eye and piqued my interest. I had to go in. There I met Gabriel, the owner of the establishment and a huge fan of Americana, which made up the majority of the items he had for sale.

He showed me around and I met his two lovable, languid dogs, who also spoke (well, understood) only French. Thankfully, my French was strong enough that day to converse a bit with them as well as their owner. I was even able to understand Gabriel when he explained how he wants to go to the US to buy an Elvis-era Cadillac convertible. He already was the owner of an extended-cab pick-up truck, which he had parked out front.

Gabriel was what could best be described as a French good ol' boy, and he shared his thoughts on the world with me. Turns out, it would be one of the best conversations in French I would have with anyone. Not only because I wasn't really called upon to have to speak much myself, but also I managed to grasp a lot of what he was saying. It was all about French politics and what was currently happening in the country. "Les jeunes sont perdus" ("the young are lost"), he kept saying. I was thrilled I could understand this.

"Finally," I thought, "I've made it to France". It was one of the most rewarding moments of my entire trip.

Back on the road, I discovered as I approached my destination, that I had booked a hotel not in Deauville, but in the neighboring area of Villiers. So I missed the glamorous, cool resort town and ended up in a new-ish-looking sort of suburb town, with mostly self-catering holiday makers and not a lot of nightlife.

After exploring the area for a while in search of a place to have dinner, I ended up back at the hotel "restaurant" which was the name they'd given to an area where in the mornings they served that staple known as the "continental breakfast". While I was grateful the hotel offered something in the way of evening fare, I wasn't exactly smacking my lips over the frozen lasagna with hot chocolate to drink.

My travels in France were definitely proving not to be about the food.

Chapter 28

The next day, it was time to take Claire the Car back to Rouen, and meet up with the girls. This wound up being the diciest part of the week's travels for me. There were numerous slow-speed rural roads and delays along the way, and it took me two and a half hours to drive 130 km (80 miles). Still, I managed to turn in the car exactly at 10AM, right on time.

Claire the Car had made it safely home, not a scratch on her. I had driven for seven days in a foreign country, all by myself (albeit with help from the navigation system), and I was proud of that.

I would be staying overnight in Rouen, just as Emily and Cornelia had done, so after saying my goodbyes and thank yous to Claire, I liberated my big suitcase from the car trunk for the first time in a week, and walked with my bags to the hotel a few blocks away.

In 1922, the girls had left all of their luggage at the train station. But then they weren't exactly traveling light. At this point in their journey, Cornelia and Emily boasted between them two steamer trunks, at least half a dozen suitcases and a multitude of parcels containing purchases they had made along the way.

The prospect of moving around Europe with that amount of luggage would've caused me no end of angst, but it was nothing to the girls. They were fortunate to live in a time when there were always scores of lovely porters at every station, ready to help whisk the luggage from one place to another. Cornelia and Emily could accumulate as many heavy, bulky and breakable items as they wished, with nary a thought that they might ever have to tote any luggage around themselves.

Anytime I was having to cope with my suitcases, I would think about the girls and their steamer trunks, and the porters, with envy in my heart.

Rouen is one of my favorite parts of *Our Hearts*, mainly because a wide array of noteworthy things happened to the girls during their brief, overnight stay, as they explain:

"… why our experience in that historic town didn't leave its mark on the rest of our lives is proof positive that there must be a special Providence set apart to watch [over] the faltering steps of such ninnies as we."

I was eager to join up with Cornelia and Emily – I had very much been missing my travel gal pals. Luckily, the girls' account of their visit to Rouen is extensive and detailed, which meant it would be easy for me to track them down and spend a good amount of time with them.

I started my visit with a walking tour through the medieval streets, just as Cornelia and Emily had done, who

"… with Baedekers in hand, open like hymn books, went on foot about that lovely ancient city."

It was not Baedekers, but my copy of *Our Hearts* I carried as I retraced the girls' path, beginning at Ouen Church and the Hotel de Ville, where I found that the, "little shops nestled under the overhanging eaves of ancient buildings" had vanished, probably during World War II. But most of the Place de l'Hotel du Ville was still as the girls recalled it.

From there, I followed the girls' route to the Vieux Marche, or Old Market square, where Joan of Arc was burned at the stake in 1431. This had been one of the most powerful, profound moments of Cornelia's and Emily's journey.

"… at last we were in the old Market Place, standing on the spot where that guileless girl from Domremy was burned to death. It was Emily's first experience of the sort. She stood in the center of that beautiful and heartbreaking square murmuring, 'This is the place. This is the very place.' And quietly, unpremeditatively, we both stooped down and touched the cobblestones."

The square has changed a bit since the girls had been there. A church stands in its center now, along with a graceful, towering cross which reaches way into the sky. Gardens have replaced those cobblestones that the girls had bent down to touch. In the heart of those gardens is a placard marking the location where Joan of Arc was executed. Yes, it has definitely changed since Cornelia's and Emily's visit, but that isn't by any means a bad thing.

I continued our tour down Rue de le Gros Horloge (Street of the Big Clock) to the magnificent Rouen Cathedral, where I discovered it was closed until 2PM. An ideal window for grabbing something to eat, and seeking an answer to a question I had.

I started with lunch, a surimi baguette purchased from a food truck, the first one I'd ever had (or even heard of). In a small garden area next to the cathedral, I perched myself on a low stone wall under some shade trees, and enthusiastically consumed my new favorite sandwich.

It took me some time to fully take in my surroundings, and realize that scattered around this garden were pieces of the cathedral which had been blown off during World War II and never put back. The cathedral had taken a major hit on April 19, 1944, and two buttresses were all that had kept the whole thing from collapsing.

I started to consider the open-air square in front of the cathedral, which I had just passed through. In the girls' day, it had looked different. It was where "the little thirteenth century houses nestle, as if for sanctuary, about the great Cathedral." Vintage postcards I'd come across on the internet verified the girls' recollection: up until the 1930s, Rouen Cathedral had been ringed by humble half-timbered medieval cottages. Those 700-year-old homes must've been destroyed in that same World War II air raid. Sickening.

After my lunch in the garden, I went to the tourist office, and lobbed a question at the staff which I'm fairly certain they'd never been asked before:

Did they know where the red-light district of Rouen was located a hundred years ago?

The reason for my crass question stems from one of the most hilarious parts of *Our Hearts*, involving a mistaken address which landed the girls at the doorstep of a house of ill repute. Cornelia and Emily, in their naiveté, believed it to be a respectable pension in which they intended to stay the night.

Astonishingly, the madam of the establishment provided the girls with a room.

Remember, Cornelia's and Emily's book is a work of non-fiction. This really happened.

> "... beckoning us to follow, [she] led us down a hall. It was lined on either side with smallish rooms, rather elaborately decorated. Some of the doors were open, and we caught glimpses of the other guests who seemed quite surprised to see us and we were indeed surprised to see them. They all appeared to be young women in very striking evening dresses. This was certainly unusual, but we concluded they must all be waiting to go out to a dinner-party... I couldn't help thinking that this was an eccentric sort of pension, and Emily remarked that it lacked the 'homey' quality of the one in St. Valery."

That night, blissfully unaware that they were bedded down in a brothel, Emily and Cornelia, "slept the sleep of babes". Babes is right. It's hard to fathom two young women being so utterly guileless. But they were.

"As for the infamous brothel itself," I queried the tourist office staff, "where would this place have been?" To my delighted surprise, they seemed to know the answer to my question... or else they had been trained to tell the tourists anything just to appease us, seeing as how we won't know any better.

(It's the same sort of thing we Angelenos do when people come visit us in L.A. We drive them through Beverly Hills and say "Clark Gable lived here" as we blithely point to some random house that may or may not have existed during his time. Karmically speaking, I certainly had no room to be upset if this is what these folks were pulling with me.)

Whatever the truth was, I chose to believe the tourist office staff, and went down to the area they had marked on a map for me, east of the Cathedral and past another impressive church.

I arrived in a neighborhood which did appear to be a bit rough, well, by French standards – meaning it wasn't travel-magazine beautiful and dripping with charm.

Another thing which pointed to it being the right area was that it was close enough for the girls to have walked from the train station with their overnight cases, which they described doing. I couldn't know which building had been the brothel they stayed in, but I was pretty convinced I was treading along Cornelia's and Emily's path. I took a few photos before heading back to the cathedral.

On the way there, walking just ahead of me, an English woman was calling out something to her friend about how they "just had to go see this very interesting place". Needless to say, I made a beeline over to her and latched onto her group of four with only the barest of introductions.

I followed them into a courtyard of an immense half-timbered building which was presently being restored, to be used as a school. There appeared to be construction work going on in the middle of the courtyard, but on closer inspection, it turned out to be an archaeological excavation. I had never seen a dig up close. An unexpected first.

Standing in a three-foot-deep trench was a young woman looking over piles of bones, measuring each of them, while another young woman crouched next to a full skeleton in a grave, examining it and making notes.

Wow, now this really was a first.

I had never seen human remains before, let alone any dating back to the great plague of 1300-something, as I was informed these were.

Bless their poor souls.

I spent a while taking pictures and listening in on a tour being given to some other English-speaking visitors, then started again towards the cathedral.

Once more, I was waylaid, drawn into a dress shop, which was unlike me, but I had spotted a sundress in the store window that I felt an inexplicable, overwhelming compulsion to purchase. The dress was blue and baggy, sort of like a big cotton sack with straps, and it was wildly comfortable.

With my purchase in hand, I set out yet again to the cathedral and finally made it. My first order of business there was to locate the Joan of Arc chapel. Cornelia and Emily had each lit a candle here, which Cornelia recalled:

> "I placed [the candle] on a little spike beside the others which flickered before the shrine of Joan. She hadn't been canonized for very long and it was sweet to think of her coming into the eminent name of St. Joan. For all my Universalist forbears, I went down on my knees to thank her and France and God for letting me be there."

Of all the moments in *Our Hearts* I wished to capture for myself, this was the one I felt most deeply. I lit a candle for Cornelia and Emily, and placed it on a small altar with some others. While I didn't drop down on my knees, I did sit down in a chair in front of the shrine of St. Joan and gave thanks to her and France and God for letting me be there, and to Cornelia and Emily for leading me into this joyous adventure.

The other item on my Rouen Cathedral checklist took a bit of searching around, but I managed to locate the door to the belfry tower, the one the girls had been forced through by an "old harpy" who had insisted they climb to the top of the tower.

This is, again, one of the funniest passages in the book, and I had been planning to make that same climb up the tower with the girls, but it was not an option.

Perhaps it was damage from the war, or else it was that the climb up to the top of the tower was now deemed too dangerous (from Cornelia's and Emily's description, it sounded precarious at best). But for whatever reason, clearly a decision had been made not to allow tourists into the tower anymore, and the entrance to it is locked up tight.

At Rouen Cathedra: The door to the Belfry Tower, flanked by statue guards; **Our Hearts** *at the Chapel of St. Joan.*

It was a disappointment, not so much because it sounded like fun, but because I had once read a sort of spoof travel guide called, *Let's Blow Through Europe*, where they had explained how in every country you should climb one tall thing.

It may have been intended as a joke, but in my travels I had sort of adopted this notion as a rule. This was to be the designated Tall Thing

To Climb for this journey, so I was none too pleased about being thwarted.

Also, I had very much wanted to see the view which the girls had described. Or, more accurately, alluded to:

> "We came out into fresh air and a dazzling sunset. I guess there must have been a magnificent view too but we didn't dare look. However, we gazed with delight at the sky and some charming carvings in the balustrade…"

That view from the tower is one which probably next to no one besides the drones gets to see now. Maybe on a subsequent visit, if I know better French, I can sweet talk someone into letting me go up there. Because it feels like unfinished business. A hole in my journey.

Still, I headed back to the hotel with a sense of great satisfaction for how the day had gone. On arrival at the hotel, I was informed by the staff that at 11PM that evening, there would be a light show at the cathedral, and I really should see it.

So at a few minutes before 11PM, I returned to the cathedral where a large number of people of all ages was gathering. Soon the program began. It was one of those shows where gigantic images and animation are projected onto the side of a building. I had heard of them, but this was the first time I had ever experienced one.

Set to classical and medieval music, this production told the story of France. It was luminous, breathtaking, indescribable. And it was a beautiful, warm evening in which to enjoy the show, just to make it perfect.

A marvelous bonus to end a very interesting day.

I found myself fervently wishing that the girls could have seen such a spectacle when they were here. Oh, what would they have thought of that! But it was close to midnight now. At this point, Cornelia and Emily would already have been tucked up for the night in the brothel down the road, sleeping that sleep of babes.

After my own good night of sleep and another breakfast of fruit and to-die-for croissants, I checked out of the hotel and arrived at the train station in plenty of time to look around and reflect on when Cornelia and Emily had been here, catching their train to Paris.

It hardly goes without saying that, after their eventful stopover in Rouen, they couldn't depart the city without incident.

This time, it involved Emily's handbag.

> "Her pocket book was a grey suede 'envelope' fastened, not too securely, with a blue enamel clasp… Shallow and not very large, the thing was intended to hold only a few bare necessities. But that day Emily had rammed it to bursting point…"

Which it did, spilling its entire contents down into the tracks just as a train was pulling in. Her passport, traveler's checks, jewelry, letter of credit, along with a cigarette case and some fancy cosmetics became trapped under the train, just as Cornelia's and Emily's train to Paris arrived on the other side of the platform.

Mercifully, a station employee was able to crawl between the train's wheels and retrieve most of Emily's belongings, though he scavenged a fifty franc note for himself, presumably for his troubles.

This episode has always given me more of a sense of anxiety than amusement whenever I've re-read it – a sensation akin to that feeling one gets when they think they've misplaced their wallet or keys… or, these days, their cell phone.

But…

The Spilling of the Purse didn't actually occur in Rouen, according to Emily's recollection of events. She writes in her draft of the book that this unfortunate occurrence instead took place on the last day of their journey together, when they were saying their goodbyes at the Gare de St. Lazare in Paris.

Cornelia was leaving Europe a couple of weeks ahead of Emily, who had been invited to go on a motoring trip in Italy.

Their respective trains were scheduled to leave five minutes apart and from adjoining platforms.

Cornelia was on her train, presumably speaking with Emily through an open window, and as the train began to move, Emily waved with her clutch purse, which is when the Spillage happened.

Everything fluttered onto the tracks mere moments before her train pulled in on top of her possessions, sending Emily and a few nearby passengers and station attendants into a panic.

All of this Cornelia witnessed from a growing distance as her train pulled out of the station.

Cornelia and Emily, the authors, conclude their book before their parting at the Gare de St. Lazare, but knowing a good story when they had the misfortune to fall into one, they made room in Rouen for what was in reality the closing mishap of their journey together.

Part 5

As If Monet Had Painted It

Paris

Chapter 29

"The sloping [Champs-Elysees] rose before us in a soft, blue haze, as if Monet had painted it..."

It wasn't long before the train from Rouen to Paris reached the Gare de St. Lazare. On my arrival, I couldn't help but once again think of Emily's purse exploding as I stepped off the train and onto the platform.

It had been at least twenty years since I had last paid a call on Paris. Before then, I'd had the good fortune to visit a few times, spending a total of about six weeks here, which meant I'd already covered a lot on the tourist list of must-dos.

I had selected a hotel right across from Gare du Nord, from where I would be leaving in seven days on the Eurostar to London. The area around the Gare du Nord isn't the most fashionable or charming, which is to its advantage, in my thinking, as it provides an escape from the crowds which clog the more touristy areas of the city.

The girls, on the other hand (along with Otis and Maud, when they arrived a few days later), stayed in the Rue St. Honore, which is much more in the middle of the action.

Cornelia and Emily had come to Paris right at the dawn of one of the most colorful, captivating periods in the city's history. Known as *les Années Folles* ("the crazy years"), it was the French counterpart to the Roaring 20s in America. The austerity of the Great War had given way to the burgeoning prosperity of the 1920s. With it came an explosion of culture, from Gertrude Stein and her Lost Generation of literary compatriots, to modern painters like Picasso, Chagall and Mondrian. It was the era of Art Deco and flapper fashion and jazz, with Jean-Paul Sartre offering controversial new ways of looking at the world, while the dazzling Josephine Baker was singing and dancing to packed houses beginning in 1925.

(Fifteen years on, Baker would join the French Resistance during World War II, for which she was later awarded the *Croix de Guerre* and made a member of the French Legion of Honor. She spent her whole life being courageous. Serious guts and sand. She is my hero.)

While Cornelia and Emily would end up doing their fair share of mingling with stars of the French theatre, it's unlikely they ever brushed up against much of the "crazy years" culture. Still, the girls certainly did seem to sense the spirit and energy of those heady, happy days.

The best I could figure from *Our Hearts* was that Cornelia and Emily spent somewhere between four and eight weeks in Paris. I had decided to stay for only one. It would make my journey rather lopsided, much more England than France, but there was no changing it now. I was already scheduled to return to the States sooner than I would have liked, but I had managed to score a killer deal on the August 4 *Queen Mary 2* transatlantic crossing to New York – which, wonderfully enough, had worked out to be cheaper than buying a one-way airline ticket.

I couldn't pass up the opportunity, but it meant shortchanging Paris.

In truth, I hadn't really planned on duplicating this part of the girls' story, even though it is as lively and humorous as the rest of their tale. This was mainly due to Cornelia and Emily spending a large part of their time taking courses at the Sorbonne and seeing plays at the Comédie-Française, neither activity of which appealed to me, my French still being pretty darn atrocious.

Almost a quarter of *Our Hearts* takes place in Paris, so there was a lot of ground for me to cover, literally and figuratively. I wasn't sure where to start, so I headed first to the heart of the city, Notre Dame Cathedral.

I was within a block of the cathedral when I came upon some police pulling an irate woman off a bus. I couldn't be sure what the woman was being accused of, but from the few words I caught, I surmised that they thought she was a pickpocket. There were five officers – beautiful beings, they were – young and chiseled with shaved heads and scruffy beards, dressed head to toe in black. As a couple of officers were putting the woman in handcuffs, one of the others lit a cigarette and started smoking as he continued interviewing a witness.

Ah, France.

Arriving at Notre Dame, I discovered, even late in the afternoon, there was a massive line to get into the cathedral. I had visited it a few times in the past, and though I would have loved to have seen it again now, it wasn't worth that hideous queue. I was just thankful Cornelia's and Emily's only mention of Notre Dame was about admiring the rose window. It may have been a cheat, but that was something I could do from the outside, and I figured it counted.

Done and checked off the list.

Next, I meandered over to the Right Bank and walked along the Rue de Rivoli towards the Louvre, being wildly thankful I wasn't going to have to take on that behemoth of a place. A person could spend a month in there and still be far from done. I have a vague recollection of doing the tourist hustle through there with my fellow study abroader Stephanie, during our between-terms backpacking trip all those summers ago. We made the requisite visit to the Venus de Milo and the Mona Lisa, and skipped over most of the other 380,000 art objects housed in the former palace.

Another time, for sure. Preferably in the off-season. Even the colossal Louvre can get crowded.

I had synchronized my promenade so I would arrive at the Place de la Concorde as the sun was beginning to set, just as the girls had done on their first evening in Paris. On the way there, I walked through the Tuileries, where I discovered I had forgotten an unappealing aspect about the City of Lights' parks.

Most Paris "green spaces' – including the famous Tuileries – aren't actually that, but rather just large patches of dirt with trees and benches scattered about them, with very little paving and nary a blade of grass in sight. It can be like walking on an unpaved country road in the summer when it's dry and dusty.

No biggie, except when one is in open-toed shoes. I just wished I had remembered this before I'd worn my sandals.

At the Place de la Concorde, I took some pictures of the Paris skyline and of

> "… those seated heroines, the cities of France – Metz and Strasbourg, so long in mourning, now festive with wreaths."

Cornelia and Emily had been speaking of the statues of ladies who represent the French cities of Metz and Strasbourg. The pair had been "in mourning" after their two cities had fallen under German rule during the Franco-Prussian War in 1871, but were "now festive" because Metz and Strasbourg had been returned to France after WWI.

In 1942, those words must've been difficult for Cornelia and Emily to write, because at the time they were put to paper, the Germans were once again in possession of Metz and Strasbourg. The cities would eventually be liberated by the Allies in 1944, and have remained a part of France to this day.

I awoke the next morning to find it was blazing hot in Paris. Figuring it was better to be hot outside of the city, I decided this would be the day I made my visit to the Palace of Versailles.

It was a heady day for Cornelia and Emily when they visited the most famous palace in France. Those nice young doctors from the ship, Paul White and Joe Aub had come to Paris and invited the girls to lunch at Pre Catalan, a swanky restaurant in the Bois de Boulogne, followed by the afternoon at Versailles, and then back to Paris for an evening of dinner, dancing and a show.

Versailles ranks right up there with the Louvre in being massive enough to run a person ragged – even the young! – so the itinerary Paul and Joe had planned seems unfathomable, but according to Cornelia and Emily, they did all of those things in that one day.

Presumably in heels.

I elected to skip the part about going to lunch at Pre Catalan, which is still in operation today. Harboring some residual effects from my meltdown at Mont St. Michel, I just couldn't bring myself to dine in all that elegance alone, when the girls had been there on dates with their doctors.

So I hopped on a train and headed straight out to Versailles. I had been there once, with Stephanie. It had been cold and rainy that day, and Stephanie and I had pretty much skipped the gardens. Now I was eager to poke around the grounds on a day when – though hot – the weather was cooperating.

Emerging from the train station along with what seemed like a thousand other people, I made the short walk over to the palace, where to my happy surprise, I was able to quickly and easily buy a ticket.

And then I stood in line for an hour and a half to get in.

The lines at Notre Dame the day before should have clued me in. No more simple ticket taking and in you go. There was high security, with a preliminary bag checkpoint, a metal detector/body scan, and another bag check through a conveyor belt scanner before one can gain entry to the palace.

Completely understandable these days, and sadly necessary.

But an hour and a half...

"This is for the girls," I said to myself. "This is their day, and it's a big one." And seeing as how I had nowhere else I needed to be, I could and would tough it out.

During that hour and a half in the snaking line, I got to know the lovely women from Long Island, New York who were standing behind me. They had come over for a party being given in honor of one of their daughters, who had married a Frenchman. The young man's family is from Normandy and it was they who were hosting the party at the weekend, but in the meantime, the Long Island Ladies had a few days to themselves to roam and play.

The women were fun and funny and made the time pass quickly, and I was so thankful to be in line with them.

Once I'd finally made it inside, I filed in with the enormous herd of tourists plodding through the palace. Every room was packed wall-to-wall with people, and it was impossible to get a good look at anything.

The third and last leg of the line into Versailles; the breathtaking view of the famous Hall of Mirrors.

It became almost comical, the size of the crowds and the unsavoriness of the situation.

What a huge disappointment it must've been for all the people who were visiting for the first – perhaps the only – time.

I was just grateful that I'd toured the palace before, and could focus on wiggling my way through the rooms and escaping to the gardens as quickly as I could.

Outside, the revitalizing fresh air and influx of personal space put a spring back into my step, and I started the one-and-a-half-mile hike to Marie Antoinette's Petit Trianon and hamlet.

The day which had started out so beastly hot had turned partly cloudy and cooler, so I felt certain my goals were within reach.

But first, I needed to meet up with the girls and their dates.

I had on my phone a copy of the picture of Cornelia with the doctors, from Paul White's photo album. With this, I was able to locate the spot in the gardens where presumably Emily took the picture of the other three, and I got my picture made there.

I knew from *Our Hearts* that, on their day at Versailles, Cornelia had worn a knitted dress she had bought in Dieppe:

> "… for very little, which was not surprising. In those days, size 14 was big on me, and my model was an ample 40, but I'd taken for length and because it was marked down."

Which explained why Cornelia, devotee of the slinky vamp look, is wearing such a surprisingly baggy dress in Paul's photo.

For my day at Versailles, in anticipation of sweltering heat, I had worn the baggy sundress I bought in Rouen.

And just like Cornelia, I had brought a straw hat along with me. It hadn't been intentional, but it pleased me greatly that I'd mimicked her attire that day.

It was one of the top, best, closest moments of being with the girls, in their footsteps, matching their experience, that I would have. This was only one of two occasions where I had photos to confirm I was standing precisely where they stood (the other photo of the girls was the one taken in Mr. Wells' garden, in an area which I hadn't been able to access).

There was also another happy part of that moment in the garden, which was that I was getting to spend some time with Joe and Paul. I had gotten to know something about them through the research I'd done at Harvard, but I hadn't yet had the pleasure of really being around them until now.

Such fine young men, and I was tickled to be grabbing a few minutes with them before I continued my tour.

The Petit Trianon is a small chateau situated within the grounds of the massive Versailles estate, where Marie Antoinette would take refuge from court life. It was interesting and I was glad I got to see it. But, French history not being an obsession of mine like English history, I didn't connect with the ill-fated queen, nor Madame Pompadour, nor any of the other famous figures who passed through the chateau's doors. Unlike that day at Hampton Court, I couldn't feel the energy or presence of those who in centuries past had inhabited the rooms and walked the halls here.

I then went on to The Queen's Hamlet, a fabricated village surrounding an artificial lake, constructed in the 1780s by order of Marie Antoinette. The pretend cottages and windmill seemed rather otherworldly, but it was all quite picturesque.

Museum legs were coming on so I sat for a bit by the lake and got pictures of the carp. In actuality they were catfish, but I like to think of them as carp, descendants of the ones Cornelia and Emily saw on their outing to Versailles:

> "… we wandered about the parks, and took snapshots
> of ourselves feeding the carp."

There were still roughly four hundred square miles of gardens left to cover (okay, a slight exaggeration), but I'd had enough. Time to retreat to the palace and their enticing gift shop.

I made it as far as the prodigious Apollo fountain at the base of the grand canal, where I sat down on its edge, took my shoes off and put my feet in the water. It wasn't as cold as Lake Michigan or the Thames, but about ten minutes of soaking my feet did a world of good, and I felt revived enough to continue my walk.

On the way to the palace, I took a few photos of exhausted tourists who had conked out on the grass and benches lining the path.

Defeated by Versailles.

Upon finally reaching the top of the long sets of steps leading to the palace, I ran into my Long Island Ladies sitting in a crumpled heap. They said that when they saw me, I looked as tired as they felt.

Versailles defeats everyone.

The Long Island ladies, foreground, holding up better than others.

How on earth did Cornelia and Emily go out for an evening of dancing after this, when they'd spent hours here trekking around *in heels*?

Seriously, how?

Having been vanquished at the Battle of Versailles, I had no desire nor intention of following in Emily's footsteps, and visiting the Chateau de Fontainebleau, as she had done one day with John Mason Brown, an acquaintance of hers and Cornelia's, who was visiting Paris at the same time as the girls. Emily wrote about their experience in her draft of *Our Hearts*:

> *"We were peopling those stately, beautiful rooms, and the ghosts were pressing in on us... we could hear the brush of their stiff brocade over the floor, and the echo of their quick, high voices."*

This bit of the story was left out of the final version of *Our Hearts*, and I had to wonder if it was because Cornelia and Emily worried their readers would find it silly or kooky-sounding. I, myself, was overjoyed to discover Emily had recorded her encounter with the otherworldly occupants of the chateau. Her words affirmed that we are indeed compadres.

Chapter 30

Prior to arriving in Paris, I'd had all sorts of ideas about how I would spend my time. I had most certainly intended to look up Stacey from Dieppe, and go hang out with her and her family. I'd also considered having a day of adventure, and taking one of the bullet trains from Paris to Frankfurt to meet up with Tamara, a friend of mine going all the way back to junior high school, who was on her own travel adventure through Germany.

But by the time I'd reached the city, I was running out of steam, and I found it was taking all I had just to get through the laundry list of places I needed to visit and things I needed to do.

In hindsight, perhaps a break from my personal journey and spending time with friends, either old or new, could have recharged my batteries. But in those last days in Paris, I just couldn't muster the strength to see people.

I was starting to feel the melancholy of my grand adventure ending, and I knew myself well enough to know I would be dreadful company.

Besides, I needed to spend this time with Cornelia and Emily. These would be our last days together, and I wanted to focus on the girls and the book. Though I wouldn't be doing proper justice to them or *Our Hearts,* and genuinely immersing myself in Paris as they had, I would give it my all as a tourist.

Thursday proved to be a challenging day, and a rather dismal one, with the sun incessantly fighting – and failing – to break through heavy graphite-colored clouds.

Starting at the Sorbonne, I snapped a few cursory photos of its façade, taking a moment to picture the fresh, eager faces of Cornelia and Emily, hurrying to their French lessons.

It was then a two-minute walk over to the Cluny Museum to piece together the bits of what would prove to be a seminal moment for Emily. For it was here in the Cluny that Emily "learned about Life," all thanks to museum's art and antiquities:

> "Wandering there one day in an aimless fashion, gazing
> at the same exhibits for the third or fourth time,

> something caught her eye. It was that exquisite but frankly realistic carving of Leda and the Swan. She had looked at it often, but now she looked at it again. For a moment the world stood still, then knowledge began to dawn, and she was like a pinwheel that had just been touched off… when her eyes focused it was upon one of those well-known medieval objects adopted by the Crusaders as a measure for preserving the sanctity of the home… "So that's how it is!" she exclaimed…"

I had gone to the Cluny that day because for decades I'd wondered how a carving of a woman and a swan, paired with a medieval chastity belt, could possibly have spelled out for Emily how human procreation works.

But my visit would be for naught. I didn't find Leda and the Swan. And there certainly were no chastity belts on display. There was no learning about Life for me that day.

From the museum, I walked over to Les Invalides and took pictures of the magnificent dome. Part museum, part hospital, part retirement home for war veterans, this was where Cornelia and Emily occasionally came to pay visits to a veteran of World War I. They don't explain how they came to do this, or how they became acquainted with the former soldier, but it doesn't really matter. It's just a lovely, sweet part of the girls' story, in which they befriended this man and his family, and came away with some of the most poignant memories of their entire journey.

Already feeling a bit deflated from the Cluny experience, I just couldn't bring myself to explore the museum, or check out Napoleon's tomb in the church crypt, or even wander around the gardens. I sat on the wall awhile and thought about Cornelia's and Emily's soldier. It was comforting to know he had been honored and looked after here in this pretty place.

Then I was off to the Eiffel Tower. Though the girls make no mention of touring the tower, they write about it affectionately (which is only right and natural). I walked to the end of the long park at the base of the tower where Stephanie and I had lunched on the grass all those years ago, after we'd made the expedition to the top.

I settled onto the grass, watching and listening to the families who were picnicking around me. Most were speaking English, and from what I could glean, almost all of them seemed to be in the throes of one parent being irritated with the other parent for not helping with the tired, impatient children.

Those families who were speaking other languages also appeared to be at odds and complaining.

I found this strangely reassuring. It was a lovely, crazy reminder that, in the end, people are exactly the same the world over.

Just as it had happened so many times before, I found myself filled with a sense of deep contentment that my day belonged to me, and how I was unfettered and free to enjoy it as I liked.

After the sucker-punch I'd received at Mont St. Michel, I relished this moment.

Turning my attention to the Eiffel Tower, I noticed that the entire base of it was encircled by high, ugly, utilitarian security fencing. I thought back to my past visits to Paris, and how visitors had been able to walk up and under the tower from any direction. Now the only way for tourists to stand under the tower involved passing through one of two security checkpoint tents.

It shook me out of my contentment and made me feel as gloomy as the sky.

I started to think perhaps all of this heightened security was adding to the weariness I was feeling. Paris had changed, not just from Cornelia's and Emily's time, but from mine as well, and it was not for the better.

Perhaps it was like my experience in Cambridge – the change wouldn't seem so startling if I had visited it at other times in the last twenty-plus years, like I had with England.

It was also possible I was projecting my gloominess onto the city.

But – to me – The City of Lights seemed sad. It wasn't teeming with the resilient, "carry on" spirit of London. The city and its people had been through a lot in the last few years, and it felt worn down by its troubles, as if it had lost a little of its vigor.

I was maybe not being my best self in Paris, but it was not its best self either.

There was something especially demoralizing about this notion. After all, the title of Cornelia's and Emily's book is a play on the lyrics of the song, "The Last Time I Saw Paris":

> "... the last time I saw Paris
> Her heart was warm and gay
> No matter how they change her
> I'll remember her that way."

The song came out in 1940, and by December of that year, with the Nazi occupation of Paris in its sixth month, it had become a favorite on the music charts, with no less than a half-dozen singers recording versions of the tune. That song provided Cornelia and Emily with an ideal title for their book – light and happy, with a potent subtext.

Like Cornelia and Emily, I had numerous joyful memories of Paris from my first time abroad, and from subsequent visits. And now it seemed as if the words to that bittersweet old song were resonating as they had in 1940, albeit to a far lesser degree.

Or was it just me?

I just couldn't get perspective enough to know for sure.

Friday was the second day of my crusade through the streets of Paris. I started it with a ramble down le Boulevard Haussmann, along the Rue de la Paix to the Place Vendome, walking the same route the girls had taken in their taxi from the train station to their hotel. Arriving in the rue St Honore, I located the Hotel Costes, formerly the France et Choiseul, where Cornelia and Emily had first stayed in Paris.

> "... sooner or later nearly every itinerant American got there. It was hard to explain its popularity – it was noisy, the service was not over-efficient and guests were always being moved from one room to another. But it was conveniently located on the rue St. Honore. The rooms were attractive and clean, the food good, and the atmosphere pleasant... Our room overlooked the courtyard, a sweet, hidden spot, gay with potted plants. This was the main gathering place, furnished with tables and chairs where one could have drinks..."

I slipped inside and, finding that the hidden courtyard still existed, now as a luncheon spot, I grabbed a few quick, surreptitious photos of it before hustling back out onto the rue St. Honore.

Scooting over to the Place Vendome, I popped into the Ritz to search for the restaurant where Cornelia and Emily once had a most memorable lunch.

The girls had not dined alone that day, but had brought along Gamin and Lily, their newly-acquired Brussels Griffon puppies. Known as Belgian Griffons in the 1920s, these beguiling little dogs charmed every human they encountered, and the girls soon discovered "they were the means of our getting wonderful service". This emboldened Emily and Cornelia to take the pups to fancy restaurants like the Ritz, where:

> "[The maitre d'] led us to one of the best tables and seated us, all four, on chairs of pale rose brocade... He served us lunch himself and brought up dishes of chopped filet mignon for our mascots, and we ate under the rapt scrutiny of every other occupant of the dining room."

When Cornelia and Emily had finished their lunch and it was time to leave, they discovered they were unable to do so, because both Gamin and Lily had made puddles on their chairs. Horrified, the girls took their time over their coffee, hoping the stains would dry, but to no avail. Finally, after paying the bill, they dropped their napkins over the wet spots as they picked up the dogs, and scurried out of the restaurant.

The Ritz has multiple dining options, but after a quick confab with a few staff members – all of whom spoke impeccable English, and were very kind – I was let into L'Espadon, the Ritz's Two-Michelin-Star restaurant, even though it wasn't open yet. Sumptuous and elegant, it carries the stately atmosphere of an establishment with a long, rich history.

Almost as if to convince me I had the right place, the restaurant was filled with rose brocade chairs. Of course, it wasn't likely to be the exact same rose brocade fabric which had been on the chairs ninety-five years ago. But it was a happy surprise to discover everything looking much the way it did when the girls were there.

Thanking the staff for their kindness and indulgence, I made my way across the hotel to the Ritz bar, finding it also closed at that time of day. Still, I managed to snap a few pictures of its interior through the glass door. The bar was dark and intimate, and I could almost see how the girls could have described it as "the smokiest hole of Calcutta ever conjured up out of an old coat closet". But then again, maybe they were being a bit harsh. I thought it was rather seductive.

Hardly a smoky hole… the Ritz Bar, and the elegant scene of Cornelia's and Emily's crime.

By now I was ready for some lunch of my own.

Leaving the Ritz, I went a block over to the famous patisserie "Angelina", known as "Rumpelmayer's" in Emily's and Cornelia's time. Emily had once met up here for afternoon tea with Agatha Clark, a high school chum she happened to bump into just as the girls were arriving in Paris.

Breezing into Angelina, I felt as though I'd stepped inside a giant candy box. The resplendent walls and woodwork are painted in light neutral shades, with gold-colored carved accents resembling heirloom jewelry. To the left of the entrance is their gift shop, selling vintage-looking souvenir tins filled with sweets. To the right is the magical patisserie counter, where scores of mouth-watering pastries – confectionary works of art, they are – fill the cases. Past the lobby is the restaurant itself, replete with soft lighting, leatherback chairs, small round marble tables, and walls adorned with pastoral murals in tantalizing, muted hues.

Glancing around the restaurant, I thought I glimpsed Emily in the back room having tea with Agatha, before I was led by a hostess to a table of my own with my copy of *Our Hearts* in hand.

Being far too hungry to make due with a dainty pastry and a cup of tea, I ordered an open-faced sandwich which looked remarkably like a bouquet of flowers. It was really too pretty to eat, but that didn't deter me from downing the whole thing. I followed that with a cup of Angelina's famous hot chocolate, which turned out to be the best I have ever had. It's like drinking light, silky melted chocolate.

Topped with whipped cream for good measure.

Perfection.

I also couldn't resist ordering Angelina's signature pastry, the Mont Blanc, simply because it had been created at the beginning of the 20th century, which meant there was every chance Emily had tried it as well. This exceedingly rich confection is comprised of meringue, whipped cream and chestnut vermicelli, and one bite was all I could handle, but it was enough to satisfy my curiosity and my desire for symmetry with the girls.

(The rest of the pastry took a rough and tumble ride inside a "to go" box which I stuffed into my shoulder bag, but eventually the Mont Blanc made it back to my hotel room mini-fridge, and later proved to be a very satisfying after-dinner dessert.)

After my delectable lunch, I ambled over to check out the new "Canopy" on the Forum des Halles, a large shopping and entertainment complex which stands on the former site of Les Halles, the central fresh food market of Paris for almost eight hundred years.

"… in one of the worst acts of urban vandalism of the century," according to *The Guardian*, the current structure replaced the wrought-iron and glass pavilions which were constructed in the 1850s under orders from Emperor Napoleon III, and subsequently demolished in 1971. In 2016, the city revamped the Forum des Halles, adding the Canopy for visual impact. The tourist office refers to it as the "new Parisian architectural symbol," while *The Guardian* wrote it up as a "custard-coloured flop".

I'd never spent any time in and around Les Halles, but I thought I should give it a look – see what all the fuss was about – even though what I would find had to be a far cry from the marketplace Cornelia and Emily would have browsed in.

Sadly, the Canopy didn't seem to make much of an impression on me one way or the other, because my journal entry about visiting Les Halles mentioned only the Forum's open space where people were enjoying music, their pets and sunshine.

On the walk back to my hotel, I stopped at the Café de la Paix to have a drink with Otis Skinner. Located next to the Opera National de Paris, this was where Otis had taken refuge from Cornelia and Emily on the day they were driving him crazy with talk of their upcoming dates with Joe and Paul.

I had enjoyed the time I spent with Otis in London, and was looking forward to having this drink with him while I was in Paris.

The Café de la Paix is one of those classic Paris eateries, complete with sidewalk tables designed for whiling away the day and people watching.

Happily, I was able to snag one of those outside tables, joining a cosmopolitan mix of Parisians and visitors from around the world. I pictured Otis coming here, enjoying a coffee and reading the international newspapers. He was one of the thousands of famous figures who, for over 150 years, have frequented this legendary establishment. Of everyone sitting at the café that afternoon, it gratified me to think I was there in the most esteemed company.

Then again, perhaps some of the other patrons were here with their own historic favorites: Victor Hugo, Sarah Bernhardt, Gustave Flaubert, Marlene Dietrich, Charles de Gaulle. It was quite possible the place was crawling with nerds like me.

With a white port aperitif in my hand, I toasted to Otis and all those famous and not-so-famous patrons of the café for instilling this place with a treasure trove of glittering stories.

No doubt, her father's fame and prestige added a dimension of glamour to Cornelia's travels, opening doors for her (and Emily, too).

In her memoir, *Family Circle*, Cornelia wrote about a lengthy visit she and her parents had made to Paris the year before her trip here with Emily. During that visit, she first started taking acting lessons with Emile Dehelly, one of the leading men of the French theatre of the day. And because of her famous parents, Cornelia was able to mingle with numerous luminaries of the Paris stage, which she wrote about in her autobiography.

The mention of one actor in particular caught my attention.

> *"The Guitrys were at the Edouard VII [Theatre] that season and whatever may have been Sacha's subsequent behavior under Nazi influence, his plays… were a joy."*

Alexandre-Pierre Georges "Sacha" Guitry was an actor, director and writer, an icon of the French theatre and film community. What Cornelia is referencing, in regards to the Nazis, is – because he was allowed to continue working in Occupied Paris – accusations of collaboration were made against Guitry. When France was liberated, he was one of the first to be arrested and sent to a detention camp. Later he was found innocent of any collaboration, but the damage had been done, and the shadow of those accusations haunted Guitry for the rest of his life.

Certainly his tarnished reputation was something Cornelia felt she must acknowledge, even as she wrote of the man with admiration. What she didn't know at the time, and most likely never knew, was Sacha Guitry had made a significant contribution to the Allied war effort – one that he never divulged, even though it could have salvaged his reputation.

On a visit to London in August 1939, it was Sacha Guitry who had smuggled into England that replica Enigma machine which changed the course and outcome of the war.

It had been supplied by the Polish Cipher Bureau, and once inside England, the Enigma was taken to Bletchley Park, enabling them to crack the German codes – and supposedly make the discovery that *Our Hearts Were Young and Gay* was used as a codebook.

Once again, small world.

Chapter 31

Though things had brightened for me the day before (likely due in large part to that Angelina hot chocolate), I still woke up on Saturday expecting it to be a slog. I wrote in my journal:

"My third day of marching around Paris, and my zeal to follow in the girls' footsteps is starting to feel like a chore, like a have-to, and there is no joy in it.

Numerous reasons for this:

Cloudy weather, good for walking but kinda depressing.

Heaps of walking, and my body has hit the wall. There's no moving with any speed today. My body feels just so heavy and sluggish. But I have to walk. In less than two weeks, I have to be able to fit into those evening gowns on the ship!

The isolation factor – my French is still for crap.

I feel like I'm failing. I didn't expect throngs to flock to my blog, but I doubt more than a handful of people read it. I'm not getting more than a dozen or so likes on my Instagram photos, and my FB posts are pretty much ignored."

What a thing to snivel about! I found it aggravating that I was supposed to be wildly concerned over my social media stats. It had been drilled into my head during a writers' workshop that an author lives and dies by their "platform" – the new measure of a writer's value. Our worth is to be tabulated on the length of our email subscribers list and the number of thumbs up and shares which follow anything we post.

Ridiculous. And even more ridiculous was that it was screwing not just with my mind, but with my whole experience. And I was letting it.

A surefire way to reinvigorate myself, I knew, was to walk up the Champs- Elysees to the Arc de Triomphe. No one who ventures along that grand avenue can remain unmoved by it.

Cornelia and Emily had certainly sensed this on their first evening in Paris, as they traveled up the avenue at twilight in a horse-drawn cart, in awe of their surroundings.

> "We didn't talk. Conversation seemed out of place. Ahead of us rose a stolid arch."

I may have been somewhat more prosaic in my approach, strolling along swinging my purse, but I still felt the charge of being on that iconic stretch of pavement. Though the names on many of the store fronts had changed, the great boulevard of Paris was, happily, pretty much as I remembered it.

I was especially pleased to find, just as I recalled, the Pomme de Pain sandwich shop was still operating right outside the Franklin D Roosevelt Metro stop. After stopping to pick up a villageoise (French for "yummy") sandwich, I headed up towards the Arc de Triomphe, where I watched a few folks with more bravery than brains attempt to dash across the *Etoile*, before I disappeared into the underground tunnel which leads to the monument.

Although still referred to as the *Etoile* ("Star"), this vast intersection of twelve straight avenues which encircles the Arc de Triomphe no longer officially goes by the name Cornelia and Emily called it when they wrote about it in 1942.

This is because it was renamed the "Place Charles de Gaulle" in 1970 following the death of the heroic general and president of France.

When his country surrendered to Germany in 1940, de Gaulle had refused to surrender with it. Going into exile in England, he declared, "Je suis la France" ("I am France").

Over the next two years, he rallied his fellow countrymen and led the charge to get his country back.

In his fight, De Gaulle had been spurred on by memories of fighting alongside the British 51st Highland Division in Normandy, before those soldiers were cornered in St. Valery-en-Caux. In a speech he delivered in 1942, as Cornelia and Emily were penning *Our Hearts*, de Gaulle spoke of his comradeship with the 51st Highlanders, asserting how that experience,

"... played its part in the decision which I took to continue fighting on the side of the Allies unto the end, no matter what the course of events."

As if it needs repeating: Small world.

I emerged from the underground tunnel and stood the base of the Arc de Triomphe. There I took in the view of the Champs-Elysees and paid silent homage at the resting place of the Unknown Soldier, just as the girls had done. This is one of the most poignant moments in *Our Hearts*, as Cornelia and Emily, return misty-eyed to the horse-drawn cart where their driver has been waiting for them.

> "He, too, had been looking at things and had been having his own meditations. His shiny leather hat was in his hand. He observed us shrewdly for a moment and in his husky voice said, 'Je vous remercie, mesdemoiselles, au nom de la France.'"

That man, thanking the two Americans, in the name of his country, had to have struck a chord with readers in 1942, knowing so many American boys were once again "over there", trying to save France like the generation before them had. This was something I hadn't understood in my first hundred readings of *Our Hearts* – how that small, sweet incident, in context of when the story was set to paper, was profoundly powerful.

Here in this place, I now understood the full measure of it.

Off-handedly, I thought about Cornelia and Emily visiting at a much prettier time of day, and resolved that I would try to make it out one evening to see the Champs-Elysees at twilight.

It was then that I got clubbed with a sobering realization: This half-hearted attempt of mine to rush around Paris, checking items off a list as quickly and carelessly as possible, was lunatic.

I was no longer savoring a glorious, glamorous, once-in-a-lifetime journey.

I was just a tourist in a hurry.

For weeks, I had carried around smug condescension for all those visitors I saw snapping a million pictures and recording endless videos, while never enjoying or connecting to where they were. Those people, I told myself, would get home with their snapshots and feel they had seen a place, when in fact, they had only viewed it through a screen. Whereas I had often been so present in the moment, so caught up in the experience, I usually forgot to take pictures. I might not have photo evidence of being in a place, but I had actually *been* there, which was far better.

But now I was one of "those people".

Worse, actually.

At least these tourists seemed to enjoy the experience they were having, even if it didn't measure up to my oh-so-exacting, high-handed principles on how to travel.

I, on the other hand, was just a moaning mess trying to get things over and done with.

And the worst part of it all?

The girls and their book deserved better.

If my fantastical notions of Cornelia and Emily being with me on this journey were by any means true, then I owed them an apology.

For days, I'd been dragging the girls around their beloved Paris with me, which was certainly not something they'd signed up for.

I began to suspect that, if I had been paying attention that day at the Eiffel Tower, I would have heard the girls making the same complaints as were being vented in all those tired families around me.

I needed to remember I wasn't really traveling alone, and I'd better shape up and start acting like it.

Turning again towards the Champs-Elysees, I whispered, "I'm so sorry, girls. I'll make this right."

Steeled with this new determination and change of mood, I walked from the Arc de Triomphe over to the Hotel Regent's Garden at 6 rue Demours, the pension where Cornelia and Emily had stayed for most of their summer.

It was from here the girls left on their big date to Versailles with Joe and Paul – but only after a morning fraught with panic. Having spent the night in an antique bed "so enormous it looked as if it belonged at Fontainebleau with a rope around it," Cornelia awoke to find she'd been bitten by bedbugs, and her top lip had swollen to gargantuan proportions.

"The swelling took up so much of my skin, my eyes were
pulled down like a bloodhound's. Everything about my
countenance had a high gleam, especially that throbbing
upper lip which shone like a polished tomato."

Fearing their day with the doctors was in jeopardy, the girls made
a wild dash to the American Drug Store, and with the purchase of a
miracle cream which managed to deflate Cornelia's face, the day was
saved.

At the Regent's Garden, once again I got some surreptitious
pictures of the hotel's interior, notably the parlor where the girls had
learned to dance the tango from Jacques Ventadour, a fellow guest of
the hotel, and the lobby where Paul and Joe waited for Cornelia and
Emily who, after their morning's high drama,

"… swept down to meet them with beating hearts and
an air of non-chalance."

Not every day at the pension was quite as dramatic for the girls.
Their lengthy stay in Paris allowed them to settle in and establish some
routines which made them feel as if they were home.

In Emily's draft of the book, she mentioned how once a week, they
would have the same taxi driver pick them up at the door, and drive
them five francs' distance from the hotel, where they would hop out
and walk back. Each week he would drive a different direction,
allowing the girls to discover much of the city surrounding them.

In *Our Hearts*, Cornelia and Emily recall being given a room
overlooking the garden. After dinner on many evenings, the girls
would,

"… pull up chairs in front of the long window of the
garden, light cigarettes, and … we would talk about
THINGS."

These girls had set out that summer on a journey of independence.
In their travels, they had grown up, becoming women in the months
they lived in London and Paris. And a lot of that maturity had come

here in this pension, in those late night tete-a-tetes filled with the candid honesty which girlfriends always share.

Outside the back of the hotel, I took pictures of the exquisite garden, where Cornelia would do some more growing up – professionally-speaking this time – as she took her first uncertain steps in becoming both a writer and an actress.

> "… I began inventing a sort of solo act about an American girl visiting the Louvre. I wrote it down, memorized it and then with a good deal of shyness, told Emily I had 'worked up a little skit' and would she care to hear it. To my astonishment, she became almost lyrical about it and said I must do it for the family. But I said, heavens NO! They'd think I was only frittering away my time. Monologue wasn't theatre."

Even though Cornelia had already dipped her toe in the water theatrically with parts in the school plays, and a bit role in "Kismet", a film her father had starred in, she hadn't fully declared to herself or anyone her intentions of being an actress. But on that day in the hotel garden, Emily recognized that she was witnessing her friend's dream crystallize into reality. In her first draft of the book, Emily wrote about it at length and quite profusely.

> *"I shall never forget it – you were so defiant out there in the little French garden, shy about telling me, burning to try it… I had a feeling that it was important, and when you said you were not going to tell it to your family, nor do any more, I grew furious… and said why couldn't you do these in a theatre – and you said that was idiotic, and for me not to be the fool."*

Cornelia would go on to become famous for the one-woman shows she wrote and starred in, and would for decades tour the country and the world, performing in her monologue plays.

It had been a defining moment in Cornelia's life, here in this garden where I was now standing.

No doubt Emily long enjoyed the satisfaction of being able to lovingly say to her friend, "I told you so."

And Cornelia, for her part, must certainly have been happy to have been proven wrong.

I lingered in the garden for a while, imagining that pivotal moment in Cornelia's life, and feeling the magic of it, before making my way back through the hotel to rue Demours.

The hotel wasn't too far a walk from the Arc de Triomphe, and like I had for Madame Corue and those in St. Valery-en-Caux, I felt a pang of sorrow for Madame Griffe, the proprietress of the Hotel Regent's Garden when the girls had stayed here. Had she been one of those Parisians in the newsreel footage twenty years later, who had stood in the streets with tears running down their cheeks as they watched German soldiers march down the Champs-Elysees and overtake their city? Had she been in those Liberation Day newsreels, ecstatically cheering as General de Gaulle led his French troops followed by American soldiers around the Etoile and into Paris?

1922, 1940, 1944… it was all of those years as much as it was 2017, and I felt myself moving between the ticks of the clock with an erratic, disconcerting velocity. I let the sensation run its course, then settled myself back in the present and resumed my tour.

There was still time for me to get over to the Church of St. Sulpice. Cornelia and Emily had gone there one Sunday at the invitation of the great composer and organist, Charles-Marie Widor, who was scheduled to play a Bach mass.

They sat in the choir loft with him as he played, then after the service, Widor led the way to a room upstairs from the loft, which contained a small white and gold organ. Seating himself at its bench, Widor began to play it for the girls, explaining that this handsome instrument had been a gift from Marie Antoinette to Mozart.

When I first began researching *Our Hearts*, I could find no present-day mention of the organ being within the Church of St. Sulpice. My first thoughts had run to the Nazis, and the possibility they could have stolen the organ from the church. Had it been taken to Germany? If so, had the Monuments Men not been able to recover it? Or had the Church, before the German Occupation, been able to spirit the instrument away to some hidden location, from which it never returned?

Back in London on my very first night in town, I had gotten the answer during my visit with Amy and Caity. Amy, a musician, conductor and music professor, mentioned she had been to St. Sulpice, and I raised the subject of the organ with her. To my great relief, she told me she had seen it. She had somehow known of its existence, and had managed, with only limited French, to charm one of the church workers into taking her up to that same room above the choir loft to see the organ.

No question, she confirmed, it was safe and sound.

Maybe I would have that same luck today.

But inside St Sulpice, I could find no church worker to sweet talk, and no way to get to the choir loft. So a big, fat bust.

And this one stung.

In the back of my mind, this was going to be my way of making it up to Cornelia and Emily for my numerous failings here in Paris. And for myself, it was to be a bit of redemption for an otherwise non-event of an experience I was creating here.

Instead, now I was once again circling that stinkin' drain.

Fed up, I skulked off to one of the empty chapels so I could tailspin away from the other tourists, a number of whom seemed to be searching for the *Da Vinci Code*'s Rose Line, and the spot where Silas the monk supposedly breaks up the floor looking for the keystone.

St. Sulpice is beautiful in a dark, looming way – more reverence and less pageantry than other great houses of worship – and I found safe haven in its somber elegance.

I slunk into one of the chapel seats, put my head in my hands and started muttering aloud all of the ugly thoughts that were consuming me:

I'm going to fail.

I'm already failing.

It had all been a terrible idea.

And why couldn't I solve the mystery of the Great Educationalist (I was maybe a smidgen too obsessed with this)?

And then I looked at my "failure" with my social media and the thought occurred to me: maybe this wasn't failure. It was just a lot harder than I was expecting. Maybe I would just have to put a lot more work into this than I planned on. Maybe I was going to have to fight for this.

That was not the same as failure.

In the course of my life, more often than not things had come fairly easy for me, and when they hadn't, I never had the gumption to keep going with them. I did something only when it was effortless. I had worked hard in my life, but only at things I was good at. One solid obstacle, one strong "no," was all it took to make me fold up my tent and turn on my heels.

It began to seep into my brain that maybe I was merely having my mettle tested in some small measure. Because really, the only surefire way I could fail was to stop trying. To let my fear hold me back. That was failure.

I thought about General De Gaulle.

"Continue fighting on unto the end, no matter what the course of events."

And Winston Churchill.

"Never give in – never, never, never, never, in nothing great or small, large or petty, never give in…"

It may be tough, I told myself, but in the end, you just have to keep going and never give up on what you believe in, even when it's hard and even when you fail.

The dark cloud started to evaporate, and I lifted my head, noticing the statue in front of me. It was Joan of Arc. I was sitting in the chapel dedicated to her. I smiled and thanked Cornelia and Emily for having my back and leading me to St. Joan. I took it as their way of saying "It's going to be okay."

In the end, I realized, this journey was for me. This book was for me. And it was essential that I remembered all of this in these last few hours of my travels. Two months had become two days. Then it would be over. The week in England and the voyage back to New York would be nothing more than an epilogue. And I would be doing it alone, without Emily and Cornelia.

That blog of mine, those Instagram photos, the Facebook page, were there to serve as my souvenirs and reminders of this adventure with the girls. If others got enjoyment from it, all the better, but it was time to stop looking for those clicks of approval.

Before there was ever the idea for a book, there was my love for this story. And here I was, living the dream I'd had for decades.

This moment – and every bit of the last few months – had come from my desire to take this journey. I needed to let it be its wondrous self, because I would never have this experience again.

Chapter 32

Sunday, July 23 was the final day of the legendary Tour de France bicycle race. Paris had been getting itself dressed up and ready for the party, with banners and barricades, and it looked like the race would conclude on a beautiful summer day.

In the morning, I walked from the Gare du Nord to Angelina on a quick errand to buy a souvenir tin of sweets, after which I would snap a few photos of the racing route on the Rue de Rivoli. Beyond that, I hadn't given much thought to what I would do with the day.

The riders weren't due in for a couple of hours, but there were already some crowds forming along the cycle route, and the atmosphere was happy and relaxed. I found an opening along the barrier railing where I could stand with an unobstructed view, and figured I might just stick around and watch the race. I was done with checklist days.

Near my vantage point, stationed on a large concrete block which served as an anchor point for one of the distance marker banners was a group of three friends – Tracy, Jo and Lee. Tracy and Lee were English, while Jo was a transplanted New Zealander currently living in England. They told me that they had staked out the spot on "the island" early in the day, and they'd brought a bag of provisions so they wouldn't have to give up their prime real estate.

We chatted back and forth, and shared some laughs. Pretty soon, they invited me up onto their island, gave me some of their wine and snacks, and made me their friend.

Suddenly I was having the coolest morning. My new pals were zany and fun, and I ended up spending the rest of the day with them.

By the time the cyclists were closing in on the Rue de Rivoli, we were all a bit tipsy from the beverages. In a flash, brightly-colored blurs were shooting past us. Tracy, a big fan of the sport and cyclist herself, jumped up and down with excitement (no mean feat on our little island) because the blur at the front of the pack was her fellow countryman, Chris Froome.

Her elation was infectious, inspiring me to launch into a highly effusive but rather incoherent live video broadcast on Facebook, which I blamed entirely on the low snack-to-alcohol ratio.

After the race, we escaped the crowds by maneuvering into the Rue Cambon, where we grabbed dinner, complete with more wine and more laughs.

It was just coming on to twilight as we walked up to the Etoile. This topped my day, seeing the Arc de Triomphe the way Cornelia and Emily had. My race day friends were heading back to the UK in the early morning, so we said our goodbyes there, but not before we took pictures and exchanged info. They left for the Metro station, as I finished watching the lights of the Champs-Elysees wake up.

Looking down the expanse of avenue leading to the Place de la Concorde with its ancient Egyptian obelisk and effervescent fountains – where in the troubled times of the French Revolution, Louis XVI and Marie Antoinette had lost their heads – I was as much awed by my surroundings as Cornelia and Emily had been on their first night in Paris.

The street had been reopened to cars, and long red and white ribbons of taillights and headlights began to form along the grand boulevard, as misting rain fashioned halos around the streetlamps, lending a mystical quality to the twilight.

It had been a cracker-jack day. Finally I felt as though I had shown up for Paris. And in turn, she had shown up for me.

Monday, July 24, 2017, was a day I had been anticipating with a heavy heart. It was the final day of my journey with the girls. Determined to make the most of our closing hours, I planned to spend this last day doing what Cornelia and Emily did the day before their departure.

> "… we went on a pilgrimage to say good-bye to some of the places we had loved best."

After a morning of packing so I could just get up and dash for the train the next day, I proceeded to the Left Bank and the Gardens of St Julien le Pauvre, which Cornelia and Emily had spoken of as one of their favorite spots.

I could easily see why the girls loved those gardens. They are right across the river from Notre Dame, and there is something enchanting about the gentleness of their design, and how they incorporate odd remnants of ancient architecture.

As an added bonus, the gardens are right next to the Shakespeare and Company bookstore. This haven of English-language tomes had existed when the girls were here, but not at the present location. Cornelia and Emily would have frequented Shakespeare's when the store was situated near the Odeon Theatre a few blocks away.

Well, in truth, it isn't the same bookstore. It only shares a name. The original bookshop was owned by an American named Sylvia Beach, and was a popular gathering place for the literary crowd and English-speaking ex-pats. Beach developed long-lasting friendships with numerous members of the Lost Generation, from Gertrude Stein herself to F. Scott and Zelda Fitzgerald, Ezra Pound and Ernest Hemingway, who wrote with affection about Beach and her bookstore, and was an almost daily visitor to Shakespeare and Co.

In turn, Sylvia Beach was devoted to her friends and passionate about helping promote their works. She even dared to publish James Joyce's *Ulysses*, which was considered scandalous at the time. According to legend, Beach used covers from innocuous works of the day to disguise *Ulysses*, in order for American and British readers to be able to purchase the book without fear of judgment or possible repercussions.

Cornelia and Emily make no mention of the storied history of Shakespeare and Company, but then they would have visited the bookstore while it was still in its early days. It's unlikely the girls rubbed elbows with any of the literary luminaries associated with the shop. And by the time Cornelia and Emily were writing *Our Hearts*, the Shakespeare and Company they had frequented in the summer of 1922 had vanished.

Still in operation at the beginning of the Nazi occupation of Paris, Shakespeare's demise came swiftly and unexpectedly in 1941, when Beach raised the ire of a German officer by refusing to sell him a copy of *Finnegan's Wake*. The officer threatened to return and confiscate the entire contents of the shop. That evening, Beach and her friends moved everything into a vacant apartment upstairs from the store, while the name on the building front was painted out. Overnight – literally – Shakespeare and Company disappeared.

Beach saved her treasured books, but she wasn't able to save herself. The Nazis shipped her off to an internment camp for six months before she was able to return to Paris, where she found refuge in a hostel for American students (she was fifty-four at the time) until the city was liberated in 1944. By then, her zeal had been flattened, and Beach never reopened her shop.

The bookstore which exists today was opened in 1951 by an American named George Whitman, who called it Shakespeare and Company in honor of the venerable bookseller, as well as naming his daughter Sylvia Beach Whitman.

Just like her namesake, Whitman is a great supporter and friend to both renowned and aspiring authors, even allowing some writers to take up residence in the shop in exchange for working in it.

It was marvelous to find the Shakespeare's I remembered hadn't changed much since the last time I stepped inside the shop twenty years ago.

For one delirious moment, I considered checking into the possibility of becoming one of Whitman's writers-in-residence and billeting in the famous bookshop. But cooler heads prevailed.

I poked around a bit, but didn't stay long, as there was a massive crowd inside at the time. It was nice to see it thriving.

Leaving Shakespeare's I crossed the bridge spanning the Seine and walked over to Notre Dame Cathedral, finishing my visit to Paris in the place where it had started.

There was something I needed to do at the cathedral, and that was say goodbye to the girls. Or at least to our journey together.

It had to be here.

When *Our Hearts Were Young and Gay* was published, instead of using photographs from their journey, Cornelia and Emily had the book illustrated by Constantin Alajalov, a popular artist of their day, who beautifully captured the spirit of the girls and their travels in his masterful, whimsical drawings.

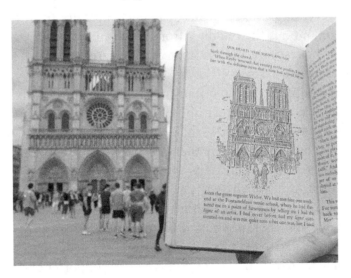

The final illustration in *Our Hearts* is of Cornelia and Emily gazing at the rose window of Notre Dame de Paris. It has always symbolized the end of their adventure for me, so I knew from that day in May when I boarded the *QM2* in Brooklyn saying, "This is it, Cornelia and Emily. Our journey has begun," we would eventually get to this day in this place.

I sat down on one of the low walls framing the square in front of the cathedral, and I really didn't care if anyone saw me mumbling to myself, or my tears.

I spoke to Cornelia and Emily, the girls, first. I thanked them for the decades of laughter, for igniting my passion for travel, for being kindred spirits, for sharing their travels with me, for being with me on my first adventure abroad, and for coming along on this journey now.

Even though I knew I would see them again at The Grand Hotel in London, and I hoped to bring them with me on the voyage home, this was where we were really saying goodbye, just as the two of them had done with each other ninety-five years ago.

> "It was the end of something and we both knew it… Our hearts were young and gay and we were leaving a part of them forever in Paris."

For Cornelia and Emily, there in 1922, it wasn't a goodbye to their friendship, but it was goodbye to an experience which could never be duplicated.

Just as it was for us now.

I then spoke to Cornelia and Emily, the women. I thanked them for writing a book with wit and style and lyricism which I could only hope to emulate. And I thanked them for being there when my faith in my book – or, more often, myself – faltered.

For getting me back on track.

For reminding me of the joy of the thing.

So many times along the way I had definitely needed those guiding spirits who were made of guts and sand.

I finished with, "I don't know how this book of mine will turn out, what it will be. I know it won't be as funny as yours. It simply can't be. But I hope it will be a credit to your legacy."

With any luck, Our Lady of Paris heard my words, and would take them as a prayer.

For a long while I sat, quiet, unmoving.

Ending the journey had been even harder than I expected.

Tuesday, July 25, a travel day and the beginning of the epilogue. I couldn't sleep knowing that I had to get up at 6AM, and so was fitful from 3AM on, after having gone to bed at midnight.

It took all of ten minutes after I was out of bed to be dressed, washed up and checked out of the hotel. I walked over to the train station to check-in forty-five minutes ahead of departure (even though Eurostar website recommended thirty minutes).

They really need to correct that on their website.

Despite careful planning and my strong determination to never cause myself to run for a train or a flight, I had to run for this train, thanks to an enormous crowd at security, and the large families of travelers who hadn't followed simple directions regarding paperwork, which held up the line.

I loathe running for trains.

I was the last person to board, and heaven help those who were in line behind me because not only did they miss it, but the next train was full as well and they would be lucky to get seats.

Meanwhile, there I was, dashing down the ramp and along the platform, pulling my two pieces of luggage, hoping to make it all the way to my assigned train car. But the attendants, who clearly saw me, were not about to delay for a moment, and began closing the train car doors. I was forced to hop on many cars from where I needed to be, just as the door slammed behind me.

Banging my suitcases down the aisle, I fought my way through the train, finally reaching my car in a hot, cranky and disheveled state. I hadn't spilled the contents of my handbag onto the train platform like poor Emily, but still, my departure from Paris was equally un-glamorous, and it was a rather pitiful showing I made aboard the sleek and sophisticated Eurostar.

I was just glad the girls weren't there to witness it.

Even though they would have understood. Symmetry.

Part 6

A Realm Of Enchantment

England Encore

Chapter 33

"… I trust the day never dawns when it ceases to be for me a realm of enchantment."

After the hurried start in Paris, it was an easy journey to London, and within an hour of my arrival in the city, I had the keys to the Chelsea flat back in my hand.

It was a joy – like coming home – but it didn't feel the same as it had the first time. These were two separate visits, not a continuation of one. To borrow a phrase from the girls, "it hadn't quite the flavor I anticipated."

Still, my enthusiasm wasn't dampened.

I arrived to a perfect day in London, almost like the first day of autumn – cool but not damp, crisp and bright. After I had unpacked (putting everything back where it had been the first time I lived in the flat), I went out and loaded up on groceries, then came straight back and did the pastiche of laundry which had built up during my two weeks in France.

I considered going down to the bar for dinner where I might find Lola the Pomeranian and the other regulars, but after a couple of weeks of eating out for every meal, I found it a treat to fix dinner for myself.

Afterwards, I settled in to get caught up on every internet-related item on my to-do list. In my emails I had a note from Sabrina, letting me know she had gone to Boston the day before, at the last minute, for her husband's aunt's 90th birthday. She wouldn't be back before I left, so there would be no hanging out with her and sweet Tigger.

Things weren't going to feel the same without them there.

I spent the next few days ticking a few boxes on my London checklist: last bits of souvenir shopping, one more walk through St. James Park, one more pub grub lunch. There was nothing novel or necessarily exciting in anything I was doing, but I took great pleasure in it. Everything was amplified, in sharper focus, because I would be gone from it soon. I was completely connected to this time and place, as I felt – and tried desperately to hang onto – every moment as it passed.

My summer had been all about the writing – both the girls' and my own – so it seemed only right I make a pilgrimage to the grave of Aphra Behn. This Restoration era playwright, poet and translator had also been a spy for King Charles II, and one of the first women to earn a living as a writer. Talk about guts and sand.

> "All women together ought to let flowers fall upon the tomb of Aphra Behn, which is, most scandalously but appropriately, in Westminster Abbey, for it was she who earned them the right to speak their minds." – Virginia Woolf, *A Room of One's Own*

Aphra Behn is not buried in the abbey's famous Poet's Corner, but outside, in the Cloisters floor. It's not really feasible to leave flowers on her grave as they would become a slipping hazard for the throngs of tourists who trample over her. Still, I visited the abbey, and stopped and thanked her, not just for myself, but for Cornelia and Emily as well. They hadn't mentioned visiting here in *Our Hearts*, but it seemed right that I should bring them along.

Another event I was happy to share with not only the girls, but Otis and Maud as well, was a trip to Shakespeare's Globe Theatre to attend a performance of "Much Ado About Nothing."

(This time when I was booking my online ticket, I brazened it out and selected the title of Viscountess for myself. Surely the Globe didn't have peerage police who would call me out as a poser.)

It would be my first visit to the Globe since the theatre had opened twenty years prior. I've always been fond of "Much Ado", but this production sounded particularly intriguing because it was set in 1914 Mexico, with Latin music and dancing.

Shakespeare really delivered that day. It was a boisterous, colorful production, and I had to think the men, especially, enjoyed their costumes. In place of the standard-issue Elizabethan frills, the actors had been outfitted as caballeros, with cowboy boots and gun belts and a scruffy appearance which added some tantalizing grit to their performances.

The Globe Theatre itself exceeded all of my expectations. The building is a meticulous recreation of the original theatre from Shakespeare's day, from the half-timbered Tudor-style structure with its thatched roof (the first allowed in London since the Great Fire of 1666), to the simple wood benches and bona fide open-air playhouse design.

The experience was as authentic as one could hope for, right down to when the "groundlings" – a.k.a. audience members standing in the ground floor area of the theatre known as "the yard" – got spritzed with light rain during the performance. But no one seemed to mind in the slightest.

And I could've sworn, the staff welcomed me with an effusive friendliness which could only be attributed to their trusting belief that I was a viscountess.

At least it amused me to think so.

Chapter 34

When I travel to England, I visit London. I visit Canterbury and Brighton and wherever else my journey leads me. But when I travel to Oxford, I am not visiting. I am returning home.

Oxford, even more than Cambridge, is part of my "first time" story. The study abroad program which brought me to England during my senior year of college had afforded me the opportunity to spend the fall term, known as "Michaelmas", studying theatre history in Oxford, and interning at the BBC in London. They were eight marvelous, memorable weeks which would compel me, upon graduation, to return to the city of dreaming spires for another twelve months.

In that second Oxford year, I would build ties to the town which would tempt me to veer off from the plans I'd already made for my life and career.

Almost thirty years later, during my first enchanted weeks in London, I had made multiple visits to Oxford.

The first time had been when I made a daytrip down to the home of Francis and Penelope Warner, the wonderful people who had developed and operated my study abroad program. They had made it possible for me, along with countless other students, to have the opportunity of studying in Oxford. It was a tremendous gift they had given me, along with their friendship.

It had been close to two decades since we'd last met, and I was looking forward to seeing the Warners again. But then it struck me, as I knocked on their front door: the last time I had stood in front of number 27, I had been a young woman.

Where had the time gone?

Penelope was the one to open the door, and welcomed me with love and a joyful smile. Together we stepped into the front room where Francis was waiting. To my heartfelt delight, his first words to me were, "Welcome home."

It was a comfort to find we were able to pick up right where we left off. I told them about my visit to Winchester Cathedral (conveniently skipping over the part involving James the dick pic guy), and how it had brought back happy memories of Francis' play.

We talked about my journey with the girls, and what a surprise it had been that *Our Hearts* was tied so closely to World War II. At that, Francis presented me with a book he had written about his childhood, in particular his memories of growing up during the Battle of Britain.

He then shared something I hadn't understood before, about the church bells.

It is part of the story of V-E Day, that church bells all across the UK rang in celebration of the war's end.

Before then, though, for the entire duration of WWII, the church bells had been silent. Which meant that for Francis and most of the children of the United Kingdom, the first time they ever heard church bells was on V-E Day.

What a memory to be given.

I had hoped that along with seeing Francis and Penelope, I might catch their daughter, Miranda, who was visiting from New Zealand, but it turned out I had missed her by just a day – she had been in Oxford, but had gone up to Scotland to see her younger brother, Benedict, and his girlfriend. I had known Miranda since she was four years old and Benedict since he was a baby. I had yet to accept that either of them could possibly be older than, say, sixteen, so I found the situation to be as disconcerting as it was disappointing.

Another of my trips to Oxford was to visit the family of my former boyfriend, Alistair. Though I had seen them more recently than the Warners, it still had been well over a decade since I'd been in the company of Bruce and Sylvia, Alistair's parents. When I first informed them of my plans to visit England, they had invited me to come stay with them, offering to put me up in "my room". This touched me deeply, that they would still refer to it that way, after all these years.

I had been twenty-two when Alistair and I met and dated for a while, before continuing on as friends. We've known each other and stayed in touch through a lot of our lives' highs and lows, first through letters and then emails, with an occasional crossing of paths here and there along the way.

During that year when we were dating, Alistair had been working and living near Windsor, but would come up on weekends and stay with his family who, as luck would have it, lived just down the road from me.

Over the course of those months, I grew close to Bruce and Sylvia, along with Alistair's brother, sisters and cousins. They were a warm, engaging lot, and I spent a significant amount of time with them, even without Alistair around.

From everyday activities like running errands, to sightseeing excursions around the neighboring villages, to dinners and the oh-so-divine Sunday lunches with friends and loved ones, the family took me in and shared their lives with me, providing me with countless happy memories.

And now, thirty years later, I am blessed that they still let me come around.

Upon my arrival at Bruce's and Sylvia's home, despite more than a few years since our last visit, they greeted me with an affectionate familiarity, calling me by the nickname "Girlie", which Alistair had given me back in our college days. Over refreshments, we began the lengthy process of catching each other up on the last decade and a half of our lives. Sylvia enquired as to whether I had been able to meet up yet with Alistair and his wife, Sue. I explained that our schedules hadn't meshed so far, but I was counting on seeing them before the summer was over.

A little while later, Alistair's brother, Francis arrived and we all had dinner al fresco in the back garden. Sylvia put on a spread of hot and cold dishes that, as always, were delicious and too numerous for a person to eat much of any one thing.

The weather and the sunlight were of the ideal English summer variety, worthy of the dinner we were enjoying, just to make things perfect.

Casting my glance around the table, it was clear that everyone was exactly as I remembered them: Francis, with whom I'd always exchanged banter, jokes and ideas, had retained his wry sense of humor coupled with the charm which all the men in the family seem to possess; Bruce, who had an enthusiasm for life and an astute interest in people and experiences which was infectious and magnetic; and Sylvia, who possessed an unshakable strength beneath her sparkling, fun-loving spirit, and who had welcomed me in as a close friend and confidante.

Being there with them in the garden felt easy and just as things should be.

Dinner al fresco with some of my favorite people; Inset: a relic from my first time abroad, circa late 1980s.

Later, when I went up to my room, to the bed I had slept in numerous times before, and climbed under the covers, I dozed off into a contented night of sleep, the kind which comes when you feel at home in your surroundings.

The next morning I met Francis' wife, Susie, for coffee and a chat before heading back to London. She and I first met each other even before she and Francis were married, and now I found her to be just as I had always known her, glowing with an ethereal quality mixed with great humor and insight.

We stayed chatting for a couple of hours, filling each other in on the happenings in our lives. Sitting and having a "natter" with Susie, I thought about how it felt so natural to be here to be in this place, with her and all of the family.

I really had returned home.

Eventually, I found I needed to "be" in Oxford for a while, and was able to procure a charming AirBnB in my former stomping grounds of Summertown, a lovely, leafy neighborhood just north of the hustle and bustle of the city. This allowed me to spend unhurried time with myriad people I adored.

There was the evening I joined half of Alistair's family in the neighboring village of Kidlington to hear Francis' band play. Sylvia and Bruce introduced me to their numerous friends who had come to enjoy the music, and I caught up with Alistair's sister, Debbie, and her husband, James, both of whom I hadn't seen in over a decade. Added to which, I became reacquainted with Bex, Johnny and Xana, members of the next generation in the family, who had all been small children the last time I'd seen them.

I spent one wonderful morning "touring" around town with Bruce, starting with tea in Blackwell's Bookshop, before visiting a few notable locales within the colleges which make up Oxford University. We snuck in a quick hello with James's and Debbie's son, Tim, who was in the midst of studying for his exams, then from there, we made a visit to the Museum of Natural History where Bruce had worked in his youth, before we headed up for lunch at home with Sylvia.

On another day, I would return to the Warners for afternoon tea. That day Penelope had outdone herself, serving homemade scones and three kinds of cake to me and their other guest: Lucy, Francis' daughter from a previous marriage. Being only days apart in age, Lucy and I had become friends during my study abroad year, but we'd lost touch once I went back to the States. A quarter of a century and a lot of living later, Lucy and I didn't miss a beat as we filled each other in on our lives. It was especially wonderful to discover Lucy was still very much Lucy – irreverent and witty, and always the brightest light in the room.

Occasionally, I was able to squeeze in some more girl time with Susie over coffee, and I couldn't have left Oxford without at least once stopping off at the Dew Drop Inn for a happy hour pint with Francis.

If I was lucky, I might catch a few minutes of a cricket match being played on the expansive, luscious grounds across from my flat, but mostly my Oxford days were filled with the delicious minutiae of everyday living – shopping errands to the drugstore and grocery store, exchanging pleasantries with the neighbors, and walking into town on the same pavement I'd traversed all those years ago. All of the little, unexciting, exquisite things which anchor a person to a place.

Now, before I left the UK, I wanted to make one more visit.

I traveled down to Oxford on a cheerful, sunny day, and after having a fashionable lunch with Lucy at Quod on the High Street, I gave myself the afternoon to stroll around my old stomping grounds, paying calls on former haunts and ghosts from my past.

In North Oxford, I dropped in on the old homestead of myself and ten other study abroad-ers, only to find the house at sixes and sevens, stripped down and undergoing a major renovation. Even in its roughed-up state, it still looked heaps better than it had when it was filled with the likes of us grotty students.

On my way back into town, I turned into a side street, one which in my student days, I had hurried down a hundred times, but which I had long forgotten about. The moment I entered the lane, the memories came rushing back, as I caught sight of my twenty-three-year-old self hot-footing it towards Summertown, on her way to Sunday lunch with Alistair and his family.

That young woman loved it here, and it broke her heart when the time came for her to leave. She could have stayed forever, with her friends and surrogate family. Maybe she could have made a life for herself in England, perhaps with Alistair, perhaps with someone else.

She looked worried, knowing that her time here was short, and uncertain of whether she should stay here or pursue her original dream of going to Hollywood.

This time I seized the opportunity I'd let slip away at Bletchley Park, when I'd encountered my pitiful, frightened earlier self. I caught up to this younger me and walked with her for a spell. Whispering, I reassured her that, in the end, she would be very glad and thankful she had chosen to go back to the States.

"You won't have what could have been a lovely life here. But the one you are headed for instead will be exciting, and beyond your imagination," I told her. "It all works out wonderfully well, and you should try to let go of the worry and doubt you are carrying."

I didn't mention anything about the hard times, the pain, the sadness which were part of the bargain in the life she was about to choose. She didn't need to know that bit of the story, because – on balance – the good would very much outweigh the bad.

Soon I started to believe that some of what I said had reached the younger me, because I began to feel the shadows of that old angst fade away.

It had been during that year in Oxford when I was twenty-three, that our study abroad group had attended a play written and performed by Penelope Warner's brother-in-law, John Kane. It was a one-man show, based on the life of F. Scott Fitzgerald and touching on his "Lost Generation" days in Paris (proving once again, in hindsight, that everything is connected).

Mr. Kane gave a mesmerizing performance, with one moment in particular resonating deeply with me. It was when Fitzgerald was expounding on the uncertainty of his youth. All these years later, I still remember him saying this (or something close to it):

"I was so young. I was twenty-three. I didn't know how sweet life could be at that point between one's dreams and their realization."

I thought of his words now, as I walked with my younger self. She had taken this wisdom to heart, and treasured this special time in her life.

What she couldn't know then, and what I was only beginning to understand, was that three decades later, my life had come full circle, and now I had returned to that exact same moment.

Here I was, making a leap of faith, and learning all over again how sweet life can be at that point between my dreams and their realization.

Had this been the reason for me turning onto the forgotten side street and running into the twenty-three-year-old me?

Was I needing to hear and heed my own advice?

I said aloud to myself, "It all works out wonderfully well. You should let go of the worry and doubt you are carrying."

We had reached the end of the lane. With mixed feelings, I bade my younger self farewell and continued on my way back into town.

Chapter 35

When I returned to London, it was not to my adored Chelsea flat, but to The Grand Hotel in Northumberland Ave, where Cornelia, Emily, Otis and Maud had stayed in 1922. It was a special treat I'd given myself to make up for the journey being nearly over.

But this opportunity came very close to not existing at all.

Constructed in 1887, the stately building which started life as the 500-room Victoria Hotel, was taken over in the early 1940s by the War Office and used by the Ministry of Defense for the duration of WWII and beyond.

Having done its part for king and country, the building's importance to the government slowly diminished over the decades, and fell into a state of disrepair. In 2006, the Ministry sold it to the current owners, a hoteliers group who did extensive renovations and restoration work before reopening the hotel in 2010 as The Grand, more than seventy years after it had been closed to the public.

It was not lost on me just how fortunate I was to still have this thread in the fabric of Cornelia's and Emily's story which I could share with them.

My plan was to remain at The Grand until the day I would catch the boat-train to Southampton and board the *QM2* back to the States.

("Boat-train" is actually an antiquated term from Edwardian times, referring to trains which ran to a port for the specific purpose of catching a passenger ship. But it applied well enough to my particular journey plans, and I found it immensely satisfying to say, "I will be catching the boat-train." After all, how often does one get the chance to utter a phrase like that? Prissy, prissy, prissy.)

On the morning of my departure from Oxford, I woke up feeling terribly ill with what was either a cold or the flu, but something which definitely had me running a fever. Up until now, I hadn't had anything more serious than a few sniffles, but the months of being on the road seemed to have finally caught up with me.

Still, I managed to get myself to London, and into The Grand Hotel. Being sick was a nuisance to be sure, but I was extremely grateful this illness was happening at the end of my travels.

I had hoped to spend my last few days in London catching some shows in the West End, and finally meeting up with Alistair and Sue, but I was simply too repugnant to inflict myself on anyone.

Hoping to curtail being sick at sea, I spent the majority of my last days in London lying in bed, in varying degrees of consciousness. My only outings were to a nearby drugstore to fetch provisions and meds.

In my waking hours, I reflected on the last few months – its ups and downs, its surprises – and I couldn't help but marvel at the numerous times I had "run into the girls", brushing against their travels.

Strange as it was, that sensation of time and space blurring – or my desire for it to be so – had not been wholly unexpected. Without question, I had actively gone looking for Cornelia and Emily, and had often met up with them.

In fact, it had become such a regular occurrence that I had envisioned myself spending at least part of my final London days gallivanting around town with the girls. But in reality, I saw very little of them.

Then again, I was rather occupied with my own time and space issues, which I had long since learned to expect.

During my "first time", my Oxford housemate Anne, a senior from William Jewell College, shared with me a newspaper article her mother had sent her. The story was penned by the legendary columnist for *The Kansas City Star*, C.W. Gusewelle, in which he described having lunch with a friend who had just come from living abroad for a year.

> "What struck me was how, sitting across the restaurant table, I had the sense that she was there only in a conditional, qualified way. It almost was as if the angle of sunlight through the window could change – just shift a little – and she might be gone from there, reappearing 5,000 miles away in the smoky companionability of some country pub.
>
> Now that the physicists' calculations of time and space have made everything negotiable, I begin to believe a thing like that could really happen."

Gusewelle himself was well-acquainted with this phenomenon. For years after he had lived in Paris, something would trigger a memory which would make him feel that he was more there than in Kansas City.

"'It's Paris now,' I will think – sometimes even say aloud. And overcome by a truth more powerful than memory, I will feel my grasp on the present moment start to slip. The temptation to let go entirely is very strong, and I am not sure what the result might be.

That's what my friend is feeling now, as she struggles with the confusion about where her heart will live. Home can be more places than one. The pity is having to choose."

After my first time abroad, I came to know this struggle for myself, never failing to grapple with that same confusion whenever I returned from a visit to England, no matter how brief it had been.

It had proven to be true, what I wrote in the back flyleaf of my journal all those years ago, as I paraphrased Cornelia and Emily: "My heart was young and gay and I was leaving a part of it in England forever."

It's never gotten any easier to leave. The pull to stay is forever strong. And now here I was, closing in fast on yet another departure, and the pain which was sure to come when the *QM2* sailed out and away from Southampton.

In taking inventory of my journey, I couldn't help but run through the list of places and things Cornelia and Emily had encountered, which I had skipped over in my travels.

The adventures which would remain undone.

All of the unfinished business.

And I should've spent more time with Maud.

The girls had made brief mentions of visits to the New Forest, Salisbury and Stoke Poges, where they "took snapshots of each other sitting with gingerly reverence on the tombstone of Thomas Gray".

And they wrote of visiting London's Inner Temple, which I hadn't ever done. But then, the Inner Temple which Cornelia and Emily visited was largely destroyed during the Blitz.

For the most part, I was at peace with what I hadn't accomplished along the way. There was just that one elusive butterfly I hadn't managed to catch in my net: the name of the Great Educationalist. As much as I consoled myself with thoughts of symmetry, and how it was only right that, like Cornelia and Emily, I should never know the man's name, it was still a source of vexation for me.

By Thursday, twenty-four hours before I would be leaving London, I was finally starting to feel better. After being cooped up for three days, I decided the best thing for my recovery and my sanity was to get some fresh air and sunshine.

I walked over to St. Paul's Cathedral, which was quite a haul, but I didn't mind – it was just good to be outdoors. I can never approach the magnificent St. Paul's without thinking of the iconic photograph from World War II, where in the midst of a German air raid, the cathedral dome is illuminated by the flames of the buildings burning around it. That photograph by Herbert Mason became a symbol of unflinching courage, stiffening the backs and strengthening the resolve of the British to fight on.

For all its storied history and grandeur, I was content to remain outside St. Paul's, taking in the sunshine and enjoying a few moments reminiscing about the first time I visited the cathedral. It had been during my study abroad year, when some of my friends and I had journeyed up from Oxford to attend a Thanksgiving service for Americans residing in the UK. It had been a lovely way to experience St. Paul's for the first time, and a great kindness bestowed upon us by our English cousins.

After my visit to the steps of the cathedral (and a quick visit to the gift shop located in the crypts), I took my time meandering back through central London, taking a circuitous route through Covent Garden, then ambling along the Strand, and up into Leicester Square where I picked up a theatre ticket for "Queen Anne" that evening.

From there, I moseyed over to the National Portrait Gallery, for what was one of the finest last moments of my summer. I was there to view the newly-installed BP Portrait Awards for 2017. The BP (British Petroleum) Award is arguably the most renowned portrait prize in the world, and is considered to be a highly-important art competition.

There was one portrait in particular I had come to see. It was of Dr. Tim Moreton, a former Registrar of the National Portrait Gallery, which just happened to be painted by my pal Lucy.

In the National Portrait Gallery: Lucy's award-winning painting; and on another day, taking tea upstairs with the artist herself.

I knew she was an amazingly talented artist, but it had been a long time since I'd seen any of her work. I studied the compelling portrait, dazzled by the palette of colors she had fused together and formed into Dr. Moreton's likeness. I then took some time to view the other BP Award winners before returning to Lucy's painting, where I hovered for a good half hour, for the sole purpose of unabashedly boasting to other museum-goers about how the artist was a personal friend of mine.

That evening, I still felt well enough to attend the performance of "Queen Anne" at the Theatre Royal Haymarket. It was the first time in twenty years I had been there, which added a little extra fizz to my last evening in London.

After the play, I walked back from the theatre through Trafalgar Square. The daytime crowds of tourists had dispersed, and the lions and fountains of the square were left to the young, flirty people.

It was just going on 10PM as I reached the Thames riverfront walk. Not far from where I stood, Big Ben began to toll the hours with its steadfast, noble chime. I held tight to each rich, resonant strike of the clock, acutely aware of the fact that in three weeks' time, the great bell would be silenced, and was expected to remain so for at least four years while repair work was done on the tower which houses it.

It made me think back to Francis Warner and the church bells, with their deafening silence during the war. In contrast, Big Ben had continued to ring throughout World War II, tolling into the utter darkness of a London in blackout, its own clock face ceasing to be illuminated. How haunting and how comforting that must have been.

I stood for a long time gazing across the river to the South Bank, which was bustling with music and voices and silhouettes, all under the watchful London Eye, with the spectacle of lights shimmering on the water as twilight disappeared into darkness.

London was as bright and sparkling as a diamond.

That tingly sensation of being young and living here had returned once again. But twinges of sadness were starting to creep in, as I could feel the final moments my enchanted summer slipping away from me.

"Indeed," I thought, "the bell is tolling on my adventure. Literally."

All that was left of my journey now was to pack my bags one last time, and leave.

Part 7

A Momentous Occasion

The Return Voyage

Chapter 36

"It was a momentous occasion and we were at that happy age when we felt momentous occasions should be reacted to with emotional respect. Oblivious to the jostling crowd, we stood gazing at the prosaic decks of the modest cabin-class liner, dewy-eyed... and holding up a line of less sensitive passengers."

Time to get back in the fancy clothes. Go to afternoon tea. Dress for dinner. Evening gowns and opera gloves. On Friday, August 4, 2017, the *Queen Mary 2* would sail from Southampton to New York, and I was to be aboard.

The night before the voyage, I slept badly. Still, I managed to get up early enough to walk my big suitcase to Waterloo Station's left luggage office, with the plan being I would collect it when I returned to catch the train for Southampton.

I just had to get the suitcase across the Golden Jubilee Bridge and to the station, but the bridge's elevator on the Embankment side was broken, and I enjoyed the pleasure of lugging my bag up four flights of steep stairs.

Suitcase in tow, I made it across the bridge to the other elevator, which mercifully was working. But when the doors opened, I discovered the elevator was already occupied by a young man in a hoodie who was passed out on the floor, snoring and sprawled across all of the available standing space. To make matters even more interesting, his jeans were down below his backside, and his hand was down the front of his pants.

Lovely.

I started to abandon my elevator plan and use the stairs, but feeling certain I would trip and tumble down the steps (still clutching my suitcase), I opted to squeeze into the elevator with ol' Hand-in-Pants. Shoving my bag next to his feet, I wedged myself inside, next to his head. As we rode down, I decided to get a picture of what I figured would make a good story.

Not tech savvy enough to remember all I had to do was swipe right to open the camera app, I pulled out my phone and began fumbling with it as I got off the elevator. Yanking my bag out behind me, I pressed the call button on the outside of the elevator so the door wouldn't close right away. As I hurried to get my photo, the young man woke up. Catching sight of me, he started yelling as he struggled to dislodge his hand. I snapped a picture and took off fast.

I managed to get to Waterloo unscathed, without him following me. His pants situation thankfully must've slowed him down.

I proceeded to the left luggage office and dropped off the suitcase, then pulled out my phone to check my camerawork.

It was gutting!

The photo was blurry, as in really blurry. It was impossible to make out an image. It seemed unfair. I had earned that picture.

Returning to the hotel, I had a leisurely breakfast then took my time finishing the last of the packing. But I couldn't stall any longer. It was time to go.

In the lobby, as I started towards the exit's revolving door, I felt a profound sense of sadness at having to leave Cornelia, Emily, Otis and Maud. They were all there in the lobby with me, and I knew this was where I had to say goodbye to them.

These would be my last moments with Otis and Maud, for certain. I was hoping I might feel Cornelia and Emily on the ship with me, but they had each traveled back by themselves to the States. So I would probably be traveling on my own as well.

I moved to a quiet corner, and pretended to be rearranging my handbag as I said farewell to all of them. I had to fight back the tears as I thanked them for all of the fun, thanked them for getting me here. And then I left them and went out the door, and into Northumberland Avenue.

It was easier getting my small bag up the Jubilee Bridge stairs, and this time I was able to make my way to Waterloo Station without incident. Once there, I picked up my large bag and, in true priss-pot fashion, hopped the boat-train to Southampton.

Two hours later, I was standing outside the proud port city's cruise terminal, peering at the *QM2* in all her splendor. It seemed like barely more than a few days had passed since I boarded the ship in New York.

Back in May, at the beginning, when I had first glimpsed the *QM2*, I felt as awestruck as the girls had been at the sight of the *Montcalm*. Seeing her now, though, my heart was glum. Even a short visit to England is usually enough to bring on tears as I'm boarding the plane at Heathrow or Gatwick – but this time I'd been here long enough to put down roots.

Or, more accurately, to nurture the roots which had been planted and firmly taken hold all those years ago.

It was going to be tough to pull up anchor and sail away.

By 2PM, I was aboard the ship. Once again, I knew exactly where to find my stateroom – a different configuration to my first single room, but also quite attractive, with the added bonus of having a most pleasing fainting couch. And there to meet me when I arrived, as promised, was my Really Big Suitcase full of evening gowns which I'd trusted to the baggage office back in May.

I did some rudimentary unpacking, then decided I should go up on the top deck and do as much texting and emailing as possible while I could still get the internet through my phone.

Standing on the twelve deck, looking back at the Southampton shoreline, I thought to myself about how my story was over, and this voyage back to the States might as well have been a flight from Heathrow, for all it mattered to the tale.

At least we were getting an extra day aboard the ship, I told myself. The *QM2* was scheduled to make a special stop in Halifax on this particular crossing. Yet even the tantalizing notion of swanning around being prissy for nine straight days wasn't enough to brighten my attitude.

As if sensing my mood, an empathetic, ominous solitary cloud began forming on the horizon and appeared to head across the sky straight towards me. Literally a black cloud over my head.

I was roused from my pout by fellow passengers who were excitedly taking pictures of themselves along the railings, glowing with radiant, enthusiastic smiles, overjoyed by the privilege of being aboard this beautiful ship and on this dazzling voyage. They made me cognizant of my own good fortune, and how I was being wildly unappreciative and sulky about it.

I really needed to not be a mopey, miserable mess, spoiling the trip for others.

At least the pressure was off, I told myself. I wouldn't have to "try". I could just lounge around and read and not talk to anyone. That's one of the beauties of travel: No one knows who you are, so you get to choose who you want to be each time you are in a new place.

This time, I would be the quiet, keep-to-myself person.

That settled, I went to my stateroom to finish unpacking, and found Rafael, my steward, there, delivering a brochure introducing seven World War II veterans who were aboard the ship as featured speakers, giving talks about their experiences.

Just when this voyage seemed destined to be a cheerless epilogue to my travels, it became the glittering grand finale of the journey. I pored over the brochure, reading it from cover to cover like I was cramming for an exam.

When it was time for dinner – the fashionable, late seating this time – I slipped into a cocktail dress and headed for the dining room, where I joined a table of seven other solo travelers, comprised of Ben the Frenchman, Robert from Canada, Roger and Janet representing England; Anne hailing from Scotland, and two other Americans – Thatcher from Virginia and Matthew from Chicago.

Matthew and I, in particular, formed a fast friendship, and would end up running around together quite a lot during the voyage. He and his husband, Harold, had sailed to Europe together a few weeks prior, but Harold had flown back to Chicago for work, which left Matthew sailing back alone, missing him terribly, and struggling to have a good time. Still, Matthew was fun and funny, and we became great friends.

They were a lively, engaging group at Table 66 and we had a wonderful crossing together, sharing lots of stories, laughs and our bottles of complimentary champagne (one of the perks of being a returning passenger) as we lingered over our desserts. Most nights, at least two or three of my tablemates would join me after dinner in the ballroom, where we hobnobbed with other passengers and danced until the band stopped playing.

So much for my plan to be the subdued, introverted passenger.

Chapter 37

Saturday, August 5, 2017, our first day at sea. I fell straight into my old routine of rising early for stretch class, followed by laps around the promenade deck, then breakfast in the buffet, loading up on smoked salmon with hollandaise sauce to the point of nearly making myself sick. Totally worth it.

As I walked through the buffet that first morning, I spotted four of the WWII veterans, who were sitting together near one of the windows. Making a beeline for their table, I barged right in, gushing like a groupie as I introduced myself to them.

Doug, an Army Airborne colonel who had served in France, Italy and Germany (then later Korea and Vietnam), was the first to take my hand when I approached them, saying it was okay for me to join their table, that they all just might be in love again.

Turns out these men are not only heroes, but charmers.

To Doug's right was Steven (Army, 29th Infantry Division, Normandy D-Day), who talked with me the most. I was thrilled to learn that, as a young soldier, he had been to New York's Stage Door Canteen – a sort of celebrity USO, where the leading Broadway actresses of the day (like Cornelia Otis Skinner) would serve drinks and sandwiches, put on performances and socialize with soldiers who were getting ready to head off to the war. Cornelia often put in hours at the famous Canteen, but Steven hadn't crossed paths with her.

Sitting next to him was a Kentucky boy named Bruce (Navy, Airborne, Okinawa), who had grown up in the same rural county as my grandparents. He mentioned my red hair, saying I reminded him of Ann-Margret, which delighted me immensely. He said I also reminded him of Bette Davis, who had been a redhead when he danced with her at the equally famous Hollywood Canteen.

Then there was Joseph (Army Airborne, 101st Division Normandy D-Day paratrooper), who I first thought of as soft-spoken, but turned out to be a real pistol. Joe possessed the sparkle and swagger of the "overpaid, oversexed, and over here" American GIs, and had married an English girl, romancing her away from his British brothers-in-arms.

Later that day, I would have the opportunity to meet the other veterans. There was Gentleman Jim (Marines, Iwo Jima) who had just lost his wife of sixty-five years the previous November. He was sad, quiet and kind. And then there were the Pearl Harbor boys, Mickey (Navy, USS Pennsylvania) and Stuart (Navy, USS West Virginia). They'd both been cheeky, charming young lads, enjoying the plum assignment of being stationed in Hawaii. And then on that day which would live in infamy, they became first-hand witnesses and survivors of the flashpoint which brought America into World War II.

Over the course of our journey together, I would get to know these vibrant, charismatic men as they graciously shared bits of their lives with me. Just as it had been for Cornelia and Emily, with their World War I soldier in Les Invalides, this would prove to be the sweetest, most profound part of my travels.

It was especially meaningful for me to befriend Joe and Steven, the men who had been there on June 6, 1944 in Normandy. More than once, we would be speaking, and I would think back to the day I had been at the American Cemetery and then at Omaha Beach, walking in the footsteps of the D-Day soldiers. I hadn't known it at the time, but Joe had dropped from those same sunny skies I had enjoyed on my day there, and on that beach, I had walked in Steven's footsteps.

The veterans would pay the price for their kindness to me – from that first morning on, I became a borderline stalker, commandeering daily "breakfast time with the boys", as I came to think of it. The vets had no chance of ditching me. In my eyes, they were the stars of the voyage.

Each day, at least one of the veterans gave a talk about his experiences in World War II, and I made a point of being in the planetarium (the ship's largest lecture and entertainment space) at 12:15 in order to get a good seat amongst the full house.

The veterans did not speak like lecturers. Rather, they shared their personal memories with the audience as if they were relating stories to old friends. Their narratives were told with an unwavering frankness, tinged with hints of residual sadness and sometimes even pain, as they shared vivid, often still-raw memories – the noise and chaos of battle, the horror of seeing young men's lives end violently, the pain of losing their friends.

The men brought the past into the present for all of us, offering glimpses of what they and their fellow soldiers were required to not only endure, but carry with them throughout their lifetime.

As hard as some of their stories were to hear, I felt it the greatest privilege to know them and understand in some small way the true measure of these soldiers' bravery and sacrifice.

At the end of their talks, the veterans were unfailingly met with standing ovations from the audience, and rightly so. Many of the passengers waited in line after the lectures to speak with them and have their pictures made with the vets. I considered doing the same, but then felt it was only fair that I "share" the veterans with the other passengers. After all, I'd already staked my claim.

Our second evening at dinner, we had a new addition to Table 66: Marianne, a therapist and widow from Manhattan. She was the quintessential New Yorker – glamorous, tough, wickedly funny and as kind as the day is long. We hit it off instantly. She informed us she would be leaving before dessert was served because she needed to be in the ballroom for when the dancing started. Marianne was passionate about ballroom dancing, and she encouraged me to come with her and give it a try.

And so I did.

Somewhere in my travels, I had shed whatever silly bashfulness had held me back from attempting to dance. That evening, I stepped onto the ballroom floor, with not the slightest clue of what I was doing, and followed my partners as they demonstrated the most basic steps of the dances we were attempting.

It didn't matter that I was terrible. All I knew was I was having fun.

I was finally getting the hang of how to do a transatlantic crossing.

I went to bed late that evening. In only a few hours, it would be time to start a new day, but I didn't mind.

I managed to garner a hurried sleep before I had to be up and stalking the veterans at breakfast.

Finding them at their usual table, I pulled up a chair and broached the subject of Big Band Night, which was the scheduled entertainment in the ballroom that evening. The boys all planned to be there. Little did they know I was secretly plotting to make them my dance partners, and inflict my three newly-learned steps on them.

Shortly after, the vets began talking very matter-of-factly about how there won't be any of them left in five years. Steven casually remarked how it was likely that at least two of them would be gone within a year's time. I excused myself to get some more tea, because I felt tears welling up in my eyes. It was a hard, ugly truth, one I certainly was aware of, but their frankness had caught me off guard. Still, I pulled it together and returned to the table with a smile. Those men didn't need my tears.

Later that morning, I came upon Colonel Doug alone in one of the lounges. He invited me to sit down (well, at least that's how I remember it) and we had an in-depth conversation about his World War II experience. He told me he had taken part in the liberation of the Flossenberg concentration camp. He recalled how they could smell the camp long before they reached it.

He spoke about how he now had German soldier friends, along with friends who had been concentration camp victims. The war was their shared experience – an unimaginable shared experience – and these survivors had found camaraderie and comfort in each other, no matter what part they played or what side they fought for.

A powerful testament to the inherent decency, kindness and the ability to forgive that we each possess.

I stayed chatting with Doug for as long as I could, until I finally had to dash off to the ship's daily ballroom dance lesson, which on this day happened to be the waltz. It seemed like a good place to begin my new dance career, and this time I wasn't shying away.

Glimmers of guts and sand.

Matthew was at the dance lesson, too, and we gave it a go together. We were by no means sensational, but we did manage to receive an approving nod from the dance teacher at one point, which puffed us both up considerably.

Even still, I knew those poor veterans were in for a rough night on the dance floor with me.

After the lesson, I did my two miles of laps around the ship. It was the best day weather-wise that I'd had at sea – clear, with sparkling water and a mirror-calm ocean. I'd never seen the North Atlantic this smooth and wave-free. There was only the slightest hint of a breeze, the sun was warm and there were a dozen dolphins swimming on the starboard side of the ship, while two spotted whales were surfacing on the port side.

Sometimes life is perfect.

On the top deck of the QM2, and the view looking down.

I settled into a deck chair and gazed at the water. I had no interest in rushing off to the next thing. Instead, I was able to really just sit, focusing on the ocean, soaking in its breathtaking beauty, letting my mind drift, but not too far afield. It was the closest I had gotten to Zen in ages.

With the weather being so lovely, it seemed like the perfect day to check out the bridge. Passengers aren't actually allowed on the bridge, but are able to step into a passageway which is separated from the bridge by a wall of glass. Here they can observe the crew at work as if they're watching fish in a tank, with the same caveat about not tapping on the glass. It was my first time in the passageway and when I went in, I happened to be the only passenger visiting. A couple of the crew noticed me and gave me a wave, which I thought was nice and made me feel quite privileged.

It still wasn't tea with the captain, like Cornelia and Emily had partaken in, but it was something.

That evening as I dressed for dinner, I thought back to what the boys had been saying about being gone soon. They – and all the brave soldiers who saved the world – would slip from being part of living history into the annals of the past, alongside the fall of the Roman Empire and the War of the Roses. It made me wish I could hold back time. These men – these new friends of mine – deserve to live on.

Happily, all thoughts of mortality vanished later that night in the ballroom, swept away in the twirl of silk and velvet evening gowns as they brushed across the dance floor.

Marianne and I, along with some of the others from Table 66, had made it to the ballroom just after the start of Big Band night. As promised, the veterans were there, seated at prominent tables facing the stage, surrounded by an entourage of admiring passengers.

The notion of sitting with them in the ballroom had never entered my mind.

I was strictly a daytime stalker.

But I did interrupt their conversations from time to time in order to ask for a dance. Bruce was the first to indulge me, and though our steps might not have been "strictly ballroom", we managed a passable glide around the floor.

I didn't venture to guess whether it was connected to my dance performance or merely coincidental, but while I was on the dance floor with Bruce, Jim (who had earlier agreed to dance with me) along with most of the other vets, decided to call it a night. Steven alone had elected to stay, and at the next slow number, he and I took to the floor.

This was when I discovered two things.

First, Steven was an excellent dancer.

And second, I'm able to let a man lead me when he knows what he's doing.

Though I was still at a loss as far as knowing the steps, I was able to follow Steven as we moved around the dance floor. It was a real boost to my confidence, and I began to believe that I might just be able to learn this dancing stuff after all.

As Steven and I traveled across the floor, I noticed a few of the other passengers looking at us with smiles which seemed almost sentimental, as if to say they found us precious, and wasn't it sweet, how I was doing a kindness in dancing with my elder. I wanted to shout to the entire room that this wasn't some favor I was doing, that in fact it was Steven who was performing the kindness.

When our dance was over, Steven walked me back to my table where Marianne was sitting. A foxtrot began to play and they stepped onto the floor. Dancing with a partner who knew what she was doing, Steven showed himself to be the dancer he is, and instantly became the king of the ballroom. The sentimental smiles quickly vanished, and now he was in demand.

For the rest of the evening, and throughout the duration of the voyage, the women on the ship were queued up waiting for their turn with the Foxtrot King. I was lucky to get two dances a night with Steven.

There could have been more, it turned out, if I had been willing to stay up until 2AM or later, gyrating in the disco. It seems that on most evenings, Steven was in there dancing until the place closed. This I learned late in the voyage from a bleary-eyed escort, who was dead on his feet after struggling to keep up with "The Legend" night after night.

Chapter 38

Even with the gift of an extra hour of sleep we received most nights, thanks to the time change, I was getting pretty worn down myself. At best I was getting six hours a night, but it was usually less. By mid-afternoon on most days, I would have a sinking spell. Afternoon tea proved a good way to amp myself back up. Usually Matthew would join me in this divine injection of caffeine and sugar, and we formed a tight bond over pastries and little sandwiches.

Matthew also accompanied me to the returning passengers party. In addition to the captain's cocktail event for all of the passengers, the *QM2* hosted a special party for folks who had sailed with Cunard at least three times, earning them the status of Gold Member. With this crossing, I became part of this elite group, and was allowed to attend the cha-cha party. I was moving up in the ranks.

The returning passengers cocktail party turned out to be a lot more fun than it probably was supposed to be. As soon as Matthew and I were in the door, he explained how we needed champagne, and felt we should try to match the quantity our tablemate Roger had consumed at the captain's cocktail party, which had been four glasses.

At the time, what Matthew was saying seemed perfectly logical to me, and we made a run at it, downing three glasses in thirty-five minutes on stomachs filled with nary a remaining crumb of scones or tea cakes.

Which was maybe not the best idea.

Matthew then suggested that when we got to Halifax in two days' time, we go to Peggy's Cove, which is a picturesque fishing village outside of town. We could even invite the others. We settled on the plan, which turned out to be a good one, even upon sober reflection the next day.

By the time the party was over and we were to go into dinner, those three glasses of champagne had been followed by a fourth and Matthew and I were both pretty lit. Still, we managed to find our way to dinner, where we had a roaring good time of it with our fellow tablemates.

After dinner, Matthew headed off to a poetry reading with Janet, and I ambled into the ballroom with Marianne for some dancing. Mercifully, the vets weren't there to see me in my inebriated state. For this I was disappointed but extremely grateful. As it was, I let the dance hosts talk me onto the ballroom floor, which I'm sure they each in turn instantly regretted.

Champagne with Matthew; dancing with Steven and Marianne.

The next morning, I once again came across Doug sitting alone. He was scheduled to speak that day, and was wearing his French Legion of Honor medal, which was beautiful. It was the first one I'd ever seen up close, and perhaps the only one I will ever see being worn by its owner. We talked for a bit and Doug got teary as he spoke about the casualties in the Battle of the Bulge, and how he lost almost all of his company.

Too often, the scope of the burdens the human heart has to bear is staggering. Yet even in a moment of pain and grief, Doug retained a strength and steadiness which left me in awe. I was in the company of a true hero.

Soon, it was time for me to go practice the waltz with Matthew. We met up at the front of the ship in the fresh air of the twelve deck, which was quiet and sparsely populated. The sun was out and it was shaping up to be quite a nice day. Matthew and I danced for a while, until we felt we knew it well enough to attempt it that night on the dance floor.

Nearby, another passenger happened to be practicing his guitar, and he played something we were able to waltz to. It formed a surprising and charming memory, and one of my favorite moments of the crossing.

Later that evening in the ballroom, Matthew and I took a few spins around the floor, and I also got Ben the Frenchman to dance with me once. By now, the word had really spread about Steven, and he was in high demand as a dance partner. It was all I could do to get an occasional turn with him. Bruce and Jim, the other dancers in the group, had gone to see either the nightly movie or musical production.

Fortunately, Stuart had come to the ballroom and I was able to convince him to dance with me a couple of times. Attired in his naval dress blues, Stuart cut a dashing figure, and I reveled in the idea of being seen "tripping the light fantastic" with him.

My tablemates and I stayed until the music and dancing finished, sharing some tremendous laughs, before calling it a night and parting company, as we each headed back to our respective cabins.

This was when the evening took a turn.

I was within fifty feet of my stateroom door when I encountered a group of six high-spirited passengers trying to find the disco. As it wasn't far from my stateroom, I offered to show them how to get there. The leader of the group, Daniel, insisted I come have a drink and a dance with them.

For some inexplicable reason, I agreed to this.

In the disco, over the blast of the music, I became acquainted with my new friends, and Daniel bought me a long island iced tea. In hindsight, that long island iced tea was a bad idea.

But then it usually is.

At some point, a large, excited Scotsman pulled me up from my chair and onto the disco floor, where he enthusiastically spun and flung me from one side to the other for a good while, until I was finally able to beg off and return to my party.

As I was taking my seat, Daniel – who, clearly, had also had a snootful – announced he was in love with me, and then leaned in and kissed me.

Up until that very moment, I had thought he was gay.

Even when he kissed me I still thought he was gay.

Even when he confessed that he was married to a woman, I was still convinced he was gay.

But the married thing put a quick and much-needed kibosh on the kissing. I left shortly after this incident, thankful that Steven and the boys hadn't been in the disco that particular night to witness my poor display.

This time, fortunately, I made it back to my room without getting sidetracked.

The disco incident had not been the most shining moment of my voyage, but I did take comfort in remembering that when the girls sailed over, Cornelia, on the night of the big gala dance, had a similar incident of her own, which she recalled with equal discomfort:

> "I also have a distinct recollection of going out on deck with that Pride of Princeton and letting him kiss me. Girls didn't kiss much in those days. Those who did were considered 'fast'... Whenever I fell from grace in this fashion (which was whenever I had the slightest opportunity), I'd go through an aftermath of abject penitence... then when the occasion next offered itself I'd do it all over again."

It had come late in the game, but here was just one more item I could check off my list of things to "accomplish" on my journey. I had at last managed symmetry with Cornelia and her Pride of Princeton.

It was a rough start for me the next morning.

The liquor from the night before had caused me to have trouble sleeping, so I was awake and watching from my bed as the ship glided along the Canadian coastline towards the port in Halifax. We were still moving when I pulled myself out of bed, flipped on all the lights, and went in to take a shower. At that time, the QM2 appeared to be docking with the other side of the ship – the starboard side – facing the pier.

But apparently the port side of the ship is called that for a reason.

Upon finishing my shower and breezing out of the bathroom stark naked, I quickly realized the ship was now anchored, and my stateroom, with all its lights ablaze, was lined up perfectly with what appeared to be the porters' break room, and I was exposing myself to about a dozen porters who were in there at the time, along with a security guard standing just below my window on the dock.

I dashed back into the bathroom and put on my robe, praying no one had noticed me. But when I came out, it was clear that at least some of them had, because everyone in the break room was looking directly at my window, and they all seemed very much amused.

That made twice I'd exposed myself during my travels. That I knew of.

Mortifying. Again.

(Later, I would learn that Amy, who was traveling in the stateroom next to me, and with whom I had become friends, had done pretty much the same thing – stark naked, she had thrown back her closed curtains and displayed herself to the porters. We were both glad to discover we hadn't been alone in disgracing ourselves.)

To paraphrase Cornelia, the memory of the disco incident the night before "was still bright within me", and compounded my feeling of embarrassment. Doing my best to shake off the humiliation – along with the budding hangover – I was experiencing, I hurried to finish getting ready.

As planned, Marianne, Matthew, Robert and I went into Halifax where we picked up a taxi which took us to Peggy's Cove. Wondrously, the hangover never materialized, it was a beautiful day, and the fishing village was a treat. We took pictures by the lighthouse, then with Matthew's help, I was able to climb on the rocks in my sandals for a while before we walked back towards an inlet lined with small, colorful boats.

Soon we went back to Halifax and consumed an excellent lunch at one of the charming dockside restaurants. Afterwards I returned to the *QM2*, where I conked out on a lounge chair in the spa and slept for the entirety of the afternoon, barely waking up in time to see us depart Halifax.

The last full day of a voyage is never really a proper day at sea. It is about prepping to leave the ship – making sure paperwork is done, getting packed, settling bills, all of the things which let a person know their divine experience is coming an end.

In the afternoon as I was getting in a few extra gratuitous laps around the promenade deck, I ran into Matthew. We walked together for a while, then went up to the top deck where it was less crowded.

We had gone up there so Matthew could show me where he had proposed to Harold, then he took me down to the Commodore Club, the swanky bar at the front of the ship, to show me where they had gotten married.

Until then, I hadn't realized that they'd been married on the ship. Turns out that, not only had they gotten married by the captain, but for one of their witnesses, they had Dr. Ruth Westheimer, the famous psychiatrist and sex therapist. She had been a speaker on their voyage, and Matthew and Harold had invited her to the ceremony, to which Dr. Ruth had graciously agreed.

In the Commodore Club, Matthew pointed out the intimate little room which sits off the main bar area. It was a pretty space, a really lovely setting for a wedding, which I hadn't noticed before.

After that, we went to tea and loaded up on the succulent sandwiches and scones.

At dinner that evening, Table 66 polished off the last two bottles of our collective champagne, toasting to the good times we'd had and the good friends we'd made. Afterwards, for the final time, I made my way to the ballroom, along with Matthew, Roger, Robert and Marianne, where I was rarely off the dance floor. I danced with the men of Table 66, along with the six dance hosts, and, of course, Steven. The other veterans had not come to the ballroom that evening, and it left just Steven to dance with all of the women in the ballroom.

Which he did.

And then it was over. All of it. The trek from California across the US, the weeks in New England doing research, sailing to England, the month in London, the fortnight in France, the surprisingly glorious voyage back on the QM2. Three and a half months of travel, finished.

Saturday, August 12, 2017 had arrived and my enchanted summer had ended.

Remarkably, I had slept well on my last night aboard the ship, waking only when the lights from a nearby freighter blazed into my room. I climbed out of bed just in time to see us pass under the

Verrazano Bridge, an event I had meant to be on deck for. But that was okay. Next time.

Coming full circle: New York Harbor, where my enchanted summer began and ended.

The last people I saw before I left the ship were the vets, who had been given a special waiting area in the champagne lounge. I stepped out of line to say one more goodbye to each of them. I remember specifically taking Joe's hand and thanking him again for all of the fun. He said to me, "Having you here made it better for all of us." I was deeply touched by his kind words, and I told him so. I squeezed his hand, kissed him on the cheek and wished him safe travels.

Lastly, I said goodbye to Steven the Foxtrot King. I had made a promise to him, one evening when we were dancing, that I would take ballroom lessons, so the next time we met, I would know the steps and be able to dance with him properly. Dancing with him and the other vets had been one of the highlights of my enchanted summer, and I was determined that not only would there be a next time, but I would keep my promise as well.

In the next moment, I was moving away from them and down the gangway.

The rest of the day was a blur of motion, in and out of airport security and boarding lines, on planes, in the air, and by 9:30pm my bags and I were in the back of my dad's SUV, and I was headed for the guest room in my parents' house in Springfield, Missouri. During the car ride, I told my mom and dad a little about my marvelous good fortune of traveling with the veterans, and the boys' stories carried us all the way back to the house.

I was ready to go directly to my room and climb into bed. Both my body and my spirit were needing for the day to end. My parents were glad to see me, but they understood. None of us were expecting to stay up late chatting. There would be plenty of time for that tomorrow.

After all, my journey was over.

Afterword

It Would Never Be The Same

"It was the end of something and we both knew it. We would come back again but it would never be the same. Our breath would come fast and our eyes smart when the Eiffel Tower rose again in the evening mist, but that would be because we remembered it from these months. There would never again be a 'first time.' Our hearts were young and gay and we were leaving a part of them forever in Paris."

On September 9, 2017, less than a month after we arrived in New York, Colonel Douglas Dillard passed away. Upon hearing this, I thought back to the vets' conversation that day at breakfast on the *QM2*, about how probably two of them would be gone within the next year. That hard, ugly truth had begun to prove out, but how could it be coming to pass so soon? Doug had been so strong and vital.

He was very fortunate, really. To have lived such a long life, to have done such remarkable things – things which made a difference, things which saved lives – and only weeks earlier have been fit and well enough to cross an ocean, speaking to crowds and having an adventure, was a blessing.

But even understanding this didn't stop me from being terribly saddened by the news.

Rest in Peace, Colonel Douglas Dillard, and thank you for your service.

I would spend the autumn after my trip in Hudson, New York, completing the first draft of my book in a funky converted schoolhouse dating back to 1900. There I would make friends with Laurie, the "headmistress" landlady, artist and sculptor.

During those months in New York, I made a daytrip to Massachusetts, and paid another visit to the Margaret Sanger papers at Smith College.

I was still flummoxed and obsessed with the Great Educationalist. I had to make one more run at finding the answer.

The first time around, I had been focused on Margaret Sanger's photos, and it hadn't occurred to me to check her papers for the identity of the Great Educationalist.

This time I learned, according to Sanger's pocket calendar from 1922, she had gone to Easton Glebe on Saturday, July 8 and stayed overnight. The calendar read "At Wells" on Saturday, and "Otis Skinner there" on Sunday, July 9.

Solid confirmation that I'd gotten the date right, but no mention of any other guests.

I then snooped around in Sanger's correspondence from that summer. There were no steamy love letters from Mr. Wells to be had, but I did come across a missive from his wife, Catherine, inviting her American friend to come stay for the weekend when she visited England that July.

From there, I moved on to Sanger's 8x11, 184-page handwritten 1922 journal. As I began turning the pages of her weeks and months, I was thrilled to find Margaret Sanger was exhaustive in recording the details of a day's events. A mention of lunch with friends would cover the occasion, who was there, who stopped by the table, and what everyone ate and drank.

No question, Sanger was sure to have named everyone who was at Mr. Wells' house that weekend. I could hardly contain my excitement as I hurriedly flipped to July.

This is where I discovered that Margaret Sanger's last journal entry was on June 30. The entry for July 1 reads,

"It is over two years since I wrote in this book. I am now here in London again to arrange for and invite persons to the International BC (Birth Control?) Conference."

And then the journal picks up in September 1924.

It took every ounce of self-control I had not to let out a sitcom-worthy, sobbing "Nooooooo!" right there in the middle of the special collections reading room of the Young Library.

I held it together until I got to the car, and then fell into an apoplectic mess on the drive back to Hudson, yelling to no one and filling the air in the car with expletives and indignant rantings at the top of my voice.

My last, best hope in the Great Educationalist mystery had been shattered. It was gutting.

The following spring, I would travel south, and push through rewrites in Laurie's art studio bungalow in Lake Worth, Florida.

While there, I fulfilled my promise to Steven the Foxtrot King and began dance lessons with Grigol Kranz, a professional ballroom dancer and brilliant teacher in the Palm Beach area. With unflagging patience and good humor, Grigol taught me the foxtrot and numerous other ballroom dances, along with many Latin dances for good measure.

I found it especially satisfying to learn the tango, just as Cornelia and Emily had in the parlor of their Paris pension. It was nice to be connecting again with them in this lovely, small way.

On March 14, 2018, Stephen Hawking passed away at the age of seventy-six. The following summer, his ashes were interred at Westminster Abbey, not long before I made a return trip to England.

Soon after I arrived in London, I visited the Abbey, grateful to be able to pay my respects. At his gravestone, I whispered how sorry I was that I would never get to ask him about the phenomenon of time and space blurring.

I can only hope that the me from thirty years ago might find a way to ask the him of thirty years ago about it, as we pass each other on the sidewalk in front of King's College, Cambridge.

Because time is not linear, and everything is happening at once.

Pressing on with revisions, I fought my way to the end of my first book. It was a long, hard slog, filled with all the angst, self-doubt and procrastination that are staples of book-writing.

But I made it to the other side.

Still, I couldn't let it go about the Great Educationalist. One night I even dreamt I was talking to Emily and asking her who the mystery man was. I woke up from that dream and implored out loud into the darkness, "Emily, *please*, tell me, who is it?"

Nothing.

"At least tell me where the answer is. Does it exist?" I begged.

I heard in my head, "Catherine Wells knows."

H.G. Wells' wife?

I started thinking about the letter I'd seen in Margaret Sanger's papers from Catherine Wells, inviting her to come stay at Easton Glebe. Cornelia, Emily and Cornelia's parents had also been invited that weekend via a letter from Mr. Wells,

> "… when the great man wrote inviting us all to spend
> Sunday at his country place."

Everything in those days was planned and arranged by written letters. And afterwards, thank you notes were always sent to the hostess.

With any luck, Catherine Wells' papers contained one of these "bread and butter letters", as they were called, from the Great Educationalist.

The University of Illinois at Urbana-Champaign may seem like an unlikely repository for the papers of an English writer with no known ties to the college, but UIUC houses an extensive collection of over 65,000 of H.G. Wells' letters.

Along with this impressive assemblage, the Rare Book and Manuscript Library also houses some of Catherine Wells' papers, including her pocket diaries.

I'd already had some luck with Margaret Sanger's pocket calendar. Perhaps lightning would strike twice.

About a week after I emailed them regarding the Catherine Wells collection, I received a reply from Taylor, a graduate student working in the library. Taylor had very kindly combed through Catherine's papers, and sent me an image of the lady's teeny-tiny 1922 pocket diary, from the weekend of July 8 and 9.

The entry for Saturday read, "Marvin" and "Mrs. Sanger". Sunday, July 9 read, "Skinners lunch".

Lightning had struck twice.

The pocket diary of Amy Catherine Robbins Wells; Mrs. Wells, circa 1925.

I'd actually found a piece of the puzzle. I had the Great Educationalist's first name!

Marvin...

I started Googling "H.G. Wells friend Marvin" and was getting nothing. I went back to the library's collection of letters for both Mr. and Mrs. Wells, and entered "Marvin". Again nothing. Mr. Wells didn't seem to have a single friend with the name Marvin.

And where was the thank you note from the Great Educationalist to Catherine Wells for the lovely weekend visit?

I studied Catherine's calendar again, looking for a hint. There had to be more – what was I missing?

Then I thought back to Catherine's letter to Margaret Sanger, someone she knew well. It had opened with "Dear Mrs. Sanger," not "Dear Margaret," even though the two women were well-acquainted. That letter was written at a time when people still used titles and last names with each other, even with friends.

Marvin wasn't the Great Educationalist's first name.

It was his last name.

Cornelia, Emily, everyone, meet Francis Sidney Marvin (1863-1943), historian, educationalist, and friend of H.G. Wells.

According to his obituary, Marvin "did much to improve the teaching of history in English schools" and "organized many courses of lectures for teachers and others". This photograph clearly predates the one of him with Cornelia and Emily in Mr. Wells' garden, but no question it is the same man.

Francis Sidney Marvin was the Great Educationalist.

Had it been Emily pointing me in Catherine's direction, or my own higher reasoning, based on two years of borderline manic research? It didn't much matter.

Either way, in the end, Catherine Wells had, indeed, held the answer.

"... some day someone may recognize the Great Educationalist and be able to enlighten us concerning his identity."

For over thirty years I had read those words, with never an inkling that I would be the "someone" Cornelia and Emily were speaking of. As John Mason Brown, their friend and fellow tourist in *Our Hearts*, would say,

"This is a tie that binds closer than the blood it draws. Friendships have been made today on a kind of bed-rock. Nothing can ever part us."

I hadn't uncovered the answer to every question, from either the girls' journey or my own, but I could live with that. I had scored my biggest prize. The other mysteries I would leave for others to work out.

And, who knows, maybe somewhere down the road (preferably around the year 2112), someone will follow in the footsteps of my story and be able to enlighten me concerning the identity of the Bafta-Winning Cross-Dresser.

I do hope they will let me tag along on their adventure.

Cornelia and Emily truly did take me on a journey that enchanted summer.

I had assumed I would spend the days slipping between 2017 and 1922. Yet often I landed in the middle of World War II, making discoveries which elevated the girls' book and the experience for me. And in those times when I crossed paths with my younger self, there was always some clarity that came with the memories and nostalgia.

Although I couldn't fully see it at the time, my travels were about a lot more than recreating Cornelia's and Emily's adventures. They would prove to be about my own journey, linking together the pieces of the path I had traversed, embracing the choices I had made.

During those months of exploring the girls' world and reconnecting to my own past, I began to make peace with some old, lingering disappointments. I developed an appreciation and even some gratitude for every experience in my life, the bad as well as the good, recognizing that both had equal hands in leading me to where and who I am now.

Like the girls, I had done some growing up during the summer.

In May 2019, I'm set to travel aboard the *QM2* with "the boys", as a number of WWII heroes sail to Europe for the seventy-fifth anniversary of D-Day. I'm eager to show off my fledgling moves on the dance floor with Steven the Foxtrot King. To him and all veterans I give my heartfelt thanks and gratitude for their service. But on a personal level, I am grateful to Steven for introducing me to the world of dancing, for it is a gift which will bring me joy for the rest of my life.

I shall return to London, where I plan to have a drink in the bar at The Grand Hotel, just so I can stop in and see Cornelia, Emily, Otis and Maud once again.

Say hello.

Let them know I'm in town.

Reconnect.

But it will never be the same.

There will never again be a first time.

ACKNOWLEDGMENTS

From the inception of this crazy adventure to the last punctuation mark of the final draft of this book, I have been fortunate to have had tremendous help and encouragement from an astonishing number of folks in all corners of the world, to whom I owe a heartfelt thank you.

Firstly, I must begin with my parents, John and Janet Crow, two unshakably sensible individuals who still managed to be nothing less than enthusiastic in their support of this madcap idea of mine, believing I could actually write a book even when I was doubting it myself. Thank you, and I love you.

Besides being my most vocal cheerleaders, my parents also saw my book through its final stages, acting as my proofreaders, along with writers and friends Allen Crowe and Betty Bowen Vega. To all four, I offer my thanks for their time, and for the excellent notes and feedback.

Additionally, thank you to Patty Swan, Kathleen Hains, Lisa Hains and Jan Jenkins, who took on an early draft of the book and gave me great notes, while bolstering my confidence with some well-timed and much-needed huzzahs.

And thank you to Daron McAfee, my longtime friend and travel buddy, with whom I have shared numerous "Cornelia and Emily adventures", for not just the pep talks throughout my travels and writing process, but also the articles, research ideas, literary contacts and anything else she could think of to help make this book happen.

To William Brandon Bowman, I offer a heartfelt thank you for introducing me to a book thirty-five years ago which would shape my life, and eventually lead me to this enchanted summer. A favorite teacher of mine and so many others, "Bucky" opened up our worlds while teaching us to speak another language -- and the value of being able to do so. I am a traveler, and now an author, and a lot of that has to do with him. Many, many thanks, Monsieur Bowman.

I owe a great debt of thanks to Linda Kimbrough and Mother Dolores Hart, two phenomenal women who were exceedingly kind and generous with their time, indulging a wannabe writer, and granting me interviews which allowed me an invaluable glimpse into the minds and hearts of Emily Kimbrough and Cornelia Otis Skinner.

A special shout-out to Mother Lioba at the Abbey of Regina Laudis, for helping arrange my meetings with Mother Dolores. I feel especially grateful that through this experience, this witty, vibrant woman has become my friend.

Also taking a chance on me were Vincent and Diana Thompson, the stellar couple who not only graciously opened their home to a stranger, but gave me one of the finest meals I had during the entire summer.

Without question, I would never have been able to put together this story without the assistance and resources of Megan Ward and Nicole Joniec of the Bryn Mawr Alumni Association; Jasmine, Amy and Nichole of the Special Collections Library, Smith College: Jessica Murphy of the Harvard Medical School's Countway Library; the Harvard Alumni Association; Karen Trop of the Houghton Library, Harvard University; all of the fantastic staff at the New York Performing Arts Library; Becky Marangelli of the Ball State University Archives and Special Collections; the H.G. Wells Society, Guy Revell of Bletchley Park, the National Archives at Kew, the Victoria & Albert Museum and Taylor Henning of the Rare Book and Manuscript Library, University of Illinois Urbana-Champaign.

I hold a special place in my heart for the majestic *Queen Mary 2* and the wonderful memories I've made aboard her. My time on this legend-in-the-making has been made all the more perfect by the exceptional captains and crew, who devote themselves tirelessly to the ideal of delivering an experience worthy of the golden age of travel.

A warm thanks to Hal Holbrook who took the time to share his remembrances of Cornelia Otis Skinner when this book was barely more than a germ of an idea.

To the talented authors and my newfound friends Kathy Kinney and Nancy Allen, I owe great thanks for not only writing wonderful endorsements of my book, but for your words of encouragement and invaluable advice on this whole daunting process.

It is no exaggeration to say I'm where I am today and who I am today in large part due to another writer – a brilliant writer – Linda Bloodworth-Thomason, who has been my role model in so many ways, both professionally and personally. She and her husband, Harry Thomason, have long since become family, and in giving me my first job in Hollywood, have brought me some of the greatest adventures of my life. Linda's marvelous endorsement of my book is just the latest in a long, long line of kindnesses for which I owe her many thanks.

I feel exceedingly fortunate in having the web design team of Theresa Galido and Adam Birnbaum, who took my rudimentary concepts and, with unflagging patience, transformed them into a website which is snazzier than I could have ever imagined, providing me with a beautiful platform from which I could share my journey.

And lastly, it is with enormous gratitude that I give unending thanks to all of my friends whose faith and support these past three years helped me make it through to the end. The list of names could fill an entire chapter of this book, but please know I remember and appreciate each and every time you asked about my travels or my writing, and then cheerfully let me gas on about it all. From the West Coast to the East Coast, from my hometown of Springfield, Missouri to distant shores across the globe, I feel blessed to call all of you my friends, and I thank you.

PHOTO CREDITS

The images contained within the story are those of the author, with the exception of the following. It is with thanks and great appreciation that I share them in this book.

Chapter 1: **Cornelia and Emily at Bryn Mawr** – Courtesy of the Alumni Office of Bryn Mawr College

Chapter 2: **Otis Skinner, Margaret Sanger and H.G. Wells** – Filename 8001, Margaret Sanger Papers, Sophia Smith Collection, Smith College (Northampton, Massachusetts). Photo is repeated in Chapter 21.

Chapter 2: **Cornelia and Emily in the garden with the Great Educationalist** – Filename 8014, Margaret Sanger Papers, Sophia Smith Collection, Smith College (Northampton, Massachusetts) Library has photo listed as: Margaret Sanger and unidentified group, but we know better, yes?

Chapter 4: **Joseph Aub, Cornelia and Paul Dudley White in the gardens of Versailles** – Paul Dudley White Papers, Harvard Medical Library in the Francis A. Countway Library of Medicine. Photo is repeated in Chapter 29.

Chapter 4: **Cornelia with Dolores Hart and Cyril Ritchard at the Music Box Theatre in New York City** – (1959) *Cornelia Otis Skinner, Dolores Hart with dog on leash, and Cyril Ritchard, full-length portrait, facing front, walking outside the Music Box theatre where they are starring in Mr. Ritchard's play "The Pleasure of his Company".* 1950 to 1960, 1959. [Photograph] Retrieved from the Library of Congress, https://www.loc.gov/item/2001697031/

Chapter 6: **The Queen Mary 2 in New York** – Courtesy of John Stoddart

Chapter 6: **Vintage postcard of C.P.O. steamship *Montcalm*** – Published by Canadian Pacific Steamships Ltd sales department, circa 1925

Chapter 11: **Otis Skinner, circa 1910** – Billy Rose Theatre Division, The New York Public Library. Otis Skinner - Part II. Retrieved from http://digitalcollections.nypl.org/items/–510d47e0-c23b-a3d9-e040-e00a18064a99

Chapter 11: **Maud Durbin Skinner, circa 1890** -- Skinner family papers, MS Thr 857. Houghton Library, Harvard College Library. https://id.lib.harvard.edu/ead/c/hou02927c00052/catalog

Chapter 32: **Author with Lee, Jo and Tracy at the Tour de France** – Courtesy of Tracy Mercer

Chapter 32: **Author with Tracy and Jo at the Arc de Triomphe** – Courtesy of Tracy Mercer

Chapter 34: **Retro photo of author from first time abroad** – Courtesy of Karen Erren

Afterword: **Catherine Wells' Pocket Diary, 1922** – Catherine Wells diaries, Rare Book & Manuscript Library, University of Illinois at Urbana-Champaign.

Afterword: **Portrait of Francis Sidney Marvin** – Desch, C. (1945). Francis Sidney Marvin, 1863-1943. *Isis, 36*(1), 7-9. Retrieved February 8, 2020, from www.jstor.org/stable/225670 (License #1019623-1)

Back Cover: **Big Ben, circa 1910** – Stereograph photograph, Retrieved from the Library of Congress, https://www.loc.gov/pictures/item/2003674147

Back Cover: **Cornelia Otis Skinner and Otis Skinner on ship deck** – Skinner family papers, MS Thr 857. Houghton Library, Harvard College Library. https://id.lib.harvard.edu/ead/c/hou02927c00052/catalog

Back Cover: **Paul Dudley White in uniform, World War I** – Paul Dudley White Papers, Harvard Medical Library in the Francis A. Countway Library of Medicine

Made in the USA
Columbia, SC
25 February 2022

56800883R00183